Anyone interested in the dynamic temperate raintorest ot the Tongass National Forest, the largest in the country, can do no better than to delve deeply in John Schoen's very personal account of the forest and the political controversies that have engulfed it. Only Schoen, who lived the controversies as nobody else did, could write such an engaging account of one of the nation's most important environmental policy debates.

GORDON H. ORIANS, Emeritus Professor of Biology, University of Washington

An odyssey is a long wandering voyage marked by exciting discoveries and activities, and often by frequent changes of fortune. This book is just that—a personal chronicle of John Schoen's lifelong voyage of discovery about the natural world and his captivating adventures as a wildlife scientist in the wildest corners of Alaska. Schoen masterfully blends field journal entries, research findings, personal reflections, and stunning photos into a first-rate memoir that informs and inspires. Readers will marvel at the unique and special ecology of Alaska's coastal rainforests, while pondering the political changes of fortune that continue to threaten the future of these priceless places. They will gain appreciation for the fine line that conservation scientists must navigate, between objectivity and advocacy. An odyssey can also be an intellectual or a spiritual quest. As readers will discover, this Alaskan odyssey is both of those things and much more.

WINIFRED B. KESSLER, PhD, CWB®

If you want to read a science book that isn't loaded with graphs and statistics and is an exciting and inspiring personal life story, I recommend John Schoen's *Tongass Odyssey: Seeing the Forest Ecosystem through the Politics of Trees.* John, a nationally recognized biologist, will take you on an odyssey of his four decades of Alaskan field research and advocacy to protect the rich ecosystem of one of the world's last temperate rainforests, the Tongass National Forest. His studies show how the engine for this amazing ecosystem is the relatively rare portion of big old-growth trees in our largest national forest. This is the primary habitat for brown bears, black bears, black-tailed deer, abundant birds, and wild spawning salmon. This old-growth forest has been and continues to be the target of clear-cutting by the timber industry. John demonstrates that the application of science and facts provide the tools for conserving this extraordinary treasure. Take the journey with John on a science thriller. You'll be glad you did.

TONY KNOWLES, Governor of Alaska 1994–2002; Pew Oceans Commission 2000–2003; Chair of National Parks Advisory Board 2009–2017

John Schoen, it turns out, is not just a pioneering Alaska wildlife researcher and a lifelong advocate for science-based conservation. With the soul of a poet, he is a clear-eyed and engaging storyteller. *Tongass Odyssey* is conservation history at its best, told with honesty and insight by someone who participated in a half-century of scientific discovery and resource policy-making. It should be adopted as an essential text for informing future decisions about the Tongass, forest management, wildlife conservation, and sustainable living in a world facing increasing limits and losses.

NANCY LORD, former Alaska writer laureate and author of
Fishcamp, Green Alaska, and *Early Warming*

WOW! I was absolutely amazed at the amount of research John and his colleagues have done and gathered about the animals and their environment in the Tongass National Forest and elsewhere in Alaska. It is a wonderful example of how the continued efforts of dedicated people can make a big difference. His writing at a personal level and the inclusion of his family and friends make it easy and fun to read. And having what is known about the Tongass well documented and in one place is great.

BOB ARMSTRONG, Alaskan biologist, writer, and photographer,
author of *Birds of Alaska*

John Schoen has hit it out of the park with his memoir, which manages to be three books in one. It is a lively recollection of a life well-lived, beaming a gritty spotlight on Southeast Alaska over more than four decades. It is a swashbuckling yet humble account of beauty and joy in scientific fieldwork during a golden age of wildlife ecology. And it is a principled, informed rumination on how evidence can help drive public policy, decisions, and local and global well-being. Schoen's voice is a gift, and we should heed it.

DAVID L. SECORD, PhD, Barnacle Strategies Consulting;
Affiliate Faculty, University of Washington; Adjunct Faculty,
Simon Fraser University

TONGASS ODYSSEY

TONGASS ODYSSEY

Seeing the Forest Ecosystem through the Politics of Trees

A BIOLOGIST'S MEMOIR

John Schoen

UNIVERSITY OF ALASKA PRESS FAIRBANKS

Text © 2020 University of Alaska Press
Published by
University of Alaska Press
P.O. Box 756240
Fairbanks, AK 99775-6240

Cover and interior design by Kristina Kachele Design, llc.

Library of Congress Cataloging-in-Publication Data
Names: Schoen, John W., author.
Title: Tongass odyssey : seeing the forest ecosystem through the politics
of trees : a biologist's memoir / John Schoen.
Description: Fairbanks, AK : University of Alaska Press, [2020] |
Includes bibliographical references and index.
Identifiers: LCCN 2019058800 (print) | LCCN 2019058801 (ebook) |
ISBN 9781602234260 (paperback) | ISBN 9781602234277 (ebook)
Subjects: LCSH: Schoen, John W. | Alaska. Department of Fish and
Game—Officials and employees—Biography. | Audubon Alaska—Officials
and employees—Biography. | Ecologists—United States—Biography. |
Forest ecology—Research—Alaska—Tongass National Forest. | Forest
conservation—Alaska—Tongass National Forest—History. | Environmental
protection—Alaska—Tongass National Forest—History. | Tongass National
Forest (Alaska)—History. | Tongass National Forest
(Alaska)—Environmental conditions.
Classification: LCC QH31.S36 S36 2020 (print) | LCC QH31.S36 (ebook) |
DDC 577.309798/2—dc23
LC record available at https://lccn.loc.gov/2019058800
LC ebook record available at https://lccn.loc.gov/2019058801

Contents

For Our Grandchildren

For millennia, the Earth has provided people with life-giving resources. But the Earth's resources are finite. There are few places left in the world today where large, intact ecosystems still function with all their natural parts much as they did centuries ago. Alaska is one of those places where we still have the opportunity to apply our knowledge and science to ensure that future generations can also use and enjoy these natural treasures. It is our responsibility as good stewards not to let short-term economic gain foreclose our ability to maintain the long-term sustainability and integrity of our natural ecosystems. History will judge us on how well we exercised wisdom, generosity, and restraint to endow our grandchildren with their rightful natural heritage.

Foreword

The subtitle of this book describes it as a memoir. It is that, and an inspiring one. The timeline tracks a boy as he grows up exploring the outdoors, a youth eager to discover more about how nature works, a student focusing his skills to earn advanced degrees in biology, and a man pursuing a career of exciting field research amid the grandeur of Southeast Alaska. Yet as soon as we begin traveling through that setting's old-growth temperate rainforests alongside Dr. John Schoen, *Tongass Odyssey* turns into much more than a memoir. It becomes a story about the fate of one of the wildest, biologically richest, and rarest ecosystems on Earth.

Alaska has more miles of marine coastline than all the rest of the United States combined. A large proportion of those miles are concentrated in the state's Panhandle—a mix of more than a thousand islands, steep mainland mountainsides, great glaciers, and countless rivers, streams, inlets, and estuaries. This is one rugged jumble of country. Working as a wildlife biologist for the Alaska Department of Fish and Game, Schoen covered an impressive amount of it on foot with a lot of bushwhacking; by water, navigating through fogbanks and often unruly seas (he's a boat skipper); and by air (he's a licensed plane pilot as well), surveying habitats and tracking radio-collared animals from an eagle's perspective and using beaches for remote landing strips.

About 80 percent of Southeast Alaska lies within the Tongass National Forest, the largest national forest in America. During the modern era, old-growth temperate woodlands of almost every kind have become scarce. Old-growth temperate rainforests were uncommon to begin with. The largest remaining stronghold for this type of ecosystem grows along the western edge of North America, primarily in northern British Columbia and Alaska's Panhandle. While seals, sea lions, orcas, humpback whales, and gray whales swim close to the shores, tremendous numbers of Pacific salmon surge up the Tongass waterways past mossy, lichen-draped cedars, hemlocks, and spruce 600 to more than a thousand years old. These spawning fish nourish some of the densest populations of brown/grizzly bears ever documented. In fact, it was Schoen who carried out that documentation for several areas, most notably on Admiralty Island, called Kootznoowoo—Fortress of the Bears—by the native Tlingit people. The old-growth habitats are important as well to black-tailed deer, coastal wolves, bald eagles, marbled murrelets, and even coastal populations of mountain goats at different times of the year.

We follow the author onward as he builds a home in the region at the ocean's edge, starts a family, and shares his knowledge of this special place with children of his own, coming full cycle. In the meantime, Schoen is also sharing what he learns with government policy-makers and the public at large. His studies were revealing serious problems for the forests' wild residents caused by the clear-cut logging, underway across the Tongass in grab-all-you-can-as-fast-as-you-can frontier fashion.

Powerful economic and political interests promoted this agenda of harvesting the old growth at unsustainably high levels. To carry it out, they had a staunch ally; namely, the US Forest Service. In principle, this federal agency has a mandate to maintain the natural values of a forest while also providing opportunities for recreation and resource extraction. In reality, Tongass officials measured success by the volume of timber produced from lands under their jurisdiction, and extraction had become their overwhelming priority. Year after year, they marked out concentrations of the biggest, oldest trees left as the prime targets for removal.

The extraordinary, decades-long effort Schoen and his colleagues made to try to improve management of this forest's living resources emerges as the book's unifying theme. I won't go into details of the struggle here. Schoen provides plenty. Yet he's a scientist through and through; he deals in facts. Put another way, you're not going to be bushwhacking through opinions and impassioned rhetoric in *Tongass Odyssey*. You're getting what builds into a fascinating, trustworthy case study of biopolitics—the intersection of wildlife biology and the social, economic, and governmental forces that mold the regulatory framework which in turn shapes the chances of survival for our fellow creatures.

Tongass Odyssey would be valuable reading for any student contemplating a career tied to wildlife and the natural environment. For that matter, it deserves to be read by every American. Yeah, I know; people who write forewords and reviews overuse that phrase. But I mean it this way: the Tongass literally belongs to every American citizen. Like all of this country's national forests, it is public land. We the People own the place. It's a priceless inheritance. With it comes a responsibility to pass along the beauty and vibrant communities of life this realm harbors to future generations. The least each of us can do is find out more about the Tongass. I hope you get to do that by visiting in person one day. In the meantime, read on.

DOUGLAS CHADWICK

Douglas Chadwick—conservationist, author, and biologist—has worked as a natural history journalist, producing 14 popular books and hundreds of magazine articles, many of them for the National Geographic Society, on subjects from snow leopards to great whales to grizzly bears in the Gobi desert.

Preface

As recently as the 1980s, scientists recognized that 85 to 95 percent of the original old-growth forests in the United States had been cut. In the early 1950s, when industrial-scale clear-cutting began in the Tongass National Forest in Southeast Alaska, many forest managers considered old growth to be a nearly infinite resource. Since 1980, scientists have learned a great deal about old-growth ecosystems and the many ecological and societal values they provide. As the extent of these forests declined across the United States, clear-cutting of old growth was curtailed in all national forests except the Tongass. The scientific consensus today is that clear-cutting old-growth forests should be ended on public lands in the United States. Yet, in 2019, the US Forest Service and State of Alaska began planning to significantly accelerate clear-cutting of the remaining high-value, old-growth stands across the Tongass National Forest.

My purpose in writing this book was to document my personal experience, beginning in 1977, conducting wildlife research and advocating for stronger conservation on the Tongass Forest. I also wanted to engage readers in exploring the unique and special ecology of the rainforest ecosystem in Southeast Alaska, and to promote understanding of why these ecosystems merit long-term conservation. Finally, I wanted to offer the Tongass National Forest as a cautionary case study of the harm that can result when science is eclipsed by politics and land management focuses on short-term economic gain.

Tongass Odyssey is a memoir of my personal journey working on the Tongass National Forest as a scientist and conservation practitioner. I have written numerous peer-reviewed scientific publications over my career. I purposely chose not to write this book as a scholarly work. Instead, I wanted to reach a broader audience than scientists and have attempted to share some of my memorable field experiences working in this wild and spectacular coastal rainforest. In that vein, *Tongass Odyssey* combines personal memoir, field journal, natural history, ecological theory, conservation essay, history, policy analysis, and philosophical reflection. I believe that for the general public to support the conservation of wildlife and the habitats upon which they depend, they must first have an interest in and general ecological understanding of these special places and how they are managed in the public interest. Although I endeavored to write this memoir for a general audience, I also grounded it in factual, evidence-based information.

Old-growth forest ecosystems have become exceedingly rare throughout the world. The coastal temperate rainforest of the Tongass represents a unique forest ecosystem that has global significance and provides many important values to society at large. At what point should public-land managers conserve the remaining old-growth forests from further degradation? This is the major question that I have tried to address in this book. In addition, I discuss the evolution of my early focus on species, shifting to ecosystems, and finally to the role of science (and scientists) in informing and shaping public policy. The Tongass Forest provides a contemporary example of the tension between science and the formulation of natural resource policy. We know what is required to conserve the remaining old-growth forests. The central question now is: Do we have the political will to do so?

Acknowledgments

I am grateful to my family for providing me with an incredible childhood growing up on an island surrounded by untrammeled nature. This gave me a lifelong interest in natural history as well as many important outdoor skills. A number of professors helped me develop my scientific skills and learn to ask good questions. In particular, I thank Arthur Rempel, Murray Johnson, Richard Taber, and Gordon Orians for their patience and mentoring.

During my twenty years working with the Alaska Department of Fish and Game, many colleagues both in and outside the department were instrumental in helping with my research and expanding our understanding of the ecology of the Tongass Forest. My supervisors, the area and habitat biologists in Southeast Alaska, and wildlife technicians were incredibly helpful in sharing their local knowledge and conservation insights. I particularly appreciate Paul Alaback, Dave Anderson, LaVern Beier, Rod Flynn, Jeff Hughes, Matt Kirchhoff, Doug Larsen, Jack Lentfer, Dave Person, Chris Smith, Lowell Suring, and Charlie Wallmo. I spent many memorable hours in the field with Matt, LaVern, and Charlie, and for the last four decades, Matt helped me critically assess Tongass research and conservation priorities.

All the staff at Audubon Alaska were valued conservation partners during my Audubon years. I am particularly grateful to Dave Cline, Susan Culliney, Bucky Dennerlein, Eric Myers, Pat Pourchot, Stan Senner, Melanie Smith, Ben Sullender, Nathan Walker, and Nils Warnock for their assistance, wisdom, and commitment to conservation. Dave Albert and Erin Dovichin at The Nature Conservancy were highly valued partners during our work on the Tongass Conservation Assessment. Many other people played important roles in improving conservation measures on the Tongass Forest. I particularly thank Bob Armstrong, David Banks, Anissa Berry-Frick, Tim Bristol, Richard Carstensen, Bob Christensen, Joseph Cook, Natalie Dawson, David Klein, Laurie Cooper, Dominick DellaSala, Rand Hagenstein, Russell Heath, Marilyn Heiman, Mark Kaelke, Steve Kallick, Wini Kessler, Bart Koehler, Stephen MacDonald, Brian McNitt, Jay Nelson, Richard Nelson, Dave Secord, Marilyn Sigman, John Sisk, Iain Stenhouse, Jim Stratton, Andrew Thoms, Marlyn Twitchell, Tom Waldo, and Mary Willson.

During my Audubon years, a number of funders generously supported our conservation work. These included the Alaska Conservation Foundation, Brainerd Foundation, Campion Foundation, William and Flora Hewlett Foundation, Leighty Foundation, Gordon and Betty Moore Foundation, David and Lucile Packard Foundation, Skaggs Foundation, State Wildlife Grants from the Alaska Department of Fish and Game, True North Foundation, Turner Foundation, and Wilburforce Foundation. Without their support, we could not have accomplished our important conservation work. And, finally, a big thank you to the Campion and Wilburforce Foundations for supporting the color printing of this book.

A number of people reviewed this manuscript and offered valuable editorial suggestions. Thank you to Paul Alaback, Dave Cline, Wini Kessler, Matt Kirchhoff, Bart and Julie Koehler, Sterling Miller, Mary Beth Schoen, Dave Secord, and Lowell Suring. Thanks to Nancy Lord for her valuable suggestions and to Carolyn Servid for editing the entire manuscript. Special thanks are due to the editorial staff at the University of Alaska Press, particularly Krista West, Rachel Fudge, and Kristina Kachele.

Finally, I would like to thank my wife, Mary Beth, for her wise counsel and incredible emotional support during the many ups and downs of scientific field research and dealing with the hard-ball political pressures inherent in conservation work. I am especially grateful for the patience and support that she and my children, Erik and Sarah, have provided me over these last four decades.

Photography by John Schoen. Wildlife photographs are from Southeast Alaska except for Figures 2.25, 2.41, 2.52, 2.72, 3.34, and 4.6 which were taken in Southcentral Alaska.

BECOMING A BIOLOGIST
(1947–1976)

INTRODUCTION

I have enjoyed living an outdoor life. I grew up on a rural island with a saltwater beach in my front yard and a hundred acres of forest and fields out back. All my life, my happiest times have been outdoors, where I'm surrounded by nature and open spaces. Watching a family of river otters swimming along the shore delights me. Listening to the cries of gulls as sunlight streams through a broken overcast after a hard rain refreshes my psyche. Following a game trail on an alpine ridge in the late afternoon while the sun slides slowly over the western horizon fills me with passion and hope for the future and gratitude for the magic of nature.

During my life, I have had the wonderful opportunity and good fortune to realize my dreams—dreams that began to take root more than seventy years ago and have been shaped by a lifetime of remarkable outdoor experiences and defining relationships with family, friends, and mentors. I liken the building of a life to building a fire. First you gather the fuel and construct a proper foundation, arrange your kindling, and carefully ignite your creation. As your fire grows, you must nurture it and stoke it with suitable fuel to keep it burning brightly.

The spark for my life was lit in a sailboat on sparkling blue waters somewhere in the Canadian Gulf Islands or American San Juans in July 1946. My parents, both from Seattle, were on their honeymoon on my father's thirty-two-foot cutter, *Chantey*. My mom had been a nursing student at the University of Washington and my dad had recently returned home from the war in the South Pacific, where he operated a Coast Guard tug. Although Dad was expected to join his brothers in running a family business in Seattle, that changed when my parents set anchor in Deer Harbor and fell in love with Orcas Island. My parents decided to chart a new course for their lives in these stunning but then isolated islands in northwestern Washington—much to their families' displeasure. With a business degree from the University of Washington, Dad took on a variety of jobs, from digging septic systems to cleaning salmon in the Deer Harbor Cannery. They first lived in a rented cabin in Eastsound. Dad had a pilot's license, and soon he passed his commercial pilot check ride, bought a 1946 Stinson Voyager, and started the first scheduled air service in the San Juan Islands.

THE EARLY YEARS

I was almost born on a US Coast Guard cutter between Orcas Island and the Anacortes Hospital on Washington's Fidalgo Island. Because the weather was particularly nasty that evening and Dad couldn't fly Mom to the hospital when her contractions started, he called the Coast Guard and they transported my mother to Anacortes. We got there in time, and I began my life in mid-April amid apple blossoms, daffodils, and wildflowers in a glorious island spring.

Growing up on a rural island is in itself a unique experience, and one that helped mold my childhood and adult life. Boats and airplanes were part of my life like bicycles and cars are for most American kids. I explored the beach at low tide with my brother, Steve, and our dog, Paddles, a slobbery springer spaniel (Fig. 1.1). We rolled over rocks and collected crabs, limpets, and chitons; prodded sea anemones; and pulled purple sea stars off the rocks and touched their hundreds of wriggling tube feet. We explored the forest behind our house and built forts and hidden trails through Douglas fir forests, thimbleberry bushes, and bracken ferns. Life was a never-ending series of explorations and new discoveries.

Professor E. O. Wilson of Harvard University says, "Hands on experience at the critical time, not systematic knowledge, is what counts in the making of a naturalist. Better to be an untutored savage for a while, not to know the names or anatomical detail. Better to spend long stretches of time just searching and dreaming."[1] My childhood certainly encompassed the hands-on experience of an "untutored savage." And I really don't ever remember being bored when I was a kid on the loose. I believe those early experiences were an essential part of my education that eventually led me to a career in wildlife biology.

My early life on Orcas was shared with a menagerie of animals, from dogs, goats, chickens, and ducks to cattle, sheep, and horses. From my earliest memories through high school, my ambition was to be a cowboy—and frankly

FIG. 1.1. My brother Steve and me exploring Orcas
Island's shoreline in our small skiff (ca 1957).

FIG. 1.2. With my horse Ginger at our home on
Orcas Island when I was about ten years old (ca 1957).

there are still moments when swinging into the
saddle and riding a trail into the sunset sounds
pretty appealing. I had a life-size poster of Roy
Rogers and his horse, Trigger, on the back of my
bedroom door, and according to my mother, there
was a time when I only answered to "Roy." An early
entrepreneur, I collected large butter clam shells at
low tide, bleached them, and sold them to tourists
at the Orcas ferry landing for a nickel. With that
money and what I was able to save from my meager
allowance, I bought my first horse for $90 when I
was nine. Ginger—an old gray mare of nondescript
heritage—added a new dimension to my island freedom and dreams of being
a cowboy (Fig. 1.2). We lived on an old 100-acre farm in West Sound at the end
of a mile-long road. My parents bought this place in 1948, built a small cabin
on it with an outhouse, then built our main house in 1955. We had an ancient
barn and fenced-in pasture that Ginger called home. With a horse, I was able to
explore more of the island. One of my favorite rides was up through the open

meadowlands of Turtleback Mountain overlooking the islands and waters of West Sound, Deer Harbor and Canada to the northwest.

I remember getting a Winchester Model 66 .22 caliber rifle for my tenth birthday. Expanding on my entrepreneurial spirit, I hunted rabbits, cleaned them, and sold them to our neighbors for a dollar apiece—clear evidence that even market hunters can, in time, turn into conservationists. Life was good. Of course, being a cowboy with a gun meant I also indulged in collecting a few birds on the side, even though my mother strongly objected. But perhaps that gave me the same kind of experience and enthusiasm for studying birds—close-up—that John James Audubon gained a century and a half earlier. Little did I know then that I would one day work as a scientist for the National Audubon Society.

My family always took vacations on our boat during the month of June. My folks would gather up my little brother Steve and me, load our food and gear onboard, and head north up the wild British Columbia coast. Our family cruises were real voyages of discovery and adventure. In some measure, our cruises were not unlike the coastal explorations of Cook and Vancouver— except I'm sure our bunks were softer and our food was orders of magnitude better. Without radar or GPS plotters, we explored new coves, hiked into lakes, fished and snorkeled for our dinner, and beachcombed to our hearts' content. In the 1950s and early '60s, there were few pleasure boats along the west coast of Vancouver Island, so we were truly on our own.

I have fond memories of getting under way early in the morning for big open-water crossings before the winds came up. Nestled cozy in my bunk, I could hear the rumble of the engine and the water burbling along the hull, and feel the gentle rhythm of the swell as our boat headed to a new anchorage with pristine beaches and forests to explore. In the evenings, at anchor in a quiet, secure cove, we would sit on the afterdeck and listen to the flute-like songs of hermit thrush and the trill of varied thrush drifting out of the forest and across calm waters. Wildlife watching was always a major goal of our daily adventures, and it was not uncommon to see bald eagles and common ravens in abundance as well as whales, harbor seals, and a variety of waterbirds. But our favorite sightings were furtive black bears that would unexpectedly appear grazing along tidal sedge meadows in the evenings and then melt back into the dark, concealing conifer forest.

Growing up on Orcas Island provided many wonderful experiences for a young boy (Fig. 1.3). Exploring beaches and roaming forests on my own, I learned about nature through trial and error. I also gained a good sense of direction out in the backcountry. But, at the same time, many common urban activities—such as using public transit, finding my way around big cities, or dealing with large crowds of strangers—were unfamiliar and even stressful experiences for me.

FIG. 1.3. Our family home in West Sound on Orcas Island in Washington's San Juan Islands (ca 1965).

Early on, my mother, concerned about my spiritual training, insisted that I attend Sunday school, and in the sixth or seventh grade I even served a short stint as an altar boy in the local Episcopal Church. However, these formal religious experiences were too stilted and unnatural to me. My most spiritual awareness was actually attained from my father. I recall a conversation we had one Sunday morning—I must have been around twelve—when I was helping Dad paint the bottom of our sailboat *Chantey* on a beach grid at low tide along the shore of West Sound. "John," he said looking around the bay, "this is my church—the beach, the forest, the ocean, and all that comes along with it. I don't need to attend an organized church service to feel a spiritual connection to the world." I have always remembered that fatherly sermon with great affection. My dad imparted to me a sense of spiritual awareness, a love of the outdoors, and a responsibility to be fair and honest. My mom instilled the principle of living by the Golden Rule and the importance of kindness. My dad also carried with him a love of life and a passion for living on Orcas Island and contributing positively to his community. His love of boats, knowledge of sailing, and skill as a pilot were gifts that he passed on to my brother and me in ways that we didn't clearly appreciate until much later in our lives.

How can a boy go to school when there is so much adventure and learning to be found on an island? That is a question I frequently pondered as I was growing up. I did well in school, when I paid attention. But paying attention was easier said than done. I remember the huge broad-leaf maple tree that was just outside the fifth-and-sixth-grade classroom at Nellie S. Milton Grade School in Eastsound. If I became bored with a subject, I would look out the window at that tree, the daydreams would overcome me, and any discussion sailed smoothly through one ear and out the other. Later, in college and graduate school, I would have to guard against such ingrained behavior when attending a dry and boring lecture.

I loved summer. The freedom and adventure of learning and exploring and just plain having fun was inextricably linked to summers on Orcas Island. I recall one evening walking up to the barn to feed my horse. I may have been in the seventh or eighth grade. It must have been around the first of September, and I could feel fall in the air. Tears came to my eyes as I knew that summer was over and, once again, I would become a reluctant prisoner of school.

During my early years, my maternal grandfather, Pop, played a big role in my life and had an early influence on my interest in cowboys and horses and hunting and fishing. He was from Butte, Montana, and had a horse and small farm outside of Seattle. He was an enthusiastic hunter and fisherman, and I can remember going camping with him and my grandmother, Nana. I recall one camping trip on the eastern slope of the Cascade Mountains. We camped in an old army wall tent and fished for trout, and I hunted chipmunks with my .22 rifle. That evening we enjoyed fish and chips (i.e., chipmunks) for dinner. Around that time, Pop gave me a bison skull from Montana. Inscribed on the front of the skull in black ink was "Nature writes with an invisible hand so that those who understand may read."

HIGH SCHOOL

Orcas Island High School was located in Eastsound—actually on the second floor of the same brick building as the grade school. There were about eighty-five students in the high school and eighteen in my graduating class of 1965. I still loved my summers, but school took on a new dimension. High school was pretty easy for me, and once again, when I paid attention, I did well. But it was sports—the teamwork and competition—that really captured my inter-est. Orcas High was a small school by Washington standards. We fielded teams in just three sports—football, basketball, and track—and I participated in all three. In a small school, if you wanted to play, you made the team. If you worked at it and trained hard, you could even work up to being a starter on the varsity team. My freshman year, I started as an offensive center and middle linebacker on our eight-man football team. Yep, eight-man—no tackles or fullback—but this was tackle football, and we played just as hard as any eleven-man team, and in those days, we played both offense and defense. It's amazing how quickly you adapt and learn when you are on an offensive line against older kids fifty pounds heavier than you are. Once football came to an end in October, it was time for basketball. I played guard and was a defensive specialist. I contin-ued playing basketball into my early fifties, when my knees and surgeries said it was time to move on. Our team success in high school football and basketball was average overall, but we won some big games and the value of teamwork has stood me well throughout my life. I look back at my experiences and friend-ships going to school on Orcas Island with the fondest of memories.

I also recall an ironic "political" experience my sophomore year in high school. One noon while we were milling around the halls during our break, someone pushed a heavy roll of construction material down the stairs. It crashed into the wall and did some damage. The superintendent was very angry and wanted the students to come forth with the name of the perpetrator. No one came forward, so our big school dance was canceled. We thought it was unfair to penalize the entire student body. Several of us called a student assembly, and nearly eighty students politely raised our grievance with the superintendent. I was taking biology at the time, and our biology teacher—a retired career military man—came into the room and ordered his students back to class. He called me by name, but I stayed, along with most of my classmates. In retribution, the biology teacher gave a pop quiz worth 200 points, and those who missed it failed biology that quarter. I can proudly say I overcame that F in high school biology to later become a professional biologist. I also learned that sometimes standing up for your principles can be costly. But I don't regret my actions.

Growing up in a small community has both advantages and disadvantages. I knew everyone on Orcas Island in the 1960s and, of course, they also knew me and all the things I did—both good and bad. Orcas was typical of many small rural communities. It had a very conservative perspective, politically, as did my family. The community was very homogeneous, and all problems had simple black-and-white solutions. This was the sociopolitical context that I grew up with, and many of my early political perspectives were challenged later in college and graduate school.

COLLEGE

In late summer of 1965, I left my island home and headed east across the Cascade Mountains and Columbia River to Whitman College, a small liberal arts college on the edge of rolling wheat fields in Walla Walla, Washington. College opened a whole new world of challenges, launched me on my life's work, and also connected me with my life partner and best friend.

FIG. 1.4.
I played football at Whitman College for two and a half years until knee surgery forced me to give it up in 1967.

I arrived at Whitman in August prior to classes to participate in early football practice (Fig. 1.4). It was there, lying on a small bunk in the football dorm—attempting to regain my strength and hydration between daily double practices in 100-degree heat—that I realized what a unique and incredible childhood I had had growing up on Orcas Island. But at that time, my primary goal was simply to survive what was probably the closest thing to boot camp I would ever endure. I enjoyed playing small-college football until knee surgery ended my football career during my junior year. The physical discipline and teamwork I experienced, as well as the friendships I developed, remain an important part of my college experience.

It is no exaggeration to say that my freshman year was a significant wakeup call. School had always been easy for me, but Whitman was a new ballgame. All the students were bright and most worked hard. In my first semester, I became abruptly aware that my high school preparation left much to be desired. Initially I thought I would be an economics major, but after earning an unglamorous D in economics, I adroitly adjusted my academic path. Biology was my best subject and the most interesting, so a biology major I became.

At Whitman, we studied a classical biology curriculum, including core classes of biology, zoology, botany, comparative anatomy, vertebrate embryology, cell physiology, and chemistry. The majority of biology majors were on a premed track and, as a result, competition for grades was intense. I was not interested in medicine and was not sure where biology would take me, but I knew it would lead to brighter horizons than economics. Then, in my sophomore year, I enrolled in a marine biology class. We spent much of the semester studying the classic book *Between Pacific Tides* by Ed Ricketts—an old pal of John Steinbeck—and Jack Calvin, a conservationist from Sitka, Alaska. During spring break, we headed to a field station at Deception Pass on the Washington coast for a week of collecting marine invertebrates and classifying and studying them in the lab. We worked hard and combined fieldwork, lab work, and evening campfires on the beach. Now, this was more like it. I did well in this class and absolutely loved the combination of outdoor adventure, scientific discovery, and camaraderie drinking beer around the campfire—consumed in the spirit of Doc (real-life Ed Ricketts) from Steinbeck's classic novel *Cannery Row*.

During my junior year, I worked hard in comparative anatomy, vertebrate embryology, and organic chemistry. Then, in the spring of my senior year, I enrolled in natural history of the vertebrates, taught by revered professor Dr. Arthur Rempel. We studied the taxonomy and natural history of freshwater fish, amphibians, reptiles, birds, and mammals of the Pacific Northwest. Every Saturday morning, we went on a field trip—mostly birding. In this class, we were required to collect and make museum specimens of ten different mammal species. I loved this class and poured my heart and soul into it. We would take off at first light in an old ten-passenger limo. Dr. Rempel drove while spotting and identifying a variety of birds and other wildlife as we lumbered down the back roads of southeastern Washington. It was astounding what he could spot at great distances while still driving us in reasonable safety on our wildlife odyssey.

Most of our mammal collecting was by trapping small mammals like shrews, voles, deer mice, and ground squirrels. This was hard work, but it's amazing what you can learn about an animal's habits and habitats when you actually try to catch them. There were only eight of us in the class, and the one-on-one transfer of information from Dr. Rempel to his students was extraordinary. If someone was late for our field trip, Dr. Rempel would call their dorm, worried that they might be deathly ill. It didn't occur to him that a late Friday-night party might necessitate a few extra hours of sleep on a Saturday morning.

Although I enjoyed my biology classes, particularly the few field classes that were offered, I still had no idea what I would actually do with a biology degree when I graduated. I recall watching a *National Geographic* television program with a few of my buddies in the spring of my senior year. The show was about the Craighead brothers' grizzly bear research in Yellowstone National Park. When the show was over, I knew what I was going to do. I was going to be a wildlife biologist and explore the wilderness by airplane and boat. Little did I know that seventeen years later I would be starting my own grizzly bear study on Admiralty Island in Southeast Alaska, where airplanes and boats were important tools of our wildlife research. A few years after that, I even participated in a National Geographic grizzly bear film. I was also invited back to Whitman in 1990 to present that year's Arthur G. Rempel Lecture on Wildlife of Alaska's Coastal Rainforest. Dr. Rempel was a great inspiration to me; during my bear research he actually visited our home and I was able to take him into the field on my research project when he was in his eighties.

FIG. 1.5. My college sweetheart, Mary Beth Lewis, and me in the San Juan Islands (ca 1969).

My four years at Whitman College were transformative. This small liberal arts college opened my eyes to the larger world and to a host of new and challenging ideas and ways of looking at the world. I made lifelong friends at Whitman, and my education was equally divided between classroom courses and discussions with my peers. This was a challenging time, and Whitman helped me learn how to think for myself. In contrast to my simple life on Orcas Island, I also began to understand that most issues involving politics and personal relationships were often more gray than black-and-white.

Of course, it would be impossible to leave my college years behind without describing the most significant consequence of my college career. It was fall of my senior year when Mary Beth Lewis walked into the library and asked me out to a sorority function. Mary Beth was a sophomore and a year younger, but had finished high school in Vienna, Austria, and then spent an extra year in Geneva before starting college. And she was smart, beautiful, and enthusiastic, and she loved the outdoors. We spent a lot of time together my senior year and built a friendship based on a shared philosophy of life that has been growing stronger each year for over fifty years (Fig. 1.5).

EDUCATION BEYOND THE CLASSROOM

Now that I knew what I was going to do, I realized graduate school was a necessity—heaven forbid. I could hardly believe that the same guy who found elementary school such a pain in the ass was actually going to extend his academic endeavors. But before I head down that trail, I need to catch up on a few more details regarding the rest of my education that would be so important to my later work as an Alaska biologist.

FIG. 1.6. With my 1947 Stinson Voyager in the foothills of the Blue Mountains in Eastern Washington (ca 1969).

I literally grew up on and around boats. My dad was a skilled sailor and taught both Steve and me to sail. Our family vacations centered around cruising the British Columbia coast in sailboats and workboats. We learned to tie knots, read charts, navigate, and find protected anchorages. Growing up on Orcas, I learned to handle a variety of boats (from small outboards and forty-foot sailboats to sixty-foot workboats). In my first graduate program, I used boats for transportation during my field research.

When I was sixteen, my dad started teaching me to fly in a two-seat Aeronca Champ with a joystick. I built up a few hours, but just before I was going to solo, I got sidetracked with high school sports and other school activities. It wasn't until the summer of 1966, when I came home after my first year of college, that I realized I definitely wanted to be a pilot. My dad started me flying again in our 1947 Stinson Voyager. Now I was committed, and that summer and fall I followed through with enthusiasm. I remember my solo flight out of the Eastsound airfield on Orcas Island on a calm, sunny day in the middle of July. We had been practicing touch-and-go landings, and Dad told me to pull off at the end of the runway. Dad got out, shook my hand, and said, "You're ready—it's all yours." Wow, I knew I was ready, but this was the real deal. I taxied back, made a clearing turn to check traffic, then poured the coal to her, rolled down the runway, and gently lifted off. What an incredible feeling of freedom and accomplishment. I was jazzed. Flying has been part of my life ever since (Fig. 1.6).

Because I had flown with my dad in small planes—"puddle jumpers" he called them—all my life, I had virtually no fear of the air. This emotion was soon to change to deep respect. On July 31 of that same summer, with about nineteen hours of flight time under my belt, I was flying solo and practicing simulated emergency landings over Lopez Island. I was climbing up through four hundred feet when, all of a sudden, there was total quiet. This was not a good sign. At that low altitude, everything happens quickly because the plane is now a glider. It was headed toward the ground—fast. I was forced to do a real emergency landing in a cow pasture next to an apple orchard. I was fine, but the landing gear of our old Stinson took a bit of a beating. A local farmer drove over and picked me up, and I called Dad on Orcas. The first thing he said was, "Are you OK?" This airplane was his pride and joy, but his concern was exclusively focused on me. I'll always remember where he set his priorities and how important that was to me. He flew to Lopez within the hour in a borrowed plane and put me in the left seat and had me fly it back to Orcas. These were life lessons. When you fall off, get back into the saddle and carry on. That one incident absolutely changed my attitude about flying. I went on to complete my pilot training and received my FAA check ride in November of that year. I now have a deep-seated respect for the inherent risk of flight, and to this day—with a commercial license, an instrument rating, and 3,600 accident-free hours logged, mostly in Alaska—I always know where I'll put the plane down in case of an emergency. Being prepared and keeping your options open is a great rule to live by.

Operating boats and planes became essential tools in my career as an Alaska wildlife biologist. Other outside-the-classroom education was essential as well. That included raising animals, hunting, backcountry hiking and camping, exploring nature, scuba diving, and learning the value of teamwork. All of these experiences have been critical in my education, personal growth, and success as a field biologist.

POSTGRAD

After graduation from Whitman, I hitchhiked around Europe for a month. As luck would have it, Mary Beth and her family were in Vienna, and I ended up staying with them for another month. Arriving back home near the height of the Vietnam War, and having a low draft number, I faced the certainty of getting drafted. I looked carefully at my options: entering a five-year Navy flight program, enlisting in the Army for three years, or getting drafted. At that point, I knew I wanted to pursue my interest in biology. A Navy flight program—in which I had been accepted—would be too long a wait. Instead of getting drafted, I enlisted in Army intelligence. Somehow, I had the naïve impression I would be learning new languages, wearing street clothes, and driving around Europe in a sportscar. While being processed at the Army induction center in Seattle in the fall of 1969, the Army determined I was physically unfit for military duty because of a congenital back defect. This ailment has literally

FIG. 1.7. Mary Beth and me in the summer of 1970 in front of the Columbia Glacier in Prince William Sound. This was our first trip to Alaska, and we knew we would come back.

been a pain in my back for over fifty years, but the military's acknowledgment of it clearly changed the course of my life and limited my military experience to an x-ray, a ham sandwich, and a friendly chat with an Army sergeant.

Free now to pursue another path, I worked in Walla Walla for a short stint, and coincidentally continued my budding relationship with Mary Beth, who was still in school. Later that fall, I moved back to Orcas and went to work for the Orcas Power & Light Cooperative while commuting over the mountains to Whitman on weekends. Mary Beth and I were engaged that spring.

In late spring of 1970, I met a wildlife photographer from Victoria, British Columbia, and signed on to be his assistant on a wildlife photography expedition to Alaska (Fig. 1.7). Mary Beth had planned to go to summer school at the University of Washington and then finish her degree at Whitman in December, at which point we planned to be married. However, before I left for Alaska, she came to Victoria to say goodbye. Much to our surprise, the photographer and his wife suggested Mary Beth come along on our photo expedition. Delighted, we both decided this was a capital idea. We took the ferry back to Orcas, informed my parents, and called Mary Beth's folks in Vienna—about three in the morning their time—with our news. Although it made complete sense to us, I think both sets of parents were less than thrilled but not necessarily surprised. We would go to Alaska for the summer and come back and get married at the end of summer at the University of Puget Sound, where I would start graduate school to work on my master's in biology and Mary Beth would finish her last year of college.

Traveling the Alaska Highway from Vancouver to Valdez is a long trip. But this was our first trip to Alaska, and we were psyched. We worked long, hard days traveling, hiking, camping, carrying tripods, and doing the photographer's bidding. We carried two Avon rafts and outboard motors on our crew cab truck. We launched the rafts in Valdez and explored Prince William Sound for a couple of weeks—it rained every day. I recall waking up in the early morning camped on a gravel beach in front of the Columbia Glacier listening to the explosive cracking sounds as ice broke off the glacier and plunged into the sea. This country was big and it was wild, and we loved it.

Mary Beth and I were in a twelve-foot raft with a twenty-five-horsepower outboard. To say that this was minimal equipment for Prince William Sound would be an understatement. One evening we were headed out the sound to Hinchinbrook Island. The skies were dirty, dishwater gray with hard rain coming at us sideways as the wind strengthened from the southeast. Growing up on boats, I could recognize a bad situation developing. As the waves started building, I told our expedition leader that we damn well needed to find some shelter. We got to Hinchinbrook after dark, pulled our rafts above the tideline, and set up our tents to spend a cold, wet, and windy evening on the wild Alaska coast. The next morning, we traveled on to Cordova, where the photographers left us to travel south on a Canadian research vessel. Mary Beth and I headed back up the sound to Valdez, stopping nearly every half hour or so to blow water out of our fuel line. We were delighted and thankful to reach Valdez, wet and tired, but basically safe and ready for our return trip down the Alcan to Victoria and then on to Orcas Island. Our first trip to Alaska nearly fifty years ago clearly whet our appetite for the wildlife and wildlands of the far north, and we knew we would come back for more.

MARRIAGE AND GRADUATE SCHOOL

Mary Beth and I were married in September 1970, and we both began classes at the University of Puget Sound (UPS), she to finish the last year of her bachelor's degree in sociology while I began a two-year master's degree in biology. My course work included more chemistry, microbiology, and my most interesting classes of mammalogy, ornithology, and ecology. My thesis research was an investigation of the distribution and colonization of native land mammals in the San Juan Archipelago. The project was greatly facilitated by an invitation to skipper a forty-eight-foot sailboat at Camp Nor'Wester, a summer camp on Lopez Island (Fig. 1.8).

FIG. 1.8. Mary Beth and I skippered the *Katie Ford* for Camp Nor'Wester on Lopez Island in the San Juan Islands the first summer we were married. We used this boat to teach natural history and conduct field research for my master's degree on the mammals of the San Juan Islands (ca 1971).

Mary Beth and I signed on as naturalists and used the boat as our research vessel and educational platform for sharing our knowledge of natural history with kids ranging from eight to sixteen years of age. On our cruises, we helped the kids discover the beaches and forests of the San Juan Islands. We also laid out traplines for small mammals, and I began collecting deer mice, meadow voles, and shrews for my master's research. As a group, ten-year-old boys were really game for exploring the shorelines and forests, unfazed by the typical teen pressure to be cool.

Dr. Murray Johnson was the chairman of my graduate committee at UPS. A thoracic surgeon, he was also an internationally respected mammalogist. Dr. Johnson became a good friend and patiently helped me learn technical writing. I also benefited personally from his unbridled enthusiasm for fieldwork and exploratory research, and his skill at building relationships with colleagues. He was an important mentor in my professional and personal development. I have never heard a negative comment about Murray Johnson. He was revered and respected by everyone who ever knew him. Under his guidance, my graduate work at UPS expanded my biology vocabulary beyond taxonomy, anatomy, and memorizing scientific names to learning about more advanced ecological theories like island biogeography.

With a master's degree under my belt, I once again violated my inclination of avoiding more school and started a PhD program in the College of Forest Resources at the University of Washington in Seattle. Dr. Richard Taber was the chairman of my dissertation committee and was, for nearly forty years, a valued mentor, colleague, and close personal friend. When I started at UW, there was interest and money to study the growing population of Rocky Mountain elk that had been introduced forty years earlier on the western slope of Washington's Cascade Mountains. My study area was the Cedar River Watershed, Seattle's major water supply. We were interested in learning about the habitat use and seasonal distribution of elk, and how they were affected by forest management. We planned to put radio collars on elk and follow their movements throughout the year. Dr. Taber said, "John, it's pretty simple: just go out and capture some elk, fit them with radio collars, and let them show you how they make their living." OK. With Mary Beth's help and Dr. Johnson's guidance, I had become proficient at capturing deer mice and voles. I figured that since elk were forest mammals—but just a little bit bigger—this should be a piece of cake (Fig. 1.9).

Elk, not surprisingly, are not as easy to catch—or handle—as deer mice. I searched the scientific literature and found plans for an elk trap that was developed in the Rocky Mountains. Recruiting some undergrad assistants, I built a wooden corral trap and baited it with alfalfa hay and a touch of molasses for good measure. About a week after setting the trap, I captured my first elk. I snuck up on the trap, stuck my capture gun through the slats, and darted her

FIG. 1.9. Putting a radio collar and ear tags on a captured elk in the Cedar River Watershed of the Washington Cascades as part of my PhD research at the University of Washington (ca 1973).

in the rump with an immobilizing drug (M99). When she started to get groggy, I opened the door and slipped in. Suddenly, I had an *oh no!* moment. When an elk heads your way at a dead run from thirty feet away, it's fight or flight. I dropped my gear, aggressively threw my arms up, jumped forward, and yelled. She stopped. Next I tried to scale the corral, but it was too high. One of my colleagues opened the door, and I squeezed out. Then, we prudently waited for the drug to really take effect and finally outfitted our first research subject with the instruments that would provide the data we needed. It turned out this huge elk that literally put fear in my belly was a relatively small yearling cow. But she sure looked big with her head down and ears back, charging me at a gallop.

As it turns out, most of our research elk were captured by driving around the extensive network of logging roads in the watershed—which was closed to public access—and darting them from our university van. From 1973 to 1975, we captured fifty-three elk in the Cedar River Watershed. During that time, Mary Beth and I hiked and skied in pursuit of our quarry, observing hundreds of elk and deer, as well as cougars, bobcats, coyotes, black bears, and other wildlife.

One crisp fall afternoon, we had an interesting experience when we darted a large bull. After tracking it back into the woods, we found it lying down immobile. I wanted to keep it quiet and relaxed while we worked on it—drawing blood for analysis, extracting a small tooth for aging, taking a variety of body measurements, and fitting it with a radio collar—so I covered its eyes with my favorite Cowichan Indian sweater. When I gave it the antidote to reverse the effects of the immobilizing drug, this large bull with a massive rack of antlers got up and charged off before I was able to retrieve my sweater. This big bull was really stinky because it was the fall rutting season. By the time my sweater fell, he had rolled and urinated on it. During the autumn rut, bull elk pee in a wallow and roll in the wallow presumably to better attract cows. Later, when I wore that sweater around campus, I imagined receiving admiring looks from my female classmates. Mary Beth, however, assured me that this was entirely my warped imagination. She declared that white wine and candles were much more romantic.

The fieldwork for my PhD was exciting and rewarding. Classroom work, studying for my comprehensive exams, analyzing data, and writing my dissertation was far more challenging and burdensome. My time at the University of Washington was a valuable part of my academic experience and professional growth. Dick Taber was a great committee chair. He gave me much independence but was there when I needed advice and guidance. I recall a time midway through my studies when I was frustrated with the bureaucracy and academic pretentiousness of grad school. Dick calmly told me a story, and said if you want to have influence on things you care about, you need to have either lots of money, political power, or knowledge. He suggested I should endure the academic BS, get my union card, and then go out and make a difference. After some reflection, I took his advice and never regretted it.

Dick and his lovely wife, Pat, became good friends. They hosted wonderful grad student parties and provided us all a sense of community and family. Dick helped me tremendously with my writing and scientific approach to solving wildlife problems. He also had a great wit and sense of humor. We remained friends and stayed in touch after graduate school. He contributed much to our profession, and I know his grad students all hold him in the highest esteem. As I was finishing my PhD, Dick asked me if I would be interested in doing a postdoc under him at UW. I declined without a second thought. I was ready to get out in the real world, get my hands dirty, and get on with my life outside academia.

Another memorable University of Washington professor was Gordon Orians. His advanced ecology course still sticks in my mind. Although I had taken an ecology class at UPS, Gordon's class was much more theoretical, and our reading list consisted of key papers dealing with cutting-edge ecological theory. Gordon's class opened up a new way of thinking about ecology and the evolutionary theory driving the patterns and processes we observe throughout the natural world. One of the things I recall about Gordon was his remarkable, wide-ranging knowledge of natural history and field biology, and how he integrated this into his lectures on ecological theory. It was both inspiring and humbling.

In the fall of 1976, I made one final trip to the computer center to grab my last data analysis. Then Mary Beth and I headed to the Seattle Ferry Terminal in our 1969 Ford pickup truck jam-packed with most of our worldly possessions, and boarded the ferry bound for Haines, Alaska. From Haines, we drove north through stunning fall colors to Anchorage, where I started a new job with the Alaska Department of Fish and Game. It was only a temporary job, but I had confidence that this would be a valuable foot in the door for acquiring a permanent position. Thus, we took our chances for the opportunity to get back to Alaska and begin our new life in the far north. That winter, I worked at Fish and Game during the day and finished writing my dissertation during the evenings and weekends. I successfully defended my dissertation the next spring. In April 1977, we moved to Juneau, where I started a new job with the Alaska Department of Fish and Game as a research wildlife biologist studying deer and mountain goats in the rainforests of Southeast Alaska.

TONGASS FIELD RESEARCH
(ALASKA DEPARTMENT OF FISH & GAME 1977–1996)

MY INTRODUCTION TO THE TONGASS

It was June 1, 1977, and we were flying under a heavy, gray overcast through scattered showers in a de Havilland Beaver floatplane over the north end of Admiralty Island in Southeast Alaska. This was my first field trip to Admiralty since I had moved to Juneau in mid-April to take a newly established permanent position with the Alaska Department of Fish and Game (ADF&G) as their research wildlife biologist. I was hired specifically to study the effects of logging on Sitka black-tailed deer in the temperate rainforests of Alaska's Panhandle—locally known as Southeast.

My colleagues and companions were Dr. O. C. (Charlie) Wallmo and Gordon Fisch from the US Forest Service's Juneau Forestry Sciences Lab. We three immediately hit it off and became scientific colleagues in a collaborative research investigation of Alaska's diminutive black-tailed deer—the northernmost subspecies of North America's mule deer. Working together with Charlie and Gordon my first few years in Juneau was a valuable learning opportunity as well as downright fun.

⚜

Charlie was an internationally recognized deer biologist with the research branch of the Forest Service, and he was the editor and major author of a new book, *Mule and Black-tailed Deer of North America*.[1] Early in his academic career, Charlie had studied under Aldo Leopold—considered by many to be the founder of wildlife biology—and his conservation ethic clearly reflected

FIG. 2.1. Charlie Wallmo, research scientist at the US Forest Service, was my colleague in my early deer research in Southeast Alaska.

Leopold's influence. Charlie had arrived in Juneau about a year earlier from the Rocky Mountain Research Station in Fort Collins, Colorado. He was of medium build, gray-haired, and in his early sixties. He was very fit, had an extraordinary intellect with a heavy dose of scientist's skepticism, and a bright twinkle in his eye. His personality teemed with enthusiasm and camaraderie (Fig. 2.1). Those were early years in my career as an Alaska wildlife biologist; I was still maturing and developing my personal code of ethics. Charlie was an important guide and mentor, and he and his wife, Lela, became close family friends. Later, after Charlie left Alaska, I continued to value his advice and professional "compass" as our research results stirred up strong currents of political pressure.

Our flight that day took us through Hawk Inlet, over an old abandoned cannery perched on wooden pilings, and down the heavily forested west side of Admiralty Island. Chichagof and Baranof Islands lay nestled beneath low clouds seven miles west across Chatham Strait. Admiralty, Chichagof, and Baranof—often referred to as the ABC Islands—are inhabited by deer and brown bears as well as other smaller mammals. Wolves and black bears, however, are absent on these northern islands. They instead inhabit the southern islands, where brown bears are absent.

Southeast Alaska's Alexander Archipelago encompasses over 5,000 islands and about 18,000 miles of irregular shoreline and glacial fjords. Its unique island biogeography reflects the dynamic geological and glacial history of this northern temperate rainforest. For example, the retreat of coastal glaciers and sea level rise have created barriers to the dispersal of many plants and animals, isolating some species and subspecies and altering their evolutionary trajectories. This has resulted in many interesting differences in the colonization and distribution of species on individual islands of the archipelago, which are spread like a jigsaw puzzle along the coast of Southeast Alaska (Fig. 2.2).[2]

Off the left side of the floatplane, we watched thickly forested slopes and the ragged canopy of their ancient, old-growth trees disappear into the gray overcast a few hundred feet above us. Snow-covered mountains over 3,500 feet above sea level climbed through a veil of steel-gray clouds. Admiralty Island was named by Captain George Vancouver in 1794 during his explorations of the North Pacific Coast, but the indigenous Tlingit Indians who have lived

Topography

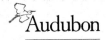

Southeast Alaska is naturally fragmented by islands and steep glacial terrain. The complex, high-relief topography is a product of intense mountain building energies generated at the suture zone of the North American and Pacific crustal plates. Glacial fjords and major river systems dissect the mountainous mainland region. The Coast Mountains form the eastern border of the state's panhandle with peaks that rise to about 5,000–9,000 feet. On the mainland west of Glacier Bay is the Fairweather Range, the tallest coastal mountains in the world. Mount Fairweather rises from sea level to over 15,000 ft in the span of only 12 miles. Across the region the action of past glaciation can be seen in the u-shaped valleys and steep-walled coastal fjords.

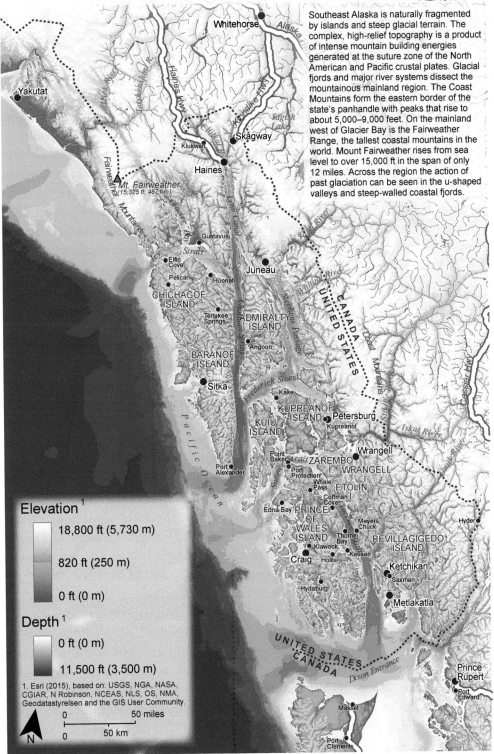

FIG. 2.2. Topographic map of Southeast Alaska and the Alexander Archipelago (courtesy Audubon Alaska 2016, *Ecological Atlas of Southeast Alaska*).

here continuously for 10,000 years call it *Kootznoowoo*—roughly translated as "Fortress of the Bear." About one hundred miles long and twenty-five miles wide, Admiralty encompasses over a million acres and supports some of the highest-density brown bear and nesting bald eagle populations on Earth. About halfway down the island we passed Kootznahoo Inlet and the ancient but still occupied Tlingit village of Angoon. A few miles farther south, we turned left into the mouth of Hood Bay and the destination of our exploratory expedition, where ADF&G had a research cabin (Fig. 2.3).

I vividly remember flying into the south arm of Hood Bay that morning. As we flew up the bay, we saw a small pod of humpback whales, likely feeding on dense schools of Pacific herring. Throughout the upper canopy of the shoreline's forest fringe, white spots dotted the trees like Christmas ornaments. These bright beacons, scattered across a dark sea of green, were the white heads of mature bald eagles perched on large, sturdy limbs of ancient Sitka spruce and western hemlock trees. As our pilot throttled back the big Pratt and Whitney engine and banked to the right, gently touching the floats down on the gray-rippled surface of the upper bay, I watched an eagle lift off the top of a spruce and glide along the shoreline. Then we taxied to a small gravel beach near the mouth of a clear creek. A trail along this creek led inland to our small research cabin.

Stepping off the floats onto the beach, we saw immense bear tracks imprinted in the soft intertidal mud. Farther down the beach, a pair of Vancouver Canada geese were grazing on newly emergent sedges near the upper tide line. We unloaded our gear, including sleeping bags, gas cans, an outboard motor, food, Scotch—the beverage of choice of both Charlie and Gordon—and other miscellaneous field supplies. Once all of our gear was stacked in the tall beach rye grass, the floatplane taxied out and took off down the bay toward Juneau about an hour away. As the steady rumble of its radial engine faded into the mist and scattered fog, a chorus of bird songs drifted out of the beach-fringe forest. We could hear the distant hooting of sooty grouse, the trill of varied thrushes, and the lyrical songs of hermit thrushes—one of my favorite melodies. And everywhere we could hear the calls of common ravens, bald eagles, northwestern crows, and a variety of gulls that seemed always to be scattered along these productive marine shorelines. Standing on that beach at Hood Bay, I had an intense feeling that I had arrived. I remember thinking, "Oh my God, John, this is work, and I'm getting paid to do this? Unbelievable."

The wildness and beauty we routinely encountered took on a different perspective the next week, however, when I flew from Sitka to a proposed logging site on Catherine Island near the southeast entrance to Peril Strait that separates Chichagof and Baranof Islands. I had been invited by the Forest Service to represent ADF&G on an interdisciplinary team (IDT) tasked with laying out a new

FIG. 2.3. Looking southeast up Hood Bay, on the southwest side of Admiralty Island.

timber sale on Southeast's Tongass National Forest. The IDT was made up of diverse specialists, including foresters, road engineers, timber managers, geologists, and fish and wildlife biologists. I was introduced to the team leader— a big, friendly forester wearing a hard hat, rubber boots, Carhartt pants with Alaska Logger suspenders, and a green Filson jacket. I can't recall his name, but in his introductory remarks, he stated that this project was focused on timber and "getting the cut out." The not-too-subtle message to our field crew was that fish and wildlife biologists were in a purely supportive role. We were not to get in the way.

This was an abrupt wakeup call to a young, idealistic scientist. Although I liked the IDT team leader personally, and respected his local knowledge of Southeast, I thought, "This is a strange way to manage a *national* forest in the best interest of all the American people." By the mid-1970s, it had become increasingly obvious to most natural resource managers across the country that wildlife, fisheries, and outdoor recreation were forest resources highly valued by the American public, and that these resources merited equal consideration, along with timber, for multiple use management. In Southeast, that approach significantly lagged behind the rest of the country.

⚜

The Tongass National Forest—at nearly seventeen million acres—is the largest national forest in the United States (see Appendix 1, Southeast Alaska and Tongass National Forest Facts). It was originally established by President Theodore Roosevelt in 1902 as the Alexander Archipelago Forest Reserve (see Appendix 2, Historical Benchmarks in Southeast Alaska and the Tongass National Forest). It lies in the northern portion of the Pacific coastal temperate rainforest—the largest temperate rainforest on Earth—which extends from Northern California through coastal British Columbia and Southeast Alaska to Alaska's Kenai Peninsula.[3] Temperate rainforests are generally defined as mid- to high-latitude forests with high rainfall, winter snow at higher latitudes, and cool to moderate temperatures.[4] Other temperate rainforests include those in Norway, Great Britain, eastern Canada, Japan, Korea, Chile and Argentina, and Australasia (i.e., New Zealand and Tasmania). Compared to tropical rainforests, coastal temperate rainforests are relatively rare (occupying less than 2 percent of forest land globally) and have been substantially altered by logging and development.[5] The northern portion of coastal British Columbia and Southeast Alaska includes the largest tracts of undeveloped old-growth temperate rainforest on Earth, and the Tongass alone represents about one-third of the global extent of this rare coastal forest.[6]

The indigenous Haida and Tlingit Indians have lived continuously in Southeast for nearly 10,000 years.[7] They still use the natural resources of the forest and the sea to help meet their subsistence needs. Salmon are a dependable and abundant source of food; their importance is demonstrated in the rich culture and art forms of both the Tlingit and Haida. These Indigenous people also made extensive use of the region's timber resources, particularly western redcedar, Alaskan yellow-cedar, and Sitka spruce, for many utilitarian and culturally significant items. Spruce roots were used for making ropes, fishnets, and baskets. Cedar bark was used for clothing, baskets, and mats. Cedar and spruce were used for houses, canoes, totem carvings, and other everyday implements.

During the period of Russian settlement in the early 1800s, and following the US purchase of Alaska in 1867, the forests of Southeast Alaska were harvested on a small scale for local use. This changed radically in the early 1950s, after Congress passed the Tongass Timber Act of 1947. This bill led the way to establishment of two fifty-year timber contracts between the US Forest

FIG. 2.4. Ketchikan Pulp Company Mill at Ward Cove in Ketchikan, Alaska (ca 1980).

Service and Ketchikan Pulp Company (KPC) and the Japanese-owned Alaska Pulp Corporation (APC) in Sitka (Fig 2.4). Pulp mills and sawmills were built in Ketchikan and Sitka and operated until the mid-1990s. The Forest Service had planned a third large timber contract for the west side of Admiralty Island, but US Plywood Champion and the Forest Service abandoned the sale in large part due to public concerns about the potential impacts to wildlife.

Despite the challenges of high costs of doing business and a location far from most markets, lumber and pulp production became a significant Southeast industry. The peak years of timber production were from 1960 through the mid-1990s, and the numbers tell the story. In 1971, sixty-nine logging companies, two pulp mills, and nine sawmills operated throughout Southeast.[8] In 1973, nearly 600 million board feet of timber were cut from the Tongass National Forest during its peak harvest.[9]

In 1971, Congress passed the Alaska Native Claims Settlement Act (ANCSA) to resolve aboriginal claims to Alaska lands. This act authorized Alaska Natives to receive title to forty-four million acres of land in Alaska as well as a cash settlement of $962 million. ANCSA also created a system of regional and village Native corporations. In Southeast, the Native corporations were allowed to select over 500,000 acres from the Tongass, including much of the best timber.[10] Native corporation logging began in 1979, and since 1986, timber harvest on Native lands has generally exceeded Forest Service timber harvest. The peak of annual timber production in Southeast (nearly one billion board feet) was around 1990, when logging occurred on both the Tongass Forest and Native corporation lands and employed nearly 4,000 workers.[11] Both Native corporation and national forest harvests began to decline sharply after that peak.

Nearly 800,000 acres have been logged in Southeast on all land jurisdictions, including national forest, state, and Native corporation lands.[12] Although these clear-cut acres make up only 5 percent of the total land area, that logging targeted the most productive forest lands, and the ecological impacts have been significant.

In the mid-1970s, when I arrived in Southeast, timber was a major economic driver, and the industry had a close working relationship with Forest Service leadership in Alaska. The prevailing attitude was that logging was essential to the local economy and beneficial to the other resources and uses of the forest. Logging roads were considered advantageous because they created an important transportation infrastructure throughout the region; clear-cuts were thought to provide valuable wildlife habitat for deer and other species. Excerpts from an advertisement in a regional Southeast publication by the Sitka-based Alaska Lumber and Pulp Company in the spring of 1979 exemplify industry attitudes:[13]

Why clearcutting in Coastal Alaska is Nature's way!

It is the most desirable silvicultural system for use on Alaska's coastal forests because it insures good natural stocking and rapid growth of conifer regeneration. . . . It is the most economical and efficient because of the steep and rocky land. Other types of logging methods are not feasible for selectively harvesting the timber. It is compatible with other forest uses: provides bush browse for wildlife, access for recreational opportunities on the forest roads, and an access to salmon streams for rehabilitation work.

A managed and supervised clearcut harvest follows Nature's methods of renewing a forest. Why clearcut in Alaska? It's Nature's way.

DEER RESEARCH: PHASE ONE

It was just after noon on October 12, 1977, on a rainy, overcast fall day, and we were headed south down Chatham Strait along the southwest side of Admiralty Island. I was operating a small, thirty-foot Fish and Game research boat headed from Hood Bay to Whitewater Bay to conduct fieldwork on southwest Admiralty Island. This trip was part of our new deer research project to evaluate the effects of logging on deer habitat. The field crew I was leading included three young wildlife technicians. When we left anchor that morning, the moderate wind and seas were acceptable for our fifteen-mile run down to our next study site. But an hour later, off Distant Point, the wind had picked up and was blowing at least twenty-five knots out of the southeast with higher gusts and seas building to over four feet. For the second time in two days, I made the decision to turn around and head back to our protected anchorage off Cabin Point in Hood Bay. Doing research in Southeast Alaska—unlike other states where you can jump in a pickup truck and drive to your study site—requires different tools of the trade, including boats and airplanes, as well as a lot of patience. I was still new to Southeast, and although I had a lot of experience with boats, I had not fully recognized that October was typically the monsoon season with heavy rain, gusty winds, choppy seas, and fog the norm. Our month-long field trip cruising around Admiralty Island in a small, cramped boat whose cabin dripped with moisture and lacked adequate heat was challenging, to say the least.

BACKGROUND AND HISTORY

For a number of years, local hunters, big-game guides, and wildlife biologists had expressed their apprehensions about the effects of logging on wildlife in Southeast. Big-game guide Ralph Young voiced strong concerns about logging on Admiralty Island and its impact on fish and wildlife in the May 1964 issue of *Field and Stream* magazine.[14] In his book *My Lost Wilderness*, Young wrote about a return trip to Kupreanof Island, where he had hunted in the past:[15]

> Each day I walked along miles of beach and roamed the woods and muskegs but saw nary a deer. Worse yet I didn't see even the track of a deer. I couldn't believe it. Only a few years ago when I used to hunt that area, deer were abundant. Now there were none. Perhaps it's a coincidence but it's a fact that the decline in the deer population of southeastern Alaska has been in direct ratio to the increase of clear-cutting of the forests. The well-known maxim that the deer follow the ax may be true in Pennsylvania, Wisconsin and Alabama, but not in Alaska.

In 1964, Frank Dufresne, a former director of the Alaska Game Commission, flew over Whitewater Bay on Admiralty Island with Ralph Young. This was an area Dufresne and Young had visited to watch brown bears thirty years earlier. Dufresne stated:

It wasn't pretty any more. It was as ugly as only man could make it, defiling a wilderness. The entire green valley of towering virgin trees had been felled by logging crews, dragged down to the bay, and towed away to the pulp mill.[16]

These opinions—although from seasoned veterans of wildlife work in Alaska's backcountry—were anecdotal and descriptive, and not the result of rigorous, scientific data collection. However, they provided a preliminary and significant warning for wildlife and forest managers to be cautious and vigilant.

Early wildlife research on the Tongass in the 1950s and 1960s included important studies of deer by David Klein, Sig Olson, and Harry Merriam. In the early to mid-1970s, biologists also began collecting data on the relationship of logging to deer. Merriam compared snow accumulations under the forest canopy with accumulations in the open. He concluded that snow depths beneath the forest canopy were about one-third to one-half of that found in open areas.[17] Early on, he was concerned that clear-cut logging posed a long-term risk to the continued welfare of Southeast's deer populations.

Two other scientists, Starker Leopold and Reginald Barrett from the University of California, Berkeley, took Merriam's concerns one step further. Based on their surveys on Admiralty Island, they stated:

On Admiralty Island, the key winter ranges are generally situated in mature conifer stands that have opened up enough to allow the growth of Vaccinium (blueberry shrubs) and other browse plants. To this extent, Alaska deer may be considered affiliates of climax forest vegetation rather than subclimax as is their normal relationship in more southerly ranges.[18]

This study—part of the assessment of the US Plywood Champion timber sale planned for Admiralty Island—helped set the stage for canceling this massive timber sale. In 1975–76, Art Bloom, from the Forestry Sciences Lab where my colleagues Charlie and Gordon worked, conducted a study of winter deer use of forests in the Kadashan Watershed on Chichagof Island. Bloom concluded that if large blocks of low-elevation timber in his study area were clear-cut, the carrying capacity of its winter range for deer would decline.[19]

In a paper describing early deer research in Southeast Alaska, ADF&G research chief Don McKnight stated:

FIG. 2.5. Sitkoh Lake clear-cut on southeastern Chichagof Island adjacent to Peril Strait (ca 1977).

We are fortunate in Alaska that the habitat base for our deer resource is still largely intact. It is apparent though that over much of this deer range unregulated timber harvesting could perhaps largely eliminate the species in harvestable or even observable numbers.[20]

Only Leopold, Barrett, and Bloom had collected empirical data on deer habitat use related to logging in Southeast Alaska. Their work was a valuable beginning, although relatively limited in scope. By 1977, industrial logging had been occurring in Southeast for nearly a quarter of a century, and about 20,000 acres of old-growth forest (i.e., virgin or ancient forest that had never been clear-cut) were being clear-cut annually on the Tongass (Fig 2.5). Thus, an understanding of the long-term effects of forest management on deer populations—the primary big-game species in the region and one that many people depended on for food—was of substantial interest to local people as well as to forest and wildlife managers.

FIG. 2.6. A buck Sitka black-tailed deer in Southeast Alaska.

There was a major gap in our understanding of deer ecology on the Tongass and the effects of logging on deer habitat, and Charlie and I intended to fill it. In the spring and early summer of 1977, we developed a plan to measure deer use and assess how forest management might affect their populations. The objectives of that initial study were to measure and compare deer use of regrowth forest (i.e., second growth) and old-growth forests, and establish preliminary information on the diversity and abundance of deer forage in those respective forest types (Fig 2.6).

FIRST FIELD SEASON

Sitka black-tailed deer are creatures of the forest, and observing deer in a dense rainforest is difficult at best. Thus, we needed to figure out how to measure deer use without observing them directly. We determined that the best technique was using deer fecal pellets (deer poop) as an index of their habitat use. The assumption was that the number of pellet groups in a habitat type would be indicative of the amount of time deer spend in those habitat types. After some experimental work, we settled on running transects of 300 one-by-ten-meter plots in each paired regrowth and old-growth stand. We also measured the occurrence of understory (forest floor) plants browsed by deer in a sample of our plots to assess the relative amount of forage available to deer in regrowth compared to old-growth forests.

This work may sound like a simple hike through the woods, but bushwhacking through dense ten-to-thirty-year-old clear-cuts, falling through slash, and crashing through thorny devil's club—all while wearing raingear and carrying a firearm for bear protection—was no picnic. Charlie and I both knew that the density of brown bears on Admiralty was very high, and neither of us had experience working around them. I recall hiking back and forth along the trail leading to the Hood Bay research cabin, all the while talking loudly to alert bears of our presence. I later carried a short-barreled .338-caliber rifle or 12-gauge shotgun with double-ought buckshot for protection. Fortunately, I never had to use one in self-defense.

Assuming that deer seek out and spend the greatest proportion of their time in the preferred habitats, then the density of pellet groups in each habitat type provides an index of its value to deer. This was a standard technique for measuring deer and elk habitat use elsewhere in North America. After a field season of running deer pellet-group transects, I could comfortably explain to my friends and colleagues, "When it comes to deer research, I know my shit."

Our first field season ran from September through October 1977. Our field crew of six consisted of Gordon, four Fish and Game field technicians, and myself. Field sampling began at Hood Bay on Admiralty Island, where we based our work out of a Forest Service wanigan—a fifty-foot floating barge that contained a workshop, bunkhouse, and galley. We had a small skiff with an outboard that we used to access sample sites in Hood Bay as well as other sites located several miles up and down the coast (Fig. 2.7).

FIG. 2.7. Unloading the Beaver floatplane at the floating wanigan research facility in Hood Bay on Admiralty Island. Our fieldwork required access by boat or floatplane to all our study sites.

Most of the Admiralty sites consisted of older regrowth forests from twenty to 147 years old. From the outset of our field sampling, it became clear that young regrowth stands—also known as second growth—were used significantly less by deer than old-growth stands. In my field notes describing a thirty-four-year-old second-growth stand in the South Arm of Hood Bay, I wrote: "This was very difficult going. This cut was somewhat variable with dense conifer stands, brushy devil's club areas, and alder stands. There was no understory [deer food] in the dense conifer stands and very little deer sign except occasional travel lanes." The deer pellet group densities measured in the old-growth stands were five times higher than in the younger regrowth stands.

We continued our sampling of sites along Admiralty's west coast and then moved into Tenakee Inlet on Chichagof Island. Throughout our study that fall, the results were remarkably consistent. In every comparison, deer use was higher in the old growth, ranging from two to thirty times higher than young regrowth. Although these preliminary results did not surprise some of the more experienced field biologists or hunters in the region, they generated an undercurrent of concern and debate within the timber industry and Forest Service timber staff.

☙

FIG. 2.8. Jack Lentfer, ADF&G regional supervisor, was my immediate supervisor during my early research for Alaska Fish and Game.

In 1977, Jack Lentfer became my boss when he moved to Juneau to take the job of regional supervisor of the game division at Alaska Fish and Game (Fig. 2.8). Jack was a tall, lean man of Scandinavian heritage who grew up hunting and fishing in Montana. For his master's degree he had studied mountain goats in Montana's Crazy Mountains. Jack first started work in Alaska in 1957 with the US Fish and Wildlife Service (FWS) before statehood and later worked for both ADF&G and the FWS, where he conducted pioneering research on polar bears in Alaska's Arctic. I worked with Jack until he retired from ADF&G in 1981. He was an important mentor and friend, and we have stayed closely involved on many Alaska conservation issues for over thirty years. Jack's scientific integrity and honesty has always been his hallmark and an inspiration to his professional colleagues. He has courageously stood tall for wildlife conservation throughout his entire professional career and has never been intimidated by political pressure. Jack's background and experience in Alaska, both biological and political, were very valuable during these early years as we encountered the typical challenges of field research as well as the political pressure associated with discovering new ways of looking at forest management.

⚜

In February 1978, Charlie and I organized a Sitka black-tailed deer conference in Juneau that was sponsored cooperatively by the US Forest Service and Alaska Department of Fish and Game. Jack and other ADF&G biologists attended the conference. We invited a range of speakers from Alaska, British Columbia, and the Pacific Northwest who were working on black-tailed deer. This conference was very successful, and it helped us formulate important questions about deer and their forest habitat, particularly along the rainforest coast of British Columbia and Alaska. Charlie and I prepared a paper for the conference, "Timber Management and Deer in Southeast Alaska: Current Problems and Research Direction,"[21] that was well received by fellow scientists, but continued to heighten concern from within the Alaska Region of the Forest Service.

During the spring of 1978, we continued to get criticism from the timber industry and the regional office of the Forest Service—an administrative unit distinct from the Forestry Sciences Lab where Charlie worked. The regional office said our results were only preliminary and not reflective of the relationship between logging and deer habitat in Alaska.

SECOND FIELD SEASON

In March, the Southeast region game division of ADF&G held its regional meeting on the Forestry Sciences Lab's wanigan in Hood Bay. Jack convened the meeting, and Charlie joined us for part of that meeting where we discussed the issue of logging and its impact on deer and other wildlife.

On our flight back to Juneau, I recall stopping in Kanalku Bay in Kootznahoo Inlet with Jack and Charlie. We walked through a 147-old second-growth stand, the oldest regrowth stand used in our deer study (Fig. 2.9). This even-aged stand originated from a rare Southeast Alaska fire, and included western hemlock and Sitka spruce varying from twelve to twenty-four inches in diameter with spruce trees larger than hemlocks. The stand's dense second-growth canopy significantly reduced the amount of sunlight reaching the forest floor. As a result, forest floor plants were sparse and consisted primarily of mosses, a few ferns, and some very small blueberry plants that were just beginning to appear. Even after a century and a half, this stand still was not close to developing the ecological characteristics of old growth, including a diverse and abundant forest-floor plant community that provides important food for deer. After walking through this relatively sterile deer habitat, I captured Jack's initial comments in my field notes: "This makes me a believer."

FIG. 2.9. A 147-year-old second-growth forest at Kanalku Bay on the west side of Admiralty Island. Even after nearly a century and a half, this even-aged, second growth still lacked the structural diversity and abundance of understory vegetation characteristic of old growth. This was one of our Admiralty deer study plots, and we measured significantly lower deer densities in this stand compared to the adjacent old growth.

During April and May of 1978, our field crew returned to Admiralty and Chichagof Islands to replicate our fall sampling. We worked hard, collected valuable data, and enjoyed the camaraderie of exploring the wild shoreline of this incredibly rich coastal rainforest. I had also learned my lesson about using small boats to conduct Southeast field research. Thus, for our spring season, we used the ninety-foot Fish and Game research vessel *Steller*—complete with a full-time skipper, cook, and deckhand—to survey the coastal forest on west Admiralty and east Chichagof. In contrast to our past efforts fighting rough weather in our small boat, the *Steller* cruised right up the coast to our sampling sites, dropped us off to work, then picked us up and provided us a hot meal and dry bunk when we returned late in the afternoon. Now that is experiential learning.

While on the *Steller*, I also distinctly remember a young deckhand telling me quietly that he really felt sorry for Charlie. He considered that at Charlie's age—his early sixties—it was a real hardship to do this kind of rigorous field-work. That sounded funny at the time, but even funnier now that I am over seventy. I also recall Charlie describing the pleasure he derived from participating in this exciting research in such a spectacular setting surrounded by snow-capped mountains and ancient forests, and sharing the place with whales, eagles, and bears. I guess *hard* work is all in the eye of the beholder. I stand solidly behind the old adage that the worst day in the field beats the hell out of the best day in the office.

ANALYSIS AND IMPLICATIONS OF LOGGING ON DEER

After completing the 1978 spring season's fieldwork on Admiralty and Chichagof, we began analyzing our data and started preparing a manuscript for publication. The results from our fall and spring seasons, measuring summer and winter deer habitat use, were very similar. In summer and winter, deer frequented old-growth forest five to seven times more often than young clear-cuts or second-growth forests. These data diverged markedly from the conventional wisdom—derived from the lower 48 states—that clear-cutting benefited deer. So why was Alaska different?

Walking systematic transects through Alaska's coastal rainforests—including young clear-cuts, older second growth, and old growth—provided us with a well-defined representation of forest succession. Forest succession is the change that occurs over time following a forest disturbance such as clear-cutting or fire. In Southeast Alaska, old-growth forests are actually quite variable in structure with trees of all ages, from seedlings and saplings to pole-size trees and large-diameter old-growth trees. The age of dominant old-growth trees typically exceeds 300 years. In coastal Southeast Alaska and northern British Columbia, wind storms commonly blow down individual trees or small groups of mature trees (Fig. 2.10). Over many centuries of small-scale disturbances, the structure of old-growth stands becomes patchy, uneven-aged, and considerably different than that of even-aged second growth, where all the trees started to grow following a single large-scale disturbance such as clear-cutting or fire.

Uneven-aged old growth is structurally diverse while even-aged second growth is structurally homogeneous. The overhead canopy of old growth is irregular and multilayered, includes many gaps, and, from a bird's-eye view, looks shaggy and ragged (Fig. 2.11). The canopy of second growth, in comparison, appears smooth and continuous (Fig. 2.12). This structural difference significantly affects the abundance of plant life on the forest floor. The more open, ragged canopy of old growth allows an abundance of sunlight to penetrate the

FIG. 2.10. An example of a small Southeast windthrow event within old growth where several trees were blown down. These events create gaps in the forest overstory that allow sunlight to penetrate the forest. Windthrow events are very common and create a diverse patchwork of tree ages and sizes within the old-growth community.

FIG. 2.11. Aerial view of an old-growth forest canopy on Chichagof Island. Old growth has a broken, multilayered canopy. Standing dead trees (snags) are also characteristic. The canopy gaps that occur in these stands allow sunlight to penetrate the stand. The tall trees and thick limbs of the dominant trees intercept significant amounts of snow during winter, leaving low-snow or snow-free patches on the forest floor. These upper limb structures also provide important habitat for a variety of wildlife, including nesting habitat for bald eagles, marbled murrelets, and northern goshawks.

FIG. 2.12. Aerial view of a patch of old growth (center) surrounded by vast acres of second-growth forest on Koskiusko Island. Note the ragged, broken canopy of tall, shaggy old-growth trees compared to the smooth, dense canopy of the second-growth forest. Second growth is structurally less diverse than old growth as the trees are all the same age and roughly the same size. The dense canopy allows little light to penetrate to the forest floor, resulting in low abundance of forest floor plants.

FIG. 2.13. A mixed hemlock-spruce old-growth forest stand on Admiralty Island. In comparison to second growth, old-growth forests are uneven aged, with trees ranging from seedlings and saplings to ancient trees and snags that are centuries old. These forests are highly diverse with multiple layers and broken canopies that allow an abundance of sunlight to penetrate the forest canopy, resulting in a diverse and abundant understory of herbaceous and shrubby plants. Dead standing trees and downed logs are important components of old growth and provide valuable habitat. For species like deer, marten, flying squirrels, goshawks, and many cavity nesting birds, old growth provides valuable, if not critical, seasonal habitats. Riparian old growth along streams, rivers, and lakes also contribute to habitat values for many fish and aquatic organisms.

FIG. 2.14. A sixty-year-old second-growth forest stand on Admiralty Island. We measured deer density here in comparison to an adjacent old-growth stand. This is a mixed hemlock-spruce stand in which all the trees are the same age and size. Few forest floor plants occur here because of low light levels. These dark, even-aged stands have low structural diversity and provide relatively poor habitat for most wildlife species. In Southeast, it takes two to three centuries before forests that are clear-cut develop the ecological characteristics of old growth. Note the old-growth stump on the left side of the image.

forest and supports a rich abundance of forest-floor plants, including herbaceous flowering plants (forbs), shrubs, and ferns (Fig. 2.13). In contrast, very
little sunlight penetrates the dense, uniform canopy of second growth, resulting in a shaded understory and relatively barren plant community except for
mosses and a few ferns that provide little in the way of nutritious forage for
deer or other wildlife (Fig. 2.14).

In my spring 1978 field notes, I wrote: "Outer Hood Bay area: 1918 clear-cut.
We observed virtually no [deer] sign in this regrowth stand. No birds were
singing. It was a veritable desert." The difference between walking through
an old-growth forest and into a 30-to-100-year-old second-growth forest is like
walking from a spacious cathedral—with light streaming in through high,
open windows—into a small, dark basement apartment.

During our spring sampling of paired second-growth and old-growth stands,
the abundance of deer forage plants averaged seven to nineteen times greater
in old growth than in mature second growth (excluding one-to-twenty-year-
old clear-cuts). Food was the primary driver in how deer used the forest. Food
was abundant in old growth and lacking in second growth.

Another important contrast in the quality of winter deer habitat between old
growth and young clear-cuts is their ability to intercept winter snowfall. Open-
canopy habitats accumulate two to three times more snow than habitats with
a high, sturdy canopy of big tree limbs (Figs. 2.15, 2.16). Although young clear-
cuts produce an abundance of deer forage, winter snow accumulation reduces

FIG. 2.15. Charlie Wallmo standing in deep snow in a forest opening on northern Admiralty
Island. This amount of snow will bury all of the evergreen forbs like bunchberry and five-
leaved bramble that are deer's preferred winter forage. Deep snow also increases deer's
energetic travel costs. Recall how much more energy it takes to walk through deep snow.

FIG. 2.16. This photo was taken the same day as Fig. 2.15 with Charlie standing under a forest canopy within 200 feet of the previous location. Note the patchy snow cover, including bare spots where deer forage plants occur in relative abundance.

the availability of that food and also increases the energetic costs of moving through deep snow.

Charlie and I published a popular article on our initial deer studies and a brief summary of the deer conference in the ADF&G magazine in July 1978. In this article we stated:

> The general consensus of the conference members was that forest practices (clearcutting on a hundred-year rotation) in Alaska and British Columbia are permanently eliminating the uneven-aged old-growth forest on the northern coast, and further that the result will most likely be a serious and long-term detrimental impact on deer habitat and consequently deer populations throughout this region.[22]

This article further sparked concern within the regional office of the Forest Service and the timber industry. In response, Dr. Don Schmiege, director of the Forestry Sciences Lab in Juneau and Charlie's immediate supervisor, strongly defended our research. However, our research was a growing threat to the Forest Service's current management practices in Southeast Alaska, and the pressure on Charlie from the regional office was intense. Our next responsibility, however, was to publish our results in a peer-reviewed scientific journal.

LIFE ON THE HOME FRONT

As the repercussions of our research intensified within the Juneau regional office of the Forest Service and the timber industry, Mary Beth and I sought distraction and began building our first home on the water just north of Juneau. This was a welcome relief from the politics brewing over logging and wildlife.

We had been living in a duplex in a small subdivision just north of downtown Juneau and decided that we did not come to Alaska to live on a suburban lot. We had been searching for a house or property with waterfront and a natural setting. However, most of the waterfront homes and lots we looked at were far more expensive than a struggling young couple fresh out of graduate school could afford. So we searched harder and began looking at property off the road system.

FIG 2.17. Looking north over the tip of Douglas Island toward Smuggler's Cove and the south end of the Mendenhall Peninsula. Our home is on the shore along the middle of the Mendenhall Peninsula (center). The Juneau Airport is above and to the right, out of the photo, while the Mendenhall Glacier is in the upper center.

We found an acre-and-a-half lot in Smuggler's Cove on the tip of the Mendenhall Peninsula just west of the airport and the Mendenhall State Game Refuge (Fig. 2.17). The lot was not for sale, but it was owned by a couple who lived out of state. After considerable pestering on my part, the owners finally relented, and we bought a beautiful waterfront parcel in a crescent-shaped cove with a stream flowing through the middle of the property. It was backed by an old-growth forest of spruce and hemlock and had a view to the west of the Chilkat Range (Fig. 2.18). To the south we looked at the Mansfield Peninsula on Admiralty Island. In September 1978, we constructed a piling foundation on the edge of the forest just above the high-tide line. With the help of many friends, we barged in materials, and started building a 1,000-square-foot cedar chalet with a million-dollar view.

There was no electricity or phone service to the property, so we were truly off the grid. We put in an outhaul—a long loop of line with pulleys on both ends and one end anchored at the lowest tide—on our beach and one at the

FIG. 2.18. The view from our home on the southern end of the Mendenhall Peninsula looking west across Smuggler's Cove to the mountains on the Chilkat Peninsula. Our view to the south included a portion of my study area on northern Admiralty Island.

end of Fritz Cove Road, where we parked our car. We pulled our boat in when we wanted to use it, and then pulled the boat out at the other end when we left it. The tidal range was over eighteen feet from low to high tide, so an outhaul prevented our boat from getting stuck high and dry on the beach at low tides. At low tide, we had about 200 feet of beach in front of our house.

We had purchased a precut cedar home kit, so the house went up easily and quickly. After it was closed in, our next priority was running water. We built a little dam upstream on the hill and buried a pipeline to the house. The pipe had to be three feet deep to prevent freezing in winter. We installed a composting toilet, a woodstove, and an oil cooking range with a boiler for hot water. Without electricity, we plumbed in propane for lights and a small refrigerator. By the end of October, we had moved in, and then spent the next ten years completing the final details. Now we truly felt like we lived in the Alaska of our dreams (Fig. 2.19).

While we lacked a number of conveniences, we did have an active bald eagle nest just down the beach, and we frequently observed many species of coastal wildlife, from river otters and harbor seals to sea ducks and whales right off

FIG. 2.19. Our off-the-grid home on the beach at Smuggler's Cove on the Mendenhall Peninsula north of Juneau. We commuted half a mile by small boat from our beach to the end of Fritz Cove Road where we parked our car.

our beach. And we could walk on a beach or in an old-growth forest just by stepping out our door.

PUBLICATION AND THE CONVERGENCE OF POLITICS AND SCIENCE

Although our home life was a great Alaska adventure, I also had to step back into the controversial issues that had become intertwined with my job. In April 1979, Charlie and I sent our draft deer manuscript to a select group of scientists for peer review. At the same time, Charlie submitted it for internal review by the Alaska Region of the Forest Service. Although the deer experts gave the paper high marks and recommended that it be published quickly, regional forester John Sandor sent it out to a number of his regional staff, most of whom were foresters or timber managers, not wildlife biologists. In his September 5, 1979, memo to Don Schmiege, Sandor stated:

> The proposed paper does not adequately describe the situation and status of research in this and related subjects. We believe the manuscript needs substantial additions and clarifications if it is to make a positive contribution to an understanding of the present level of knowledge as well as the objectives of current research-studies of this controversial subject.[23]

The following excerpts from our solicited peer reviews offer a contrast to the regional forester's conclusion on the merits of our paper. Dr. Ian McTaggart Cowan (University of British Columbia): "I found your paper most interesting and the findings accord well with my recent observations." Dr. David R. Klein (University of Alaska Fairbanks): "I have read over the paper . . . and find it well written and a much needed contribution to knowledge of deer-logging relationships." Dr. W. Leslie Pengelly (University of Montana): "You raise some interesting questions with this study and I'm sure it will attract a lot of attention. I had hinted at some of these problems in a paper I gave at Portland in 1972." Daryl M. Hebert (British Columbia Fish and Wildlife Branch): "In general, the results are good and will be extremely useful." Dr. Reginald Barrett (University of California, Berkeley): "It looks good to me, and I agree the issues need publicity in the forestry journal." The Pacific Northwest Forest and Range Experiment Station ultimately approved the paper for submission, and it was published in *Forest Science* in 1980.

Our paper, "Response of Deer to Secondary Forest Succession in Southeast Alaska,"[24] reported what we had found in our study: deer use of old growth was significantly greater than use of younger forests. In the discussion summarizing our study, and referencing research by Forest Service scientists Al Harris and Bill Farr,[25] we postulated four major stages of deer habitat in the transition from clear-cuts into old growth.

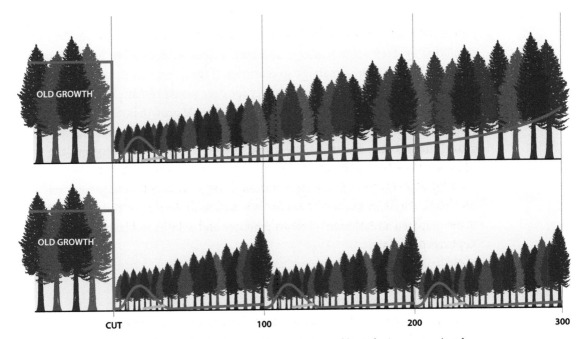

FIG. 2.20. Hypothesized changes in deer carrying capacity (red line) during successional development of hemlock-spruce forests in Southeast Alaska. Upper: forest succession following clear-cutting of old-growth forest. Lower: clear-cutting on 100-year timber rotations. In the early clear-cut stages (yellow line), winter carrying capacity may be reduced to very low levels by snow accumulation. (Adapted from Wallmo and Schoen 1980, p. 25.) Graphic by Eric Cline.

For one to two years after clearcutting, forage supplies are greatly reduced and logging debris impedes general use of the area by deer. During the "green-up" period, five to ten years after cutting, clearcuts provide summer browse for deer that diminishes as conifer stands close and browse species are shaded out. Within eight to ten years after logging conifers overtop the shrub layer and will develop into an even-aged stand . . .

Crown closure begins fifteen to twenty years after logging. . . . Twenty to thirty years after clearcutting much of the ground is in deep shade, and most understory plants have been shaded out.

Beyond age thirty, crown cover is complete; and the forest floor is in continual shade, covered with duff, and often devoid of understory vegetation. The stand offers cover for wildlife but little food. The stand may remain even aged for up to three-hundred years before gradually changing to uneven aged conditions.

Based on our deer research, we postulated that the removal of old-growth forest could be expected to decrease the carrying capacity for deer in Southeast Alaska. We presented a graph showing the hypothesized changes in carrying capacity during forest succession of hemlock-spruce forests in Southeast Alaska (Fig. 2.20). It depicted a sharp drop in carrying capacity for deer immediately following logging, then an increase for five to twenty years (unless precluded by deep-snow winters), and then a decline to very low levels that would persist for approximately two centuries. If the forest was cut again every one hundred years, the carrying capacity for deer would remain at depressed levels in perpetuity. This last concept suggests that old growth is nonrenewable when repeatedly clear-cut every eighty to 120 years. This is the reason that old-growth forests have become exceedingly rare on forestlands throughout the country and rest of the world.

In response to these concerns about the effects of forest management on deer populations in Southeast Alaska, Alaska's Joint Boards of Fisheries and Game prepared a resolution on forest practices and wildlife in Alaska in 1980.[26] Key excerpts follow:

Whereas, the present forest management practice of clearcut logging throughout Southeast Alaska on a ninety to one-hundred and twenty-year rotation is permanently converting diverse old-growth stands with high fish and wildlife values to less diverse second-growth stands of much less value to fish and wildlife . . .

Now therefore be it resolved by the Joint Boards of Fisheries and Game that:

The public be fully informed by the Department of Fish and Game and the U.S. Forest Service of the long term known and potential impacts of clear-cut logging on fish and wildlife habitat and subsequent populations levels.

The Tongass Land Management Plan be revised by the Forest Service to provide more protection for valuable fish and wildlife habitat and reflect recent research findings . . .

Our research in Southeast, although challenged aggressively by timber interests, had gotten the attention of state fish and wildlife managers. However, the 1979 Tongass Land Management Plan—the guiding document for the Tongass Forest—would not be revised for another seventeen years. This management plan did not incorporate new research results on the importance of old growth as wildlife habitat, and challenges and disagreements over research results continued unabated.

ASSESSING THE BIG PICTURE

Subsequent to our preliminary work on understory vegetation in second-growth and old-growth forests, Paul Alaback, at Oregon State University, completed his doctoral work on the dynamics of understory biomass in Sitka spruce–western hemlock forests of Southeast Alaska, and published a significant paper on this work in the journal *Ecology* in 1982.[27] Dr. Alaback observed:

> Shrubs and herbs are virtually eliminated from the understory after forest canopies close at stand ages of twenty-five to thirty-five years. . . . Maintenance of the most productive forests in (second growth) . . . will minimize the development of a productive vascular understory and thus deprive herbivores of forage during 70–80% of the forest rotation.

Cathy Rose, a graduate student working under Professor David Klein at the University of Alaska Fairbanks, conducted another important follow-up study[28] to our northern Tongass deer study. Using similar techniques on Annette Island, south of Ketchikan, Rose came to conclusions that mirrored ours:

> Uneven-aged old growth forest sites received nearly seven times more use by deer in winter than did young clearcuts and closed-canopy second growth stands from one to 270 years old. These findings support results of studies at the northern end of the Alexander Archipelago identifying old-growth forest as optimal winter range for deer.

In spite of the objections from many forest managers and timber industry representatives, the published data on the reduced deer forage resources of second-growth forests in Southeast Alaska demonstrated a common theme.

※

In the spring of 1979, we hired a young fellow named Matthew Kirchhoff as a seasonal biologist to work on our deer and goat project (Fig. 2.21). Matt was from upstate New York and had a bachelor's degree in forestry and a master's degree in wildlife from the University of Maine. He was living with his wife, Patty, in Port Alexander on the southern tip of Baranof Island. He had previously worked summers with the Fish and Wildlife Service in Alaska's Aleutian Islands and the Yukon–Kuskokwim Delta. Matt helped us with our spring fieldwork and data analysis, and then spent the summer back at Port Alexander. He came back to Juneau in the fall, and Charlie was able to hire him seasonally through the winter. Then, in 1980, I hired Matt at Fish and Game in a long-term position. Matt quickly became an important asset on our research team with his strong background in quantitative analysis and computer skills, as well as his excellent field experience and friendly enthusiasm and people skills. Matt played basketball in high school and college, and we soon started playing together at a local gym during our noon lunch break as well as in a Juneau city league. Matt and I often described our noon basketball as cheap therapy

FIG. 2.21. Matt and Patty Kirchhoff and their new baby in front of the cabin they built at Port Alexander on the southern tip of Baranof Island (ca 1980). Matt joined our deer research team in 1979.

to get us through the stress of political pressures associated with our research. Like Charlie and Jack and their families, Matt and Patty became close personal friends, and Matt and I have collaborated on conservation issues for nearly forty years.

※

In 1980, Charlie, Matt, and I, with piqued curiosity, did an extensive review of the scientific literature on old growth and its importance to wildlife, and published a paper, "Wildlife–Forest Relationships: Is a Reevaluation of Old Growth Necessary?"[29] I presented it at the North American Wildlife and Natural Resources Conference in Washington, DC. Our research revealed some interesting results. Most of the science on the relationships of wildlife and old growth had been published in just the last two decades, well after most of the nation's old growth had already been logged. Contrary to conventional wisdom, there is strong evidence that deer were abundant on the Eastern Seaboard prior to the elimination of the region's old-growth forests. In the Pacific Northwest, what biologists in the 1950s and '60s once described as old-growth were actually older second-growth forests, and these had low value to deer. In our conclusion, we stated that our purpose was to highlight

> the scarcity of old growth in North America today, and to draw attention to the need for a greater understanding of the role old growth plays in wildlife-forest relationships. Old-growth forests are today very limited and, under standard rotations, nonrenewable. Thus, our approach to forest management of old growth will have substantial and long-term consequences. . . . More research and less speculation will be required if we are to meet our responsibilities in providing enlightened and knowledgeable wildlife-forest management.

Charlie retired from the Forest Service in 1981 and moved to Bozeman, Montana. In the spring of 1982, Charlie came back to Juneau for the Northwest Section meeting of the Wildlife Society where he received the Einarsen Award in recognition of his outstanding lifetime service to the wildlife profession. Charlie was selected for this award in part for his high scientific standards and objective critical approach to research, and his honesty and integrity in expressing his findings even when they conflicted with traditional resource management philosophy and current land management practices. This was a wonderful tribute to his many contributions to wildlife research and conservation over his thirty-five-year career. And it was presented to him in Juneau where he had faced intense political pressure over the results of our research on deer–forest relationships. Unfortunately, this was the last time I would ever see Charlie. He died just a few months later after a short bout with cancer. I was asked to write a memorial for him for the Northwest Section of the Wildlife Society newsletter. An excerpt from that memorial follows:

> Charlie was much more than a productive scientist. He was a man of unquestionable integrity which was never compromised even under acute political management pressures. It was refreshing that you always knew where Charlie stood on an issue. A rigorous scientist, Charlie approached each new project with an objective, open mind free from preconceived prejudices. He was interested first and foremost in wildlife research. Charlie also recognized the importance of wildlands and wilderness and the value of this resource to future generations of Americans.

FIG. 2.22.
Looking north up the Mendenhall Glacier where we did research on mountain goats inhabiting the coastal mountains from Mendenhall northwest to Berner's Bay.

MOUNTAIN GOAT RESEARCH

Shafts of sun were breaking over the southwest ridge of Mount Stroller White as we climbed up to 3,000 feet, heading up the Mendenhall Glacier north of Juneau (Fig. 2.22). Suddenly my head hit the ceiling of the high-performance Helio Courier aircraft as we encountered mountain turbulence and abruptly lost 300 feet of altitude. The weather had been nasty the last few weeks, and my pilot, Lynn Bennett, and I were trying to get locations on five radio-collared mountain goats. I had captured them a month earlier in December (1977), near Herbert Glacier a few miles north of the Mendenhall. Today, the air was so bumpy it was like driving over huge potholes. But we had a rare window of decent cloud ceiling and visibility, and I was highly motivated to get good locations on the first radio-collared goats—three nannies and two billies—ever tracked in Southeast Alaska. As I quickly learned, doing aerial telemetry work in Southeast is challenging, unpredictable, and often uncomfortable. You spend days waiting out low ceilings and visibilities, and then need to be ready

FIG. 2.23.
A female (nanny)
mountain goat
along the edge
of the Herbert
Glacier in the
middle of our
study area north
of Juneau.

to fly at a moment's notice as soon as the weather breaks. One thing you discover about flying in Southeast is that even if it's sunny and clear, low visibility and rain are coming your way right over the horizon.

Although I was hired primarily to develop a deer research program in Southeast, when I arrived in Juneau, my supervisor suggested that I also initiate a concurrent study on mountain goats.[30] The objectives of this research were to develop capture and telemetry procedures for mountain goats, and evaluate their seasonal use of habitats in Southeast Alaska. This sounded important and exciting, so I soon began to split my time between deer research and goat research (Fig. 2.23).

My first challenge was to figure out how to capture goats in this extremely rugged mountain environment. During the summer and fall of 1977, I experimented unsuccessfully with several techniques, including using a drop net from a helicopter. I built a net using a rectangular six-by-ten-foot strip of purse seine net (used for commercial salmon fishing). This net was attached to a PVC pipe that was connected with a rope bridle to the helicopter's cargo hook.

We practiced dropping the net on fifty-five-gallon oil drums at the heliport, and then launched a capture excursion into the mountains above the Mendenhall Glacier. We made four capture attempts on real goats. The pilot flew the helicopter up behind a goat—which was running at full speed along a ridgetop—and when I tapped the pilot on the shoulder, he released the net from the cargo hook, and it was supposed to drop on top of the goat and ensnare it.

FIG. 2.24. I radio-collared this mountain goat between the Mendenhall and Herbert Glaciers at about 3,000 feet elevation. This goat was captured during winter by shooting an immobilizing dart out of a helicopter.

We had two narrow misses before a third drop that went over the top of a big billy that managed to escape. On a fourth try, we accidentally caught a very large boulder prior to the net being released. This abruptly stopped the helicopter in midflight. The pilot released the net in time to escape a serious accident, but we both decided this technique was pushing our luck, and we wisely abandoned any further attempts at netting mountain goats.

Ultimately, I decided to try darting goats from a helicopter with the door removed. Based on our netting experience, we knew we could get the helicopter close to goats, and I had substantial experience using a capture gun to dart free-ranging elk during my graduate work at the University of Washington. We used a powerful narcotic (M99) as an immobilizing drug. After test darting from the helicopter on stationary objects on the ground, we headed back to the mountains in December and successfully captured three goats, two nannies and a billy. To my knowledge, these were the first mountain goats darted and captured from a helicopter in Alaska. That first winter, we captured and radio-collared a total of five goats between the Mendenhall and Herbert Glaciers (Fig. 2.24). By the end of this five-year study, we had twenty collared mountain goats between the Mendenhall Glacier and Berners Bay.

We captured most of the goats on high, snow-covered ridges between December and April. The best technique was to find a goat located a reasonable distance away from steep cliffs. We would fly up quickly from below and move the goat away from the cliffs, and the pilot would put me in a position where I could get a shot at the hindquarters from about ten to fifteen yards. Once the goat was hit, we would move away to minimize disturbance but continue to herd it away from precipitous terrain so that after about ten minutes, when it became immobile, it would not fall and we could get to it safely. This tense, difficult work was charged with adrenaline and excitement—we were in precarious terrain, surrounded by glaciers and snowfields that overlooked spectacular fjords. Our pilots' flying skills were essential to our success.

We learned that these goats were relatively sedentary in their movements. The mean distance between summer and winter ranges was less than two miles, with males moving more than females. Several female goats had overlapping summer and winter ranges while male seasonal ranges did not overlap. Consecutive years of tracking revealed that both male and female goats maintained strong fidelity to their summer ranges. While females used similar winter ranges on subsequent years, males displayed more annual variability.

We did not detect any significant movement in or out of the relatively small range they occupied between glaciers, suggesting that the highly dissected glacial topography of this area limits dispersal. In general, the mountain goats in our study had smaller home ranges and moved about less than those reported elsewhere on the continent, perhaps because active glaciers have significantly fragmented available habitat across the landscape. One of our recommendations for wildlife managers was to carefully monitor these discrete populations and manage hunting conservatively, because if overharvest occurred, it could take many years for a subpopulation to recover, given that few goats relocate from adjoining areas.

Our observations made it clear that the most important goat habitats throughout the year were rocky outcrops and alpine and subalpine slopes, particularly those in broken terrain and in close proximity to steep (greater than fifty-degree), rocky cliffs. Cliffs provided important escape terrain from predators, particularly wolves.

We were also interested in the relationship of mountain goats to old-growth forest habitat so as to better evaluate the potential effects of logging on Southeast Alaska goat populations. We learned that from fall through early spring, mountain goats made substantial use of old-growth forests, particularly at high elevations on southern exposures near or associated with cliff terrain. During winters of deep, wet snow accumulations, steep, forested habitat generally has lower snow depths than nonforested slopes, allowing goats to find forage under the forest canopy. In some areas of Southeast, in winter and

FIG. 2.25.
An Alaska male
(billy) mountain
goat foraging
along a steep
rocky cliff during
fall. Goats
favor steep cliff
habitats to avoid
predators.

spring, goats actually move down to steep tidewater coastlines like those found in Tracy Arm Wilderness and Glacier Bay National Park.

We determined that in northern Southeast Alaska, the loss of mountain goat habitat from logging would be less of a concern than the impacts of logging on winter deer habitat. Goats used forest habitat much less than deer, and the type and location of forest used by goats was generally not scheduled for logging. However, road construction for logging or other resource development would increase human access, and thus would require more conservative hunting regulations to prevent overharvesting these relatively discrete and sedentary goat populations. The optimal approach for conserving important mountain goat habitat in Southeast is to protect entire drainages from road-building and development. All cliff terrain within a drainage is likely to be important for goats. South-facing slopes are particularly important during winter and spring. We recommended that development activities not be permitted within at least a half mile radius of such areas.

Southeast Alaska's mountain goats live in an incredibly harsh environment, especially during winter, when deep snow accumulation blankets their preferred steep habitats, and freezing temperatures and gale-force winds assault the coastal mountains. To survive these conditions, goats conserve their energy and get by on fat reserves accumulated during summer and early fall. Kids stay with their mothers through their first year of life and often continue to stay in close association with the family group as yearlings. Experience and learning from their mothers are likely key factors for successfully surviving winter and avoiding predators. It was a great privilege to have had the opportunity to study these remarkable animals (Fig. 2.25).

DEER RESEARCH: PHASE TWO

After our early research quantifying seasonal deer use of clear-cuts and second-growth forest compared to old growth, we shifted our focus to measuring how deer used old-growth forest habitats during different seasons. We also further evaluated the use of clear-cuts and old growth by individual deer. To do this, we captured and attached radio collars to a sample of deer in two study sites on northern Admiralty Island. One site, at Winning Cove on eastern Admiralty, included 1,000 acres of five- to ten-year-old clear-cuts located in long strips close to the beach and surrounded by old growth (Fig. 2.26). This arrangement of forest habitats offered a good opportunity to evaluate how individual radio-collared deer used their habitats where they had access to both clear-cuts and old growth.

FIG. 2.26. The Winning Cove deer study area on the Glass Peninsula along Seymour Canal on eastern Admiralty Island. The cove is located in the middle right below the snowcapped mountains that rise from sea level to over 3,000 feet. The light green vegetation above and to the right of the cove is a 1,000-acre clear-cut.

FIG. 2.27. The Hawk Inlet deer study area on northern Admiralty Island. This area includes a portion of the Mansfield Peninsula and Robert Barron Mountain (upper left) as well as Young's Bay, Admiralty Cove, and Greens and Wheeler Creeks drainage that extend to the right beyond this photo. Hawk Inlet is in the center while Auke Bay and the Juneau mainland lie in the background.

The other site was centered around Hawk Inlet and the southern portion of the Mansfield Peninsula on northern Admiralty (Fig. 2.27). Both sites ranged from sea level forests to alpine ridges over 3,000 feet in elevation. The Hawk Inlet site was largely old-growth forest interspersed with muskeg bogs, shrubby avalanche slopes, subalpine meadows, and alpine ridges at higher elevations. This site provided an opportunity to evaluate how deer used the natural forest mosaic throughout the year (Fig. 2.28).

CAPTURING AND RADIO-TRACKING DEER

In November 1978, Dave Beaudin and I were hiking the upper forest slope above Winning Cove, stalking deer with a capture gun. There was a light skiff of snow on the ground under the broad upper canopy of old growth, and we could hear humpback whales blowing in Seymour Canal 1,000 feet below us. Occasionally,

FIG. 2.28. Forest mosaic on Admiralty Island. Many people mistakenly think of the coastal forest as a continuous, homogeneous forest. This photo demonstrates the patchiness of the forest. In the lower right center is an open muskeg bog (open yellow areas in back of the extensive tidal area) fringed with small scrub forest. These areas have waterlogged soils that do not support the growth of large trees. Along the shoreline to the lower right is a dense, productive stand of beach-fringe forest with large, tall trees where the soils are better drained. You can also see the more productive forest stands on many of the mid-elevation slopes with better soil drainage. At higher elevations around 2,000 feet open subalpine forests and meadows occur. Above that is a band of alpine tundra and rock. To the middle right are steep avalanche slopes with shrubby vegetation. Deer and other wildlife use the forest in a highly selective manner depending on their seasonal habitat requirements.

we also heard the thunderous boom when a whale breached and its thirty tons crashed down upon the surface of water. I remember that afternoon distinctly even after forty years.

Having established that old growth was essential winter habitat for black-tailed deer in coastal Alaska, we wanted to learn more precisely how deer used different types of old growth throughout the year. On this particular fall day, Dave and I had already captured several deer by slowly sneaking through the forest, stopping every few yards to watch and listen. We used the capture gun to shoot small plastic darts containing various dosages of an immobilizing drug. The gun was designed to shoot up to forty yards, but most successful shots had to be taken at half that distance. This was just like hunting, but it took even more time and patience to get close enough to a deer to dart it in the large hindquarter or front shoulder. Once hit, it would take about ten minutes for the deer to become immobile.

November is the rut, or breeding season, for deer in Alaska. During this time, it is often possible to call them in close using a deer call that mimics the distress call of a fawn. This sound can be made by blowing on a blade of grass held tightly between your thumbs. Both does and bucks will respond to the call. However, in a place like Admiralty, you need to be very careful that you don't inadvertently call up a curious, hungry bear that has not yet denned for the winter.

Throughout that autumn day, we had come across several large bear tracks in patches of snow. For safety, the two of us worked together. I was leading the way with the capture gun while Dave followed carrying a .338-caliber rifle. We were sneaking through the upper forest, stopping occasionally on higher ground to blow the deer call and wait. This had been working well for us over the last couple of days. As we climbed up onto an open mossy knoll overlooking the inlet below, I gave a couple of loud bleats while Dave covered my back. Immediately after I called, we heard crackling noises in the brush. It was uphill about thirty-five yards away in the underbrush and it kept moving our way.

"Oh damn!" This situation was taking a turn for the worse. We stood back to back on a raised knoll and prepared for a charging bear. Then, suddenly, the animal burst out of the dense underbrush rushing our way. But it wasn't a bear. The crashing and thrashing came from two adult bucks with their antlers locked in a rutting skirmish. As they passed by us, within about ten yards, I got off a quick shot. I hit one of the bucks, but we were never able to find it. Perhaps the adrenaline of battle—shared by both deer and hunters—reduced the effectiveness of the drug. Our adrenaline was still running high, and we were thankful that we did not have to deal with a surprised or aggressive brown bear at close range.

During the winter of 1978–1979, we captured and radio-collared twenty-one deer at Winning Cove and Hawk Inlet. About half of our deer were captured by stalking them in the forest, while the others were darted from a skiff along the beach. As we had done with our mountain goat research, we aimed for weekly telemetry flights to locate our radio-collared deer and record their movements and habitat use. Our flight frequency was higher for deer than goats, since deer were distributed much lower in elevation, and ceilings and visibilities were not as restrictive for safe flying.

This research occurred before global positioning systems (GPS) were available for nonmilitary uses. Thus, during our weekly telemetry flights we recorded locations of the radio-collared deer on USGS topographic maps along with a variety of habitat and topographic features that we identified from the airplane. These data were later entered into a computer database for analysis. The aircraft telemetry system consisted of two directional antennas facing outward under each wing. These were connected to the radio through a switch box. To locate deer, we would fly over the study area while switching between antennas to identify the direction of the strongest signal from our aircraft. We then flew decreasing circles over the transmitter until we received a strong snapping sound that meant we were right over it. We measured the accuracy of this system in field trials and determined that the average error was seventy-five feet, well within the bounds of the grid system we overlaid on our topographic maps.

It was challenging to fly safely for two to three hours within five hundred feet of the ground while doing tight turns over a radio-collared deer. We also needed to pay attention to plotting the locations on the map; describing the elevation, slope of the site, and habitat type; and estimating timber volume, canopy cover and percent composition of spruce and hemlock. Safety was always our foremost responsibility. Sometimes the air was bumpy, and in combination with tight turns, this resulted in some observers coming close to losing their lunch—an occupational hazard of wildlife survey flying.

GROWING OUR FAMILY

I enjoyed the opportunity to work in the field, but I also loved coming back home. After Mary Beth and I moved into our house on the beach at Smuggler's Cove, we soon acquired our first puppy—a fluffy, white eight-week-old Samoyed. Alex provided companionship and someone for Mary Beth to talk to when I was in the field. The next inevitable milestone was a baby.

After waiting through our nine years of marriage, including graduate school and two years in Alaska, the first thing my mother said when she heard Mary Beth was pregnant was, "My God, I thought it was the mumps." Well, we proved that theory wrong. Near the end of Mary Beth's pregnancy, Juneau doctors decided that Mary Beth needed to go south in a hurry to a larger hospital. So we packed our bags and jumped on the next Alaska Airlines flight out of Juneau and arrived at the University of Washington Hospital in Seattle. Erik was born on September 25, 1979.

After bringing Erik home, Mary Beth left her job at the Fish and Game Library and became a full-time mom. This is not as easy as it sounds when you live half a mile down a beach without a road or power or phone service—though we did have a marine radio for emergency calls. The first thing we did was to buy another vehicle and a second skiff. That way, when I was at work, Mary Beth and Erik weren't completely housebound. Living off the grid is not easy, particularly with children. Everything we needed had to be brought in by boat. When winds blew or ice occasionally formed on the saltwater, it was even more of a challenge. Our unique lifestyle added many trials and tribulations to our everyday life. Looking back, however, we wouldn't have changed it for the world. What an opportunity we had living on the edge of the Alaska wilderness raising a family, and having a satisfying job that was meaningful far beyond a paycheck.

⚘

Soon after Erik was born, our friends Matt and Patty Kirchhoff moved out to a cabin just next door at Smuggler's Cove. We shared the neighborhood with river otters, porpoise, eagles, and herons, and were surrounded by stunning scenery. Now and then on Saturday nights, we would crank up the Honda generator to run the blender to make lime daiquiris. During these early days in Juneau, many of our friends came to parties at our house by walking the beach—or we would meet them at the end of the road in our skiff for a short boat ride to our home. On these occasions, there would sometimes be ten to twelve pairs of red Xtratuf rubber boots lined up outside the door.

Having the Kirchhoffs at the cabin next door was actually quite handy, since Matt and I were often out in the field together for a week or more at a time. During these field excursions, Mary Beth and Erik would have the company and support of Patty and their daughter, Rachael. Living at the end of the road sometimes prompted resourcefulness. One time an eagle flew low over the Kirchhoffs' deck with something in its talons. One of the kids shouted, and the eagle dropped its catch. It was fresh king crab legs! The smart thing to do was quickly boil some water. They all enjoyed fresh king crab for dinner that night. Matt and I were sorry we weren't there to share nature's bounty.

COLLECTING DATA FROM SMALL AIRPLANES

Our regular airplane pilot was Lynn Bennett of LAB Flying Service. He was an excellent pilot with superb bush flying skills, and he was quick to master our telemetry flying safely and efficiently. The Helio Courier is a high-performance, short-take-off-and-landing plane with a large wing and leading-edge slats that popped out at low airspeed. Aerodynamically, this reduced the aircraft's stall speed (Fig. 2.29). This airplane flew as slow as thirty-five miles per hour, making it an ideal aircraft for our kind of specialty survey flying.

One of the challenges in Southeast, however, was that when the flying weather was good, everyone needed to fly right now. Lynn was the chief pilot for his company, so sometimes when the weather broke and everyone wanted to fly, we encountered scheduling conflicts. Because I was a licensed pilot and the State of Alaska had a pilot certification program, I soon became a certified state pilot, and Fish and Game leased the Helio that I piloted for

FIG. 2.29. The Helio Courier aircraft we used for tracking radio-collared deer and mountain goats in the coastal forests and mountains of northern Southeast Alaska. This high-performance aircraft allowed us to land on beaches and was a good platform for radio-tracking and conducting aerial surveys of wildlife.

our research work. Flying this complex aircraft required significant training, so I began flying our surveys from the left seat with Lynn providing valuable instruction. I took my state check ride in the Helio in January 1980, and after that I did nearly all of my own research flying.

I distinctly remember flying back to Juneau late one December afternoon, after conducting a deer telemetry flight with Matt at Winning Cove. I was tired after three hours of rigorous flying, but satisfied with the data we had just collected. The sky was dissolving into a pale crimson as the sun slipped below Admiralty's snow-shrouded ridges to our west. To the east, up the Taku River along the mainland coast, we looked out over ragged peaks and icefields along the Canadian border. The weather was cold and the air was smooth as we flew home that afternoon, listening to the comforting drone of the Helio's powerful engine. I thought how fortunate I was—conducting my own wildlife research and piloting this remarkable aircraft over such a dramatic Alaska wilderness dominated by ancient forests and coastal mountains fragmented by deep glacial fjords. I realized I was living my dream job—a job I had envisioned when I was a senior in college.

These memories are some of the intangible bonuses that far exceed the traditional compensations of salary and benefits. These opportunities and experiences kept my internal fire burning and made me excited to get up in the morning and go to work. My dad expressed these sentiments to me when he described starting his air service on Orcas Island over seventy years ago. I'm grateful to him for teaching me to fly but perhaps more importantly, for instilling in me important values about quality of life.

NEW APPROACHES FOR CAPTURING DEER

During the early winters of this phase of our research, we were investing a great deal of time and energy trying to capture enough deer to have a reasonable sample size for evaluating seasonal habitat use. Like many hunters, we learned that most Admiralty deer migrated up into the food-rich subalpine meadows near tree line during July and August. Perhaps because of my early cowboy fantasies, I imagined lassoing or netting animals in the open alpine using a helicopter. Recalling our early experiments trying to capture goats, I decided to take a manageable piece of seine net up and try to lasso deer with it. I recall sitting on the float of an Alouette helicopter flying about ten feet above the ridges on Mount Robert Barron on North Admiralty. We saw many deer and made multiple passes, and I did my best to throw the net over several deer. We got close, but could not quite entangle a deer with the net. In the final attempt that day, we were following a big buck running lickety-split along a ridge at about 3,000 feet above sea level. I had wrapped my legs around the float like I was sitting on a horse. My left hand was hanging onto the float, and I held a big wad of net in my right hand. I was leaning over to the right where I could almost touch the deer, when it suddenly veered over the ridge and down the slope. We must have been flying at about twenty-five to thirty miles an hour, and over the edge of the steep ridge, when I looked down to the shoreline below me. "Oops!" I wasn't strapped on to the chopper. The only things that kept me on that aircraft were my legs wrapped around the float. I had a sudden adrenaline rush and wrapped myself as firmly as I could around that float until we came back to the ridge and landed. That was my last attempt at lassoing deer with a net.

A year later, however, we used a shoulder-held net gun that was developed in New Zealand to capture red deer from a helicopter. This required precision, low-level flying toward running deer. About ten to fifteen feet from the deer, we fired a triangular net, weighted at each corner, from a specialty net gun. Once the net entangled the deer, the helicopter immediately landed and the shooter and assistant would jump out and restrain the deer before it could escape. This method proved to be very successful, and in the late summer of 1981, we successfully captured fourteen deer in the alpine above Hawk Inlet (Fig. 2.30).

FIG. 2.30. Matt Kirchhoff (right) and pilot Bob Englebrecht with a black-tailed buck we captured with a net gun in the alpine on northern Admiralty Island at about 2,500 feet elevation. The red net is visible below and in front of the deer. A Hughes 500 helicopter is in the background.

SEEING THE FOREST THROUGH THE TREES

The results of our earlier deer study identifying old growth as important winter deer habitat had been challenged by the timber industry and the leadership within the Alaska Region of the Forest Service. Those results posed a risk to their logging plans. Although there were many unjustified criticisms, one of the valuable constructive criticisms of our earlier work came from Al Harris, a forest ecologist with the Forestry Sciences Lab in Juneau. Al was concerned about using a broad definition of old-growth forest. He accompanied us into the field and demonstrated how variable old growth was in Southeast. We embraced Al's suggestions to more clearly define and discriminate among the various types of old-growth forest communities.

For example, the edge of a muskeg bog is often sparsely forested by an open-canopy stand of short, small-diameter (less than twelve inches) mountain hemlock and shore pine trees (Fig. 2.31). Such forest stands may fall within the general definition of old growth, although they would be categorized as "scrub" old growth with no commercial value. But a stand of huge Sitka spruce trees

FIG. 2.31. A low-volume (small-tree) old-growth stand. Note the small-diameter trees, open canopy, and abundant shrub community in this forest. This forest stand is on poorly drained soils. Although the trees are small, the dominant trees are several centuries old. This low-productive forest habitat type is abundant across the Tongass and has relatively low commercial value. Thus, few of these forest sites are targeted for logging. These open-canopy forests also accumulate much snow on the ground, thus reducing their winter habitat value for deer.

200 feet tall and over four feet in diameter could occur less than 200 feet away (Fig. 2.32). Not only is the stand structure very different, but the understory plant community also differs dramatically. Much of this variation is due to soil drainage. The largest trees and most productive stands occur on well-drained, alluvial soils. The less-productive, low-volume, and scrub old growth is found on poorly drained, boggy soils.

Al recommended that our future studies subdivide old-growth forest habitat into discrete categories of forest community types. He also encouraged us to use the US Forest Service classification system that assigned commercial stands to one of five classes based on timber volume per acre. The Forest Service classification recognized noncommercial or scrub stands with scattered, stunted trees, low-volume stands with small trees, and mid- to high-

FIG. 2.32. A high-volume (large-tree) old-growth stand in the Kadashan watershed on Chichagof Island. This mixed hemlock-spruce stand has trees of all ages and sizes. The dominant trees are four to six feet in diameter. These stands include standing dead trees (snags) and downed logs. Much side light penetrates the broken, multilayered canopy and there is an abundance of herbs, shrubs, ferns, and moss on the forest floor. The tall forest canopy with large limbs intercept much snowfall, reducing snow accumulation on the forest floor. Such stands have high value as winter deer habitat. These large-tree, old-growth stands were always rare in Southeast and have very high commercial value. Thus, they have been heavily targeted for logging.

volume stands with larger, taller trees. Often, the highest volume old growth consisted of nearly pure spruce stands (greater than 75 percent) along the valley floodplains and riparian streambanks underlain with coarse, well-drained, alluvial gravel or karst (permeable limestone). A few of these trees measured six to eight feet in diameter and nearly 200 feet in height.

From this point on, our research focused on quantifying how deer used the variable patchwork of old-growth habitat and how their use of habitats varied seasonally and under different snow conditions. If we could accurately assess the seasonal value of different forest types as deer habitat, then we could offer management recommendations to the Forest Service for minimizing logging impacts on deer populations.

FIG. 2.33. Sitka black-tailed bucks on an alpine ridge above 2,500 feet on Admiralty Island. These extensive subalpine meadows provide abundant summer forage for deer and are used heavily by migratory deer during summer. In the background, scattered avalanche slopes dominated by shrubs are interspersed across the forested slope.

From 1979 through the summer of 1982, we flew hundreds of hours in the Helio, tracking up to fifty radio-collared deer on northern Admiralty Island throughout the year. We recorded where they moved, their elevation, and the types of habitat they were using. This was hard-earned data and very labor-intensive. Today, biologists can put GPS transmitters on animals and download location data on an hourly basis from the comfort and safety of their office. There is no doubt that the amount and quality of data generated with modern technology vastly improves the kinds of habitat analyses possible today. However, observing the habitat a deer is using under real-time environmental conditions also had its value in helping us understand the importance of different habitats under varying conditions.

From our radio-tracking studies,[31] we learned that about three-quarters of Admiralty deer migrated into the upper subalpine and alpine habitats in summer. We designated these "migratory" deer (Fig. 2.33). Others remained in forested habitats below 500 feet. These were designated as "resident" deer. Except for altitudinal movements between summer and winter ranges, all deer made relatively small movements within seasonal home ranges that averaged about 200 acres. Once home ranges were established, deer seldom strayed far from those areas over subsequent years.

Deer distribution was most limited during winter. In our unlogged Hawk Inlet study area, nearly all winter deer use was within old-growth forest habitats mostly below 1,000 feet elevation. Radio-collared deer made substantial use of mid- and high-volume old growth, and especially preferred high-volume stands with large-diameter trees. In contrast, they largely avoided stands of scrub forest and low-volume old growth with small trees and open canopies.

At the Winning Cove site, approximately three miles of shoreline was backed by a large clear-cut. Three radio-collared deer wintered in a low-elevation (less than 100 feet) strip of old growth below the clear-cut. These deer rarely moved into or above the clear-cut. In contrast, five radio-collared deer in adjacent forest areas regularly moved higher up into the forest throughout the winter. Because the three deer that wintered below the clear-cut used forest above the cut during the summer, we assumed their reluctance to move farther up during winter was due to the greater accumulation of snow in the clear-cut, the low availability of forage, and the difficulty of moving through the deep snow in the clear-cut.

During our study, we experienced two back-to-back winters of contrasting snow conditions. In 1981, snow accumulations were low, with only ten days with persistent snow at sea level. In contrast, in 1982, there were fifty-two days with greater than nineteen inches of snow at sea level. This significant

FIG. 2.34. A Sitka black-tailed doe in a mid- to high-volume (large-tree) old-growth stand on Douglas Island during a deep-snow winter. The tall forest canopy and big limb structure of the large trees intercept a significant amount of snow. Deer can travel easily through these stands and food is comparatively much more available than in the deep-snow conditions that occur in clear-cuts and muskegs as well as in small-tree old-growth stands.

contrast provided an opportunity to evaluate how deer used different types of old-growth habitat. In the low-snow year of 1981, low- and mid-volume stands— with relatively small and medium-size trees—accounted for about two-thirds of deer habitat use. The smaller area of large-tree old-growth still accounted for about 25 percent of deer habitat use, indicating it was still preferred habitat.

During the deep-snow winter of 1982, however, radio-collared deer highly preferred the high-volume old growth with large-diameter trees (Fig. 2.34). Although this forest type only represented 8 percent of the study area, 65 percent of our deer locations occurred there during the deep-snow winter. In contrast, scrub forest and low-volume old growth only received 8 percent of deer use, although it represented 59 percent of the study area (Fig. 2.35).

FIG. 2.35. A low-volume scrub stand of old growth near Juneau during a deep-snow winter. The open canopy and small trees do not intercept much snow compared to the larger high-volume old growth with tall trees and broad limb structure within the upper forest canopy. Deer avoid these small-tree old-growth stands during deep-snow conditions because most food is buried, and travel though this snow is energetically very costly.

Flying over northern Admiralty radio-tracking deer, I would bank the aircraft and look out the window below at the ragged canopy of old-growth hemlock-spruce forests. At this low altitude, I had a clear view of the landscape below. Consistently, the areas used by deer occurred in stands of large trees. Rarely did we see tracks in the open areas of deep snow. The forest that spread out below my wings was a fine-grained patchwork of stands from open muskeg bogs surrounded by scrub forest to patches of high-volume old growth with tall, large-diameter trees scattered across the landscape (Fig. 2.36). These results clearly indicated a strong preference by deer for the relatively rare patches of large-tree old growth, particularly during winters with substantial snow accumulation. By following radio-collared deer and letting them show us how they used their habitat, we inferred habitat values from their patterns of selection and avoidance.[32] Al Harris's observations that all old growth is not alike and his recommendation that we use the Forest Service inventory to define old-growth types proved most valuable.

Deer do not have a particular affinity for the big trees per se, but they are strongly attracted to the availability of food and ease of travel that stands of

FIG. 2.36. Aerial view of the forest mosaic during winter. Looking out our plane while radio-tracking deer, it was rare to see deer tracks or deer in open areas of deep snow. Most of the radio-collared deer were in the mid- to high-volume old-growth stands where snow depth was much lower and snow cover patchier than in forest openings.

large-tree old growth provide during times of heavy snow accumulation. If you have ever walked through deep snow leaving postholes in your wake, you know how much more energy it takes compared to walking in snow-free or low-snow conditions. Also, it takes only a few inches of snow to bury many of the most valuable winter forage plants like bunchberry and five-leaved bramble.

To better understand the relationship of large trees and snow accumulation, Matt and I set up a study of snow characteristics under different types of forest stands and found that stands with tall, large-diameter trees and big limbs in the overhead canopy intercepted much more snow than scrub forest or low-volume stands.[33] Deer were selecting the habitat conditions that had the most available food and required the least energy for traveling, and these areas were what the Forest Service labeled as high-volume (or large-tree) old growth.

In addition to our telemetry work, we also developed a forest sampling scheme where we measured deer pellet group densities in relation to old-growth forest characteristics on one-acre forest plots.[34] Forest community types included poorly drained bog communities; well-drained, mixed hemlock-spruce stands with an understory characterized by bunchberry, five-leaved bramble, and blueberry shrubs; and a riparian spruce community characterized by an understory of devil's club, salmonberry, and stink currants. Winter deer use, based on pellet group densities, was most strongly associated with mid- to high-volume mixed hemlock-spruce old growth on well-drained sites characterized by large, irregularly spaced trees, and an understory of bunchberry, blueberry, and five-leaved bramble—three important winter forage species for deer.

FIG. 2.37. A tame Sitka black-tailed doe (Rudy) feeding on arboreal lichen in an old-growth forest during winter. Arboreal lichens (called old man's beard) are important sources of food for deer during deep winter snow conditions.

We also found that the riparian spruce stands along the border of streams and in the floodplain received relatively little deer use during winter. Although this habitat featured large-diameter, tall trees, the spruce-dominated stands intercepted less snow than mixed hemlock-spruce. They were also dominated by less desirable winter forage species such as devil's club, currant, and salmonberry.

One winter, our colleague, Lars Holtan, worked with a hand-reared yearling black-tailed doe he named Rudy. Rudy was habituated to humans, and by following her throughout the forest, we gained insights into how deer actually traveled and foraged during winter. While closely trailing this deer through a snowy forest, we observed her moving from tree to tree, feeding on the green leaves of bunchberry, five-leaved bramble, and fern-leaved goldthread she found in snow-free patches at the base of the larger trees. She also went out of her way to eat the arboreal lichen (old man's beard) that had fallen from the forest canopy (Fig. 2.37). Occasionally, she would nip the annual growth of blueberry twigs and young hemlock boughs. Observing this deer at close range, it became clear that she moved through the forest in a nonrandom pattern to specific sites that had an abundance of preferred foods, and she consistently used the most efficient travel routes, avoiding open areas with deep snow.

The seasonal distribution of deer in Southeast is depicted on an aerial photo of a coastal watershed on Admiralty Island (Fig. 2.38). The numbers on this photo represent the types of habitats that a hypothetical deer is likely to occupy

FIG. 2.38. The annual cycle of a Southeast deer. (Courtesy Audubon Alaska 2016, *Ecological Atlas of Southeast Alaska*)

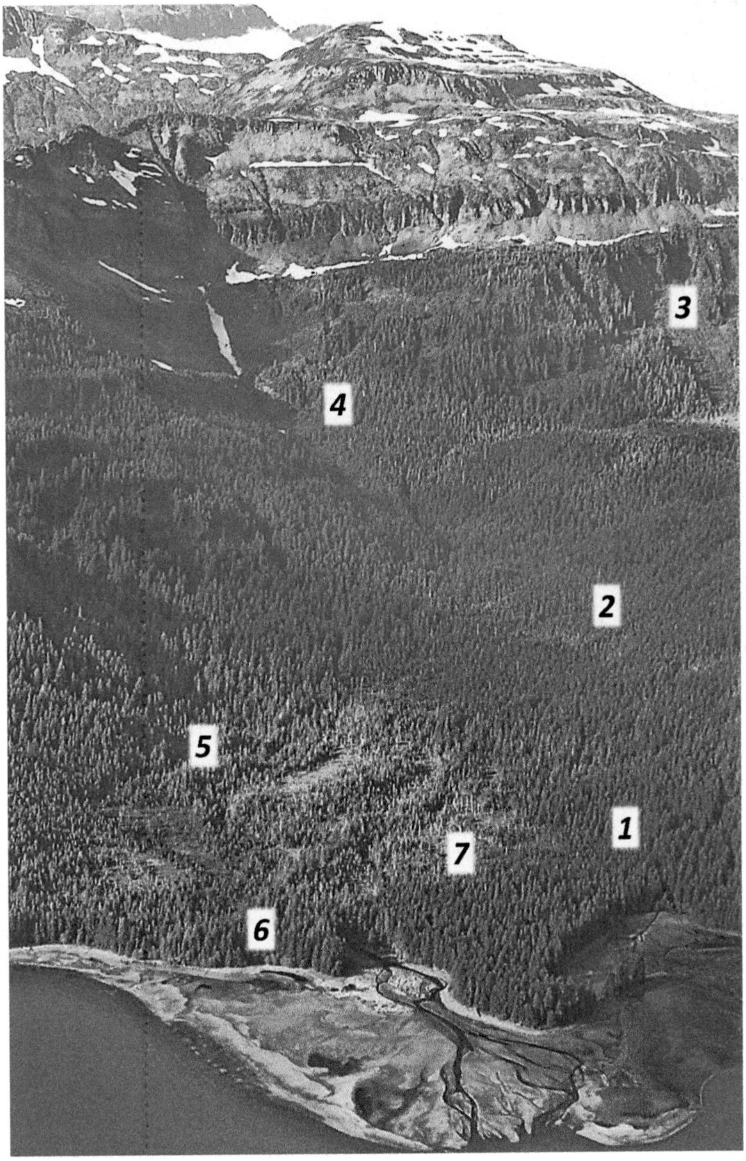

1. Fawning: In late May and early June, black-tailed does drop their fawns. During late spring, deer range from sea level to 1,500 feet in search of new plant growth. Deer use old-growth forests and increase their use of open canopy stands, fens, tidal meadows, and young clear-cuts at this time.

2. Upward migration: Throughout June, migratory deer continue to disperse off their winter ranges following the receding snow line onto upper forest slopes. Resident deer generally remain at lower elevations but use more forest openings for feeding.

3. Subalpine summer ranges: Migratory deer generally reach their summer ranges by the end of June or early July. On subalpine meadows between 1,800 and 3,000 feet, deer find abundant and nutritious herbaceous forage interspersed among stunted stands of Sitka spruce and mountain hemlock.

4. Fall migration: Following the first high-country frosts in mid- to late September, forage plants die and migratory deer move into the upper forests. Throughout the next month, many deer move down to lower elevations as snow accumulates in the high country.

5. The rut: The breeding season, or rut, begins in late October and continues through November. Deer are widely dispersed from sea level to 1,500 feet. Old-growth forests are important foraging habitats, but deer also make use of forest openings and muskeg fringes during the rut.

6. Winter range: From December through March, deer are generally confined to old-growth forest winter ranges below 1,000–1,500 feet. Southern exposures generally accumulate less snow and provide greater access to evergreen forbs like bunchberry dogwood and trailing raspberry. Deer move up and down forest slopes following changes in the snowpack throughout the winter. During deep snows, medium- and large-tree old-growth hemlock spruce forests provide the best winter habitat.

7. Spring snowmelt: Spring is a transition period as deer begin to expand their movements beyond the confines of their winter range in search of new plant growth. Wet, open-canopy forests with newly emergent skunk cabbage shoots are important foraging sites, as are upper beaches and young clear-cuts.

FIG. 2.39. Sitka black-tailed doe in Southeast Alaska. Old-growth forests provide critical winter habitat for deer throughout coastal Alaska.

throughout the year. In 1988, Matt Kirchhoff and I published an essay, "Little Deer in the Big Woods," in *Natural History*.[35] I have excerpted portions of that article below.

Our research, begun in 1977, has enabled us to put together a picture of a year in the life of a Sitka black-tail. During summer, the doe we were tracking would, like most of the archipelago's blacktails, migrate to the lush alpine ridges that form the backbone of the major islands. Here, above tree line, she feeds belly deep in meadows of succulent wildflower and green plants, particularly deer cabbage—a summer favorite. At this time of year, the high country, at least on Admiralty, Baranof and Chichagof islands, is relatively safe: the only predators are grizzlies (brown bears), and most of them move down to salmon streams far below during summer and early fall. (In the southern portion of the archipelago, the deer have to contend with wolves and black bears.) The doe is able to concentrate on eating, putting on the fat she needs to carry her through the long winter.

As alpine meadows yellow from the killing frosts of autumn, the doe begins to descend. At first, she moves just far enough to reenter the forest, where the vegetation—nutritious low-growing, broad-leaved plants such as bunchberry and five-leaved bramble—remains green and palatable. Later, as the first snows begin to accumulate, she and other deer move farther down the steep mountainsides into the heart of the rainforest.

With the end of the fall rut, or breeding season, in late November and early December, many bucks begin to lose their antlers. The yearling doe bred for the first time this year and has now descended to her winter range, the same area she wintered in last year and one that overlaps her mother's home range. Consisting of about 200 forested acres on a southwest-facing slope overlooking the frigid waters of Chatham Strait, the winter range extends from 500 feet above sea level down to the shoreline and is a complex mosaic of habitats. More than half of the range is composed of scrubby trees and dense blueberry shrubs growing on poorly drained soils. These trees, many of them 200 to 500 years old, technically qualify as old growth, but they are short and sparse, providing little protection from the elements. Snow falls unimpeded through openings in the forest canopy, burying most vegetation on the forest floor and making every step a struggle for the deer. Interspersed throughout the forest are patches of open muskeg overgrown with sedges, Labrador tea, scattered shore pines, and stunted mountain hemlocks. Less than 10 percent of the winter range contains the big trees most people think of as old growth. In these groves, the deep crowns and broad, spreading limbs of the dominant western hemlock intercept up to 80 percent of the falling snow. The old trees also bear the brunt of the frequent gales and driving rains. During the severest winter months, the doe spends nearly two-thirds of her time in these relatively rare stands.

By January, more than two feet of snow has piled up in the scrub forest and mus-kegs. Even under the old-growth canopy, the deer is faced with nearly a foot of snow. In response, she moves several hundred feet farther downhill, where bunchberry and five-leaved bramble are more exposed in snow-free patches under the largest trees. Heavy snow continues to fall, and by February, more than three feet has accumulated at sea level, forcing most deer down to the lowest portions of their winter range. Near the coast, some deer move out onto beaches, where at low tide, they feed on kelp—a low-quality food of last resort. The doe beds down beneath a large hemlock half a mile inland. Even under the big stands of old growth, the best forage is buried. To conserve energy, she spends more time resting than looking for food. When she does eat, she is restricted to the woody stems of shrubs and conifers and to arboreal lichens that are blown down out of the canopy. The doe manages to fill her rumen, but none of these foods are very nutritious. By spring she will have lost 20 percent of her summer weight.

During especially severe winters, as in 1972, snow may keep piling up for half the year even at sea level, reaching peak depths of more than six feet. At such times, more than 75 percent of the region's deer perish and beaches are littered with their car-casses. In mild winters, periodic heavy rainfall washes away the snow below 1,000 feet, and most deer find adequate food to survive until spring.

With April, come weeks of warm rain. The snow line recedes, and the doe—two months from bearing her first young—is beginning to eat well again. Now the deer prefer the scrubby old-growth forest because the relatively open canopy lets in abundant light stimulating plant growth. In addition to the low-growing, broad-leaved plants until recently covered by snow, the deer seek out the emerging yellow, candle-like spadix of skunk cabbage. At this time of year, few of the nutritious shoots escape the deer's attention. As spring merges into summer, a new crop of fawns is born, and soon the doe, this time accompanied by her first offspring, will move to the high country. The annual cycle begins again. [Fig. 2.39]

Since the mid-1980s, other researchers have also studied the habitat relationships of deer in Southeast using a variety of methods, from feeding trials and systematic observation of tame deer to additional telemetry studies of habitat use and rates of mortality, nutritional analyses of deer forage, predation risks associated with different habitats, and computer modeling of habitat carrying capacity. Key studies include those of Matt Kirchhoff, Tom Hanley, Kathleen Parker and Mike Gillingham, Dave Person, Don Spalinger, Chris Farmer, Joe Doerr, Jeff Yeo, Todd Brinkman, and Sophie Gilbert. These additional studies have helped refine and significantly advance our knowledge of deer habitat relationships in Southeast.

Converting productive old-growth forest to even-age second growth will reduce long-term carrying capacity for deer in Southeast. Although young clear-cuts provide abundant forage for deer during snow-free periods, that forage is reduced in winters with deep snow accumulation. It is also only abundant for approximately twenty-five years in a hundred-year harvest cycle, followed by seventy-five years of impoverished forage conditions.

Optimal habitat conditions in Southeast must encompass diverse habitats that provide deer with a variety of options to satisfy changing seasonal needs and variable weather conditions. Productive south-facing stands of large, old-growth hemlock-spruce trees provide optimal availability of high-quality forage during winters with deep snow.

In Southeast, large-tree old growth represents less than 4 percent of the land area, but these stands have been disproportionately cut throughout the region. The disproportionate loss of this rare but important habitat will significantly impact deer populations. To ensure that deer populations thrive across their natural range in Southeast and are available for human use and enjoyment, watersheds with a variety of high-value deer habitat should be identified and protected.

Identifying important deer habitat and understanding what is required for conserving populations proved much easier than applying this knowledge to forest management. Management application often lags behind science. In Southeast Alaska, however, politics proved to be a significant barrier to scientific management.

For nearly two decades, the Alaska Region of the Forest Service, pushed by the timber industry and its political supporters, resisted acknowledging that old growth was important deer habitat. As more wildlife managers and the public began to question Forest Service policies, the Forest Service shifted the argument. They began to acknowledge the detrimental effect of clear-cutting on deer, but argued instead that there were adequate deer to meet subsistence and sport hunting demand. In the early 1980s, the Forest Service further asserted they could manage second-growth forests to recreate the ecological conditions of old growth.

New Forest Service leadership in Washington, DC, under chiefs Jack Ward Thomas and Mike Dombeck, did have positive impacts on Forest Service leadership in the Tongass. Nonetheless, even today, within timber management staff and the timber industry's Alaska Forest Association, there is residual resistance to the concept that old growth is valuable fish and wildlife habitat and ecologically nonrenewable under standard timber rotations.

My fieldwork on deer concluded in the spring of 1982. However, Matt and I continued to analyze data and publish our deer research results throughout the

1980s. The Alaska Department of Fish and Game also continued deer research in Southeast under Matt, Ken Pitcher, and Dave Person. In addition, Tom Hanley at the Forestry Sciences Lab was expanding deer research across the Tongass National Forest.

As my deer research phased out, I recognized that the forest management issue in Southeast was about more than just deer. It was about a rare and valuable old-growth forest ecosystem that had been intensively exploited and was now greatly diminished from its historical distribution and abundance across the North American continent and throughout the world. In Southeast Alaska, we needed to learn more about the ecological complexity of old growth and its unique habitat values to additional fish and wildlife species native to this coastal temperate rainforest.

BROWN BEAR RESEARCH

Shafts of bright sunlight pierce the thin overcast, and waves of cold mist swirl across the lush alpine ridge 3,200 feet above sea level. It is late June. Several hundred yards away, a dark form appears in the dull grayness, moving slowly and deliberately along the ridge. As the apparition comes closer, it penetrates the thick fog and reveals itself to be a large dark brown female bear. Following closely behind her are two small cubs, born earlier that year in a rock cave 2,000 feet above sea level, on the steep west face of a mountain peak.

This family group is traveling a distinct trail of large, oval depressions, six to twelve inches deep and three feet apart, in the alpine tundra. These staggered depressions were first pressed into the tundra by bears following the retreat of the ice sheet 10,000 years ago. Since then, countless generations of their descendants have been stepping in the same tracks, and today, the depressions are near-permanent features of the landscape. Southeast Alaska has hundreds of such ridgeline trails, overlooking valleys of old-growth rainforest that stretch unbroken all the way to the coast.[36] [Fig. 2.40]

HISTORY AND BACKGROUND

Two hundred years ago, brown/grizzly bears were abundant and widely distributed across western North America from the Mississippi River to the Pacific Ocean and from northern Mexico to the Arctic Coast.[37] Brown and grizzly bears are the same species but are commonly called grizzlies in the contiguous US and northern Alaska, while coastal bears with access to salmon are referred to as brown bears. Following settlement of the West, brown/grizzly bear populations south of Canada declined significantly and now occupy only a fraction

FIG. 2.40. A brown bear trail embedded in the alpine tundra on a ridge next to Trap Mountain above Corner Bay on eastern Chichagof Island.

FIG. 2.41. Alaska brown bear female and cub feeding on a salmon run in coastal Alaska.

of their original range. The grizzly bear was listed as threatened in the lower 48 states under the Endangered Species Act in 1975, and today Alaska remains the last stronghold in the United States for this adaptable, large omnivore—once the undisputed ruler of its domain (Fig. 2.41).

Brown bears are indigenous to Southeast Alaska and on the northern islands of Admiralty, Baranof, and Chichagof, often referred to as the ABC Islands, where they occur in some of the highest-density populations on Earth. Hiking up a salmon spawning stream on the ABC Islands during late summer is like entering a primordial world—mist-shrouded forest laced with heavily used bear trails winding through tunnels of devil's club and stink currant shrubs beneath centuries-old, giant spruce trees. Brown bears still fish for spawning salmon as they migrate up the myriad streams and rivers that drain Southeast's rugged, coastal mountains into the Gulf of Alaska. These floodplain forests play an important role in the productivity and diversity of Southeast's temperate rainforest where bears, salmon, and big trees have been inextricably linked for millennia (Fig. 2.42).

Because of the large home ranges they require and the variety of habitats they use seasonally, brown bears represent an important umbrella species for maintaining ecosystem integrity throughout their range in Southeast.[38]

FIG. 2.42. Riparian spruce old-growth forest located along a floodplain forest on eastern Chichagof Island. The largest trees are four to six feet in diameter. The understory vegetation is dominated by devil's club, salmonberry, and currant shrubs. The unvegetated areas around the base of the trees along the streambank are the result of heavy bear use during salmon spawning season.

Coastal brown bears are also considered a keystone species because of their role in transferring marine nutrients from freshwater salmon streams into the terrestrial environment. And because human activities can have significant impacts on brown bears, their healthy survival is an indicator of a resilient wilderness ecosystem. This combination of attributes and their low reproductive rates set the stage for identifying the brown bear as an important focal species of our expanding wildlife research in Southeast Alaska and the Tongass National Forest.

Previous studies of brown bears in Southeast included early population estimates on the ABC Islands, an early Forest Service study of the effects of logging on bears, and a bear movement study on Admiralty Island. These studies provided valuable baseline data on numbers and general natural history but limited understanding on the effects of logging and mining on brown bears within the Tongass Forest.

In the fall of 1981, my ADF&G colleagues and I believed that it was time to broaden and expand our wildlife research program. We were well aware of the continued loss of old-growth habitat in the Tongass and the incremental proliferation of logging roads. In addition, exploratory work was under way to develop a major mine at Greens Creek on northern Admiralty Island. This mine would become one of the largest silver mines in the world. We knew that resource development activities by humans had played a significant role in the historical decline of the brown bear throughout its range in the western United States. We believed it was imperative to begin understanding the impacts of logging and mining on Tongass brown bear populations.

RESEARCH PRIORITIES

Our goal was to develop an ecological baseline on Southeast brown bears using study areas on Admiralty and Chichagof Islands (Figs. 2.43, 2.44). The northeastern Chichagof study area was the site of major logging activity and road building. The Admiralty study area would allow us to look at the impacts of the Greens Creek Mine. We believed that increasing our understanding of the ecology of brown bears and their relationship to these resource extraction industries could help us develop management guidelines to minimize future impacts on this iconic wilderness species.

※

I first worked with LaVern Beier in the winter of 1980, when we were capturing deer at Winning Cove on Admiralty Island. LaVern was a hardworking, woods-wise young man with black hair and a big bushy beard. He moved to Petersburg, Alaska, when he was a teenager and began trapping and hunting the wildlands of Southeast. In the early 1970s, LaVern started working as a wildlife technician with ADF&G in Petersburg and continued to expand his knowledge and wildlife skills. He later worked as an assistant guide with master guide and conservationist Karl Lane from Juneau. I hired LaVern to work with me on our brown bear research project in 1982. We worked together snaring bears along salmon streams, darting them out of helicopters, and then tracking the radio-collared bears from small planes over Admiralty and Chichagof Islands from 1982 through 1989. I greatly enjoyed working with LaVern and respected his local knowledge and wildlife skills as well as his strong conservation ethic—in part, a legacy from Karl Lane (Fig. 2.45).

※

FIG. 2.43. North Admiralty brown bear study area (bottom to center): Hawk Inlet and Greens Creek (left center), Mansfield Peninsula and Robert Barron Mountain (upper center), Young's Bay and Admiralty Cove (middle right), Chichagof Island (upper left), Glacier Bay and Mount Fairweather (upper right). Chatham Strait separates Admiralty and Chichagof Islands. This area overlapped our deer study area but was more extensive.

Our research included these major objectives:[39]

» Develop an estimate of brown bear density on northern Admiralty Island.
» Determine seasonal distribution, habitat preferences, and home range characteristics on Admiralty and Chichagof Islands.
» Describe denning ecology on Admiralty and Chichagof.
» Assess bear habitat use relative to forest management on Chichagof.
» Establish baseline data and monitoring effects of mining on Admiralty bears.

CAPTURING AND TRACKING BEARS

In Southeast, after brown bears have emerged from their winter dens, they are frequently observed grazing on the new growth of sedges along the upper edge of shoreline beaches and across rich tidal flats, particularly during late

FIG. 2.44. Chichagof brown bear study area in Tenakee Inlet looking northwest over the Kadashan River Delta. The Kadashan Watershed is largely undeveloped while the watersheds on either side of it have been heavily logged and roaded.

FIG. 2.45. LaVern Beier setting a leg-hold snare for brown bears along a beach-fringe bear trail on Admiralty Island. The red treadle is visible in the bottom right surrounded by the cable. The cable loop rests on two logs set across the trail. The cable is tied off to a tree.

evening hours. We referred to this time as the "magic hours" when bears suddenly appear like phantoms out of the shadows of the rainforest. They are also commonly seen from small aircraft foraging on high alpine ridges and subalpine meadows from mid-June through early July. Every summer and fall, millions of Pacific salmon concentrate along tidal estuaries and then migrate up their natal streams through floodplain rainforests to spawn and die. By mid-July, most brown bears fish for spawning salmon along thousands of streams and rivers that flow out of Southeast's coastal mountains and the interiors of large islands.

Because bears, like deer, spend most of their time feeding, traveling, and resting under cover of the dense rainforest—largely invisible from observation—we used radio telemetry to monitor their movements and determine what kinds of habitat they were using throughout each season. Thus, the first step of our research necessitated that we capture a sample of bears and fit them with radio collars, which we could use to locate them from small aircraft.

In late summer and fall of 1981, we captured and radio-collared our first ten brown bears on Admiralty in what would become a multidecade ecological study. Capturing and handling any wild animal can be challenging and requires learning their patterns of movements and preferred habitats. In our previous studies, we had encountered many trials and tribulations while capturing deer and mountain goats. With brown bears, however, there was also the additional hurdle of handling a large, potentially dangerous animal with a less than gentle demeanor.

We used two proven techniques for capturing bears. The first was to use leg-hold snares set along heavily used beach-fringe or streamside bear trails. LaVern had experience working with ADF&G in Petersburg to snare "problem" black bears and move them out of town.

To set a snare, we placed a quarter-inch stainless steel cable snare over a well-used bear trail with an eighteen-inch loop held eight to twelve inches above the ground by sticks, roots, or small logs. The snare had a treadle in the middle of the loop. When the bear stepped on it, the snare spring would quickly lift the loop up onto the bear's upper leg. The end of the cable was very carefully and securely double-clamped to a tree or large log. We checked the snares every day to minimize the time a bear was held in a snare. After an initial struggle, bears generally lay down and remained relatively quiet. But once we arrived at the snare site, life became very stressful and hectic for both bears and biologists. We estimated the bear's weight, and then loaded a syringe with an appropriate amount of immobilizing drug that we fired out of a capture gun. It would usually take ten to fifteen minutes for the drug to fully take effect so that we could safely handle the bear.

We also darted bears out of a helicopter when we found them in open nonforested areas such as high-elevation alpine and subalpine meadows or large intertidal grass flats along river deltas at sea level (Fig. 2.46). The advantage of this technique was that we could be more selective of the bears we captured and also minimize the amount of time they were restrained. The most effective approach for helicopter capture was to send a small plane up to survey the area and identify a likely target. Once a bear was identified from the airplane, the helicopter would approach the bear. The passenger side door was removed and a "gunner" would lean out the door and dart the bear— preferably in its large, muscular hindquarter— with a preloaded dart of appropriate dosage. We would try to get within ten to fifteen yards of the bear to maximize our success at placing the shot. Once the bear was hit with a dart, the helicopter would back away

FIG. 2.46 Darting a brown bear from a helicopter along an alpine ridge at about 3,000 feet elevation on northern Admiralty Island.

to reduce stress on the bear. The aircraft would follow the bear and call the helicopter back to the site once it became immobile.

From fall 1981 through June 1989, LaVern and I captured ninety-five individual bears, sixty-eight on Admiralty and twenty-seven on Chichagof. Of those bears, sixteen bears were recaptured twice or more and their radio collars replaced. Seventy percent of Admiralty bear captures were by helicopter—most in the alpine—while 56 percent of Chichagof bears were snared along fish streams. Once a bear was captured and immobilized, we measured and weighed it, marked it with a small plastic ear tag and lip tattoo, and extracted a small tooth for aging. Aging bears is done by counting annular rings, much like aging a tree. We also collected blood and hair samples for analysis, and fitted

FIG. 2.47. LaVern and me with a captured and radio-collared brown bear on a subalpine ridge on northern Admiralty Island above Greens Creek. This 547-pound eleven-year-old adult male bear (#46) was captured in June 1986.

each bear with a radio collar—each with a unique frequency—which we used to monitor its movements and habitat use from an airplane (Fig. 2.47).

When bears were immobile, we covered their eyes to protect them and reduce stress. We also monitored their body temperature and respiration rate. We worked quickly to minimize handling time and stress on the bear. One of the early drugs we used (M99) also had an associated reversal agent that neutralized immobilization within about five minutes after injection so we could further minimize capture stress. Later, we used Telazol as the drug of preference because it was more effective and had a wider tolerance range.

BEAR FIELD RESEARCH IN SOUTHEAST ALASKA

I awoke to sun streaming through the porthole—a most unusual but pleasing experience in the misty rainforest of the Alexander Archipelago. The water outside was flat calm without a breath of wind. It was still too early to rise from my bunk, so I lay there and listened to the rejuvenating sounds of spring. It was early May and I was anchored in Admiralty Cove off northern Admiralty Island (Fig. 2.48). From the surrounding hillsides came an almost continuous chorus of *hoo-hoo-hoots*, like the sound of blowing across the mouth of a half-empty bottle of Alaskan Amber beer. The male sooty grouse were performing their spring ritual of setting up breeding territories. I heard another familiar sound—Canada

FIG. 2.48. Looking west over Admiralty Cove on northern Admiralty Island (center foreground) and beyond to Young's Bay. The head of Hawk Inlet is just visible in the upper right with the Mansfield Peninsula above and to the right. Chatham Strait and Chichagof Island are in the background.

geese, but just a couple—probably a breeding pair of Vancouver Canada geese, which are year-round residents of Southeast. Then I heard a different, cavernous, almost explosive exhalation. Humpback whales! There must have been several, because I heard two deep blows in a row, then nothing. They seemed quite close. Then a crack and continuous rumble of an avalanche rushing down one of Admiralty's ragged, snow-covered alpine ridges. Maybe one of the ten-foot cornices hanging over the side of a knife-edge ridge had finally succumbed to gravity and warm, spring sun.

It was so still that morning that I could hear the calls and songs of many different birds. The caws and croaks of ever-present ravens and crows were obvious. But I heard a recent arrival as well: Bonaparte gulls had returned from their winter retreat along the Pacific Coast from Puget Sound south to Central America. And there were others—the rapid-fire chatter of belted kingfishers and the yodeling calls of long-tailed ducks from a large flock rafted up near the head of the bay. This was better than listening to *Morning Edition* on National Public Radio.

FIG. 2.49. An Admiralty cave den on the south side of Eagle Peak at about 3,000 feet elevation.

Suddenly, a sound not unlike the blast of a small dynamite explosion brought me out of my bunk with a start. A hundred yards off my stern, a humpback whale had breached—catapulting almost entirely out of the water. Such a multiton belly flop gets your attention in a hurry. The first whale was joined by a second, and the two whales continued breaching for several minutes. Later, the pair rolled on the surface, slapping the water with their pectoral fins. It was truly a glorious morning in Southeast Alaska with sunshine to boot.

As I scanned the mountaintop with binoculars, I saw a single set of bear tracks winding down the slope. They began just below a steep, rocky cliff at about 2,900 feet. Most likely there was a den up there somewhere, maybe in a rock cave or excavated into the steep subalpine slope. Although cave denning by brown bears is relatively unusual throughout most of their range in North America, on Admiralty Island many brown bears den in natural caves or rock crevices (Fig. 2.49). Others den under the roots of ancient large-diameter Sitka spruce trees at upper elevations below the tree line (Fig. 2.50).

FIG. 2.50.
Bear den located
under an old-
growth spruce
(bottom center)
at about 1,200
feet elevation
above the
Kadashan
Watershed
on Chichagof
Island.

LIFE BEGINS IN A DEN

For bears, after spending four to seven months hibernating, emergence from
their winter dens is the beginning of a new year. The average date bears come
out of their dens varies according to spring snow conditions.[40] A late spring
with deep snowpack above 2,000 feet means a later start for most bears. Males
are the first to leave their dens in the spring—some as early as late March or

early April. Females generally den a month and a half longer. Single females leave next, while females with newborn cubs are the last to depart—sometimes well into late May. This is not surprising since the tiny, naked cubs—weighing about a pound at birth—are born in January or February and are absolutely dependent on their mother for warmth and sustenance within the protective confines of the natal den. Some females with cubs may stay near their dens until early June.

Litter sizes range from one to four cubs and average about two in Southeast. When they leave the den, new cubs weigh twelve to fifteen pounds and are about the size of a cocker spaniel. By the first week of May, 95 percent of the males are out of their dens and on their way to recoup the fat reserves that saw them through their winter dormancy. In contrast, only 50 percent of female brown bears have emerged from the security of their winter dens by this time. Once bears leave their dens, they embrace a fresh world of spring and the explosion of new, vigorous life.

Following den emergence, many bears do not immediately head to the best food resources. Instead, it may take a week or more for them to get their metabolism ramped up. From a small aircraft, I have followed spring bear tracks for many miles on snow-covered ridges over 3,000 feet above sea level. The bears seem to be just wandering.

Once bears have become reacclimated to the world of sunlight and nutritious food, they head to the richest feeding areas. It is not unusual to see brown bears on tidal flats, where they graze on new spring growth of Lyngby sedges (Figs. 2.51, 2.52). Spring in bear country is an exciting time. Everything is happening at once—new plants bursting from the ground, hundreds of thousands of migratory birds inbound from the south to begin a new cycle of nesting and rearing their young, and rapidly lengthening days produce a fresh bounty of life from the intersection of land and sea—one of the most productive terrestrial-aquatic-marine interfaces on Earth (Fig. 2.53).

⚜

It was early June 1982, and LaVern and I had just landed a helicopter on a snow-covered alpine ridge at about 2,500 feet on northern Admiralty Island south of the Greens Creek drainage. We had marked this site with a radio collar we dropped out of the Helio Courier earlier in the winter while we were monitoring the den locations of our radio-collared bears. We were standing at the mouth of a bear's winter den as I was preparing to slide down through the snow tunnel, enter the den, and measure and describe its characteristics (Fig. 2.54). Standing there on three feet of snowpack, however, I was seriously contemplating a small complication. The bear's radio collar was still transmitting from deep within the den. This bear (identified as #60) was a twenty-one-year-old female with a two-year-old male offspring. We had seen her and her cub

FIG. 2.51. Intertidal sedge flats at Windfall Harbor on northeastern Admiralty in early May. New growth of Lyngby sedges are just turning green while there is still a late-winter receding snowpack at the forest edge. Sedge flats are some of the first places bears begin foraging after they emerge from their winter dens.

FIG. 2.52. A coastal brown bear foraging on grasses, sedges, and herbaceous plants growing near a tidal wetland area in late June. Prior to the advent of salmon runs and berry production, the new growth of succulent green vegetation makes up the bulk of the diet of coastal bears.

FIG. 2.53. King Salmon River delta on northeastern Admiralty Island. This productive estuary supports a bounty of marine and terrestrial wildlife resources, from abundant herring and salmon stocks to marine mammals, bears, deer, and forest and water birds. The snowcapped mountains of the mainland coast are visible in the background.

FIG. 2.54. The entrance to bear #60's snow-covered winter den. The snow was about three feet deep over the entrance to the rock cavity that this bear and her two-year-old cub denned in over the winter.

standing outside their den a week earlier on one of our telemetry flights, and we were relatively confident that she had shed her collar inside the den—that the den was now empty.

With a flashlight in one hand and my .44 handgun in the other, I started down the steep, narrow, four-foot-long snow tunnel to the small opening into a rock cavity. As my head went into the jagged rock entrance, I asked Vern and our pilot, who were holding my feet, to give me a few moments before I continued down into the dark, dank void. Although I was 99 percent sure the bears were gone, that 1 percent weighed heavily on my mind as I hung suspended with my arms and head just within the den entrance. Not knowing what I would find below, my fear was escalating. After contemplating this unique circumstance, I told them to let me go, and I wriggled down into the den cavity. Once in the den, I located the slipped collar, breathed a big sigh of relief, and went to work measuring and recording the den's configuration. It expanded beyond the small entrance and was about ten feet long with a nest of mountain hemlock boughs and dried heather at the far end. That was where the radio collar was lying, just outside the nest site. The cavity of bedrock and boulders was relatively small but with enough room that I could move around on my hands and knees. The den was clean with no odor of urine or fecal material. It was a secure but cramped site for a mother bear and her subadult cub to overwinter for six months.

During the course of our study, we located over 120 brown bear dens on Admiralty and Chichagof Islands.[41] Den sites generally occurred at high elevations, averaging 2,100 feet, and on steep slopes averaging 35 degrees. On Admiralty, bears preferred subalpine and rock habitats for denning, while Chichagof bears preferred old-growth forest habitat and often excavated dens under large old-growth trees. This information helped us develop general guidelines to minimize resource development impacts to denning bears.

OUR QUEST FOR THE BEAR

The spring and summer of 1982 was an exciting but hectic time for our family. Mary Beth was pregnant with our second child, I was finishing up the last of my deer fieldwork (including radio tracking and forest sampling work), and I was in the midst of our new bear research project, which involved weekly radio-tracking flights and capture work. On top of that, we were still burdened with responding to the continuous sniping and criticism by the timber industry and some of the Forest Service timber staff over our research findings.

Although our deer research had provided me significant field time on northern Admiralty, looking at the study area through the lens of a brown bear was new, and it led us to a very different assessment of seasonal habitats. LaVern and I spent much time walking up salmon streams setting and checking

FIG. 2.55. Spawning male chum salmon, also called dog salmon because many
Native people in northern Alaska fed these salmon to their dog teams.

leg-hold snares under the towering canopy of ancient spruce trees. Although
we observed a lot of bear sign and worked very hard running our snares, we
had relatively little early success. All the time we spent on the ground, however,
helped us get a feel for the country and how bears used the landscape. I recall
walking up a salmon stream in hip boots checking our snares one day, when
something grabbed my foot. I was so startled I must have jumped two feet in
the air. I had stepped near the edge of a redd—a gravel nest where spawning
salmon laid their eggs—and a large green-and-purple-banded chum salmon bit
me on the heel of my boot while defending its redd (Fig. 2.55).

During these trips, we often had use of a thirty-foot Fish and Game boat that
provided us with both transportation and lodging. This allowed us greater
freedom to roam as well as to work long days under Alaska's lengthy summer
daylight and twilight. On some days, we would fly aerial telemetry surveys
during the day, followed by helicopter capture trips up in the alpine during evening hours. Some of those days, we would start before eight a.m. and finish
around midnight. Even through those long, hard-working days, we were keenly
aware of our responsibility to collect ecological data that could help managers
conserve this national forest and its wildlife for future generations. An idyl-
lic moment on the northern Tongass is indelibly etched in my mind: standing

FIG. 2.56. Late-evening view from a subalpine slope on our northern Admiralty study area looking north over Young's Bay and Lynn Canal.

on top of a 2,500-foot subalpine ridge on Admiralty Island, surrounded by a collage of lush subalpine meadows that were home to scores of brown bear and hundreds of deer, looking north across Lynn Canal and watching the sky turn purple and pink as the sun slowly sank down behind 15,000-foot Mt. Fairweather to the northwest (Fig. 2.56). During the course of my nine years of bear fieldwork on Admiralty and Chichagof, LaVern and I handled about a hundred bears. This was difficult and often stressful work compounded by the necessity of working out of boats and aircraft in challenging weather—often climbing in and out of helicopters toed into precipitous mountain slopes. LaVern and I developed a close friendship because our lives literally depended on one another and on our pilots, Lynn Bennett of LAB and Bob Englebrecht of TEMSCO helicopters. Bob was a very good helicopter pilot and learned to anticipate a bear's behavior during our capture flights. Just as we exercised caution concerning our own safety, we were also concerned about minimizing the stress we placed on the animals we captured and handled. We were also aware of the risk of losing an animal to a drug overdose or the stress induced by the shock of capture compounded by a reaction to the immobilizing drugs.

Over the nine years of our capture work, we lost four bears (3 percent), all in the first few years of the study. As we acquired better drugs with broader tolerances for individual weights and conditions, and learned to more closely estimate dosages, our success significantly increased. I know from personal experience that it is very stressful emotionally to lose an animal you have captured. I've frequently been asked if doing this kind of work is worth the stress and risk to animals. I strongly believe that the data we gathered from our radio-collared animals in our research has significantly contributed to better conservation measures. The knowledge gained will ensure that we have the necessary information and tools to sustain the habitats and populations that underpin this extraordinary rainforest ecosystem. The key is for researchers to closely scrutinize their study plans and use the best tools and techniques available. They must also critically evaluate their goals and objectives to ensure that the stress and risk to their study animals are truly justified by the data acquired from their research. Today, nearly all agencies and research universities subject their study plans to review by an animal care and use committee. Later in my career with Audubon, I served on such a committee for the Alaska Science Center of the USGS in Anchorage.

FAMILY TIME

It was the middle of August 1982, and Mary Beth was very close to her due date with our second child. Her parents were visiting us at our beachfront home at Smuggler's Cove. I had taken the weekend off, and Mary Beth wanted to take her parents fishing, so we loaded our son Erik, dog Alex, and both of her parents in our fourteen-foot Lund skiff and headed across Stephens Passage to Bear Creek on Admiralty for a little halibut fishing. Late that afternoon, we caught a forty-pound halibut and brought it home for processing on our beach.

We finally had dinner and finished filleting and packaging the halibut. I think we headed to bed around midnight. Suddenly, forty-five minutes later, Mary Beth was pushing me out of bed, telling me we needed to go to the hospital. Her water had broken, and Sarah was on the way. We quickly dressed, packed up, pulled the skiff onto the beach, motored down to our outhaul at the end of the road, and drove to the hospital. Sarah was born at about seven thirty that morning. We attributed her prompt arrival to that afternoon's bouncy boat ride home from our halibut expedition.

FIG. 2.57. View looking north over the Kadashan Flats and Tenakee Inlet to the community of Tenakee Springs. The main channel of the Kadashan River is on the right. We routinely landed our radio-tracking aircraft on the grass flats to the left of the small stringer of spruce in the middle right.

EXPANDING OUR RESEARCH TO KADASHAN

In the late fall of 1982, I flew Jack Lentfer and Matt Kirchhoff to the Kadashan watershed in Tenakee Inlet on eastern Chichagof Island to evaluate that area as a potential study site for our research on bear habitat use and forest management. We did an overflight of the watersheds surrounding Kadashan, including Corner Bay, Crab Bay, and Sitkoh Bay. All except Kadashan had been substantially clear-cut within the last decade and also had a network of logging roads. We had previously worked in the Tenakee Inlet and Kadashan area during our deer research and knew that the brown bear densities in Kadashan were relatively high. Kadashan also had some of the highest pink and chum salmon escapement in northern Southeast. It was a roadless watershed of over 34,000 acres with a minimal history of early logging.

I landed the Helio on the beach, and we hiked up the river and into the forest. After our reconnaissance of this area and a thorough discussion with LaVern, we concluded that this was the optimal site for expanding our brown bear research. To some extent, Kadashan would serve as a natural control area compared to the surrounding watersheds with their extensive clear-cutting and network of logging roads.

⚜

On February 5, 1983, I was one of three ADF&G biologists invited to participate, along with six Forest Service personnel, in a Tenakee Springs City Council meeting to discuss the Forest Service's plans to log the Kadashan watershed. Tenakee Springs is a small Southeast village of about 100 people—mostly fishermen and retired folks living a largely subsistence lifestyle. There are no connecting roads to Tenakee, and local transportation is by floatplane, small boat, or the state ferry out of Juneau. Most of the homes line the shoreline, some set on pilings over the beach, and look directly across Tenakee Inlet at the Kadashan River delta. Many Tenakee residents used the Kadashan watershed for recreation or traditional subsistence gathering of food, particularly salmon and deer (Fig. 2.58).

Our meeting room was packed with locals, many of whom were quite concerned about the Forest Service's plans to log Kadashan. I was asked to present a slide program on old growth and the impacts of logging on deer and other wildlife. My basic message was that old growth is valuable wildlife habitat and particularly important winter habitat for Sitka black-tailed deer. I also emphasized that once clear-cut, old growth is not renewable under standard 100-year timber harvest rotations. The Forest Service spokesman assured Tenakee residents that there would be little harm to wildlife or fish and categorically stated there would be "no impact on deer." There was much discussion at this meeting, some of it rather heated. The bottom line expressed by the Forest Service was that they could not change their decision on timber sales and roads near Tenakee. They intended to construct a road into Kadashan and log the watershed. A common theme from Forest Service staff was "These decisions were made before I got here." Clearly, there was growing unrest within the community of Tenakee Springs with the Forest Service's logging and road building plan.

On May 9, 1983, ADF&G commissioner Don Collinsworth sent a letter to regional forester John Sandor stating in part:

> the State requested deferral of harvest in the Kadashan drainage until the
> Tongass Land Management Plan is scheduled for revision in 1990. . . . Kadashan
> River is among the top five producers of pink salmon, and among the top ten

FIG. 2.58. The community of Tenakee Springs on the north shore of Tenakee Inlet across from the Kadashan River on eastern Chichagof Island. Approximately 130 people live in Tenakee Springs.

producers of chum salmon in southeastern Alaska . . . commercial and sport fishing values combine to make the Kadashan one of the most valuable stream systems in southeastern Alaska. . . . Logging this watershed would introduce variables that could affect the accuracy of the data upon which fishery managers depend. . . . We think the Kadashan watershed is too valuable to expose to such risks. . . . The subsistence and game values of the Kadashan drainage are also high. . . . Research conducted since 1975 has indicated that clearcut logging reduces habitat carrying capacity for Sitka black-tailed deer.

The Commissioner's letter had little influence on the Forest Service. In the early 1980s, the timber industry was a major economic driver in Southeast, and, for more than two decades, they had largely called the shots on land-management decisions in the region. But storm clouds were building across the rainforest. Clear-cutting had left an ever-expanding footprint throughout

FIG. 2.59. Jack Lentfer and I purchased the *Orca II* in 1993 and ran it up Alaska's Inside Passage to Juneau in ten days. We often used this boat in our bear research work on Admiralty and Chichagof Islands.

Alaska's Southeast Panhandle and a significant impression on the minds of many local southeasterners, particularly hunters and fishers who were intimately familiar with the forest and its renewable bounty of fish and wildlife.

ORCA II

Boats were an important part of our family activities for both work and play, so it was just a matter of time before Mary Beth and I expanded our home vessel fleet beyond the small skiffs we used to commute from our beachside home to the end of the road. I had flown our 1947 Stinson Voyager from Washington to Juneau in the early summer of 1977. Now that I was a certified state pilot and doing much of my own research flying, I decided it was time to sell our plane and invest in a family cruising boat. My former supervisor Jack Lentfer, now retired in Juneau, was also interested in a boat. We decided to go into partnership and found a beautiful 1946 thirty-eight-foot double ender, the *Orca II*, for sale on Orcas Island in Washington. *Orca II* was a troller hull built of red cedar planks on oak frames and was a perfect family cruiser for Southeast (Fig. 2.59). It had a Chrysler Crown gas engine, cruised at seven and a half knots burning about two gallons an hour, and was very seaworthy.

On June 2, 1993, Jack and his two daughters and I departed my parents' dock on Orcas Island in the *Orca II* bound for Juneau. We pushed along rapidly because it was the middle of my field season and I needed to get back to work. Our cruise went well, and we learned more about the boat each day of our voyage. The most challenging day was our fourth day out. After leaving Alert

FIG. 2.60.
My children Sarah
(ten months) and
Erik (three years)
on the beach at
Cape Fanshaw on
our cruise up the
Inside Passage
to Juneau.

Bay and heading northeast from Port Hardy on the north end of Vancouver Island, we ran into southeast winds gusting over twenty-five knots and seas building to eight to ten feet as we crossed Queen Charlotte Strait. We were running through a low overcast with visibility down to about two miles as we approached Cape Caution on BC's mainland coast. This was a long and challenging day, but the boat handled the weather like a champ, and we anchored for the evening at Calvert Island with one of the toughest passages behind us. Four days later, we arrived in Ketchikan, where we met Mary Beth and our kids (Fig. 2.60). Jack's wife, Mary, met us in Petersburg, and we arrived in Juneau on June 10 after a glorious but short cruise through the famed Inside Passage. Now we had our Southeast cruising boat, and I used *Orca II* for several weeks each summer over the next seven years for logistical support in our bear research. The added advantage was that I was able to bring my family along during portions of the summer while I was conducting my research.

FIELD RESEARCH EXPANDS OUR KNOWLEDGE OF BEARS

Back in Juneau after our Inside Passage cruise—on which, unlike most Alaska cruises, we had no nightclub entertainment or shuffleboard but always sat at the captain's table—I hit the ground running. LaVern and I continued to capture and radio-track bears on Admiralty. We also began capturing and radio-collaring bears on Chichagof. That summer, we captured or recaptured thirty brown bears.

There has always been a strong national interest in Alaska, generated in part by media coverage of this wildest edge of the continental United States. In the summer of 1983, writer Bill Richards traveled to Southeast to research a story for *National Geographic*. He requested permission to accompany us on our bear research project. I flew him on one of our radio-tracking flights over Admiralty Island, and later LaVern and I brought his *National Geographic* photographer along on a capture trip. Bill was very impressed with the number of bears we observed foraging in subalpine meadows above tree line. He had also observed the extensive logging that was occurring throughout Southeast, particularly in the valley bottoms. In his 1994 article, "A Place Apart: Alaska's Southeast,"[42] he wrote, "They're going to cut the heart out of the forest." This was and still is one of the key concerns with forest management throughout Southeast and the Tongass National Forest. Although the amount of logging on the Tongass is small compared to its nearly seventeen million land acres, the focus of that logging and the network of logging roads is concentrated in the highest-quality, low-elevation forest land. This approach to forestry has had a disproportionate impact on wildlife, including bears and deer, as well as on important salmon spawning systems throughout the forest.

By midsummer 1983, we were working full-time on bear research and splitting our efforts between Chichagof and Admiralty Islands. This resulted in long, busy days and lots of flying. But what a way to spend our time exploring Admiralty and Chichagof Islands, capturing and locating brown bears, checking out salmon runs, and getting to know individual bears—where they traveled, what they ate, who they mated with, and how many cubs they successfully produced. And all of this research conducted in one of the most stunning laboratories in the world.

During those early years of bear research, I kept handwritten field notes in Rite in the Rain notebooks. Reviewing those notes brings back vivid memories of various excursions.

6-23-83: Kadashan, clear.

1700: After a day in the office, we departed Juneau Airfield in Hughes 500 helicopter with pilot Bob Englebrecht, LaVern, and Rod Flynn. Lynn Bennett flying the Helio Courier for air cover and reconnaissance.

1800: We flew the chopper to a subalpine ridge above Kadashan Delta. Lynn spotted a bear on upper Kadashan ridge and we launched the helicopter in pursuit.

1900: We captured a 370-pound male brown bear at the head of the Kadashan drainage above False Island. . . . Bear #88 was fitted with a radio collar.

2000: Lynn located three bears on upper ridge line east of Corner Bay. It looked like a female with two large cubs. We came in and darted two of the bears which turned out to be two adult females 375 and 500 pounds. . . . We instrumented them and marked them as #21 and #24. The bear with them was a very large male which we were not able to capture. There is much breeding activity occurring here now.

The incident above was a good example of how difficult it can be to correctly identify a bear's sex and age at a distance from an aircraft. With more experience, we learned that a large bear following a smaller bear, particularly from late May through early July, is usually a male trailing a female. In contrast, smaller bears following a larger bear are usually cubs following their mother.

2200: Lynn located another large bear on the Kadashan Delta. We flew the helicopter down to the delta and were able to get a good shot on this bear that turned out to be a 500-pound male. As the sun was getting lower, swarms of noseeums [tiny biting flies] worked us over as we processed our new bear (#23). While we weighed, measured, and instrumented this last bear of the evening's capture work, we saw a female and cub come out on the delta to graze on sedges. Compared to our study site on Admiralty Island, there was comparatively less use of the higher elevation alpine areas on this part of Chichagof while there was more use of tidal grass flats during this time of year. After a long but highly productive day, we landed back home at the Juneau Airport at 0130 in the morning.

As we continued to fly telemetry surveys of our marked bears and capture bears in the alpine, it became obvious that the density of bears was particularly high in our northern Admiralty study area. In order to further assess these relative bear numbers, I organized an early survey project whereby we launched three aircraft on one evening—when bears are generally the most visible—and completed three simultaneous survey flights, which included north Admiralty, south Admiralty, and our general study area on southeast Chichagof. These exploratory flights would be the first aerial survey we would conduct on Admiralty. It would be followed later on by more rigorous census estimates in which we captured, marked, and relocated the bears.

6-29-83: Juneau Airport, broken overcast.

1930: Departed Juneau for bear survey. LaVern and his pilot flew to east Chichagof in a Super Cub on floats. Steve Peterson and his pilot flew north to Admiralty (including our study area) in a Super Cub on floats. I flew the Helio Courier down to survey south Admiralty with George Reifenstein. Each team flew about two-hour surveys at sixty to sixty-five miles per hour and at an altitude of about 500 feet over the ground. We concentrated on the higher elevation alpine and subalpine habitats but also surveyed the larger tidal wetlands at some of the big river deltas. Schoen observed twenty-eight bears, LaVern observed nineteen bears, and Steve observed forty-two bears (in our study area). The ratio of marked to unmarked bears observed in the study area indicated that observability was roughly 16 percent suggesting the density of bears on northern Admiralty is very high and may rival some of the highest density areas on the continent.

Our two study sites on Admiralty and Chichagof provided us with an interesting contrast in resource development activity. The Noranda Mine was on Admiralty's upper Greens Creek, which drained into Hawk Inlet. The development was quite localized and did not yet have a road system. All of the construction at that time was focused on the underground mine (not an open-pit mine), with minimal activity at the staging area located about four miles away at the old cannery site in Hawk Inlet. The mining company had very stringent rules about garbage management and the kinds of activities their employees could engage in while on site. They also installed a fuel-fired incinerator for disposal of organic garbage at the old cannery facility at Hawk Inlet (Fig. 2.61).

On Chichagof, there was an active logging camp and a Forest Service facility located at Corner Bay, adjacent to and just east of the Kadashan watershed. Corner Bay was connected to Kook Lake and Basket Bay by a network of logging roads to the south, where current logging activity was taking place. West of Kadashan was Crab Bay, which had been logged a decade earlier and still had a network of old logging roads, by then inactive.

Once we began regularly monitoring the movements and habitat use of radio-collared bears on Chichagof Island, we began to see some interesting patterns related to clear-cuts, roads, and development. And the contrast with Admiralty was significant, particularly in relation to garbage management and so-called "problem" bears. Unlike the mining camp at Greens Creek, Corner Bay handled their garbage in an open pit dump, much like all logging camps throughout the Tongass.

FIG. 2.61. Fuel-fired incinerator used to burn garbage at the Greens Creek mine in Hawk Inlet on northern Admiralty Island. Incinerating garbage significantly reduced the attraction to bears and minimized bear problems at this industrial site. There were no bears killed at this site during our study.

8-7-83: Corner Bay, Chichagof Island.

1500: LaVern and I visited the Corner Bay facility and found recent bear sign in the dump. I took a series of photos. Dump is a mess—no attempt to keep it clean or to keep bears out. Two workers from the logging camp came to the dump while we were there. They told us that the camp had no problems with the bears. They described three cubs which likely belong to #24. They said the cubs are always in the dump and only occasionally come into the camp. They described several other bears that also use the dump. [Fig. 2.62]

The dilemma of this kind of situation is that once bears become conditioned to human food and garbage, they inevitably become "problem" bears. Ninety-nine percent of the time, this results in the bears being killed in defense of life or property. Killing a bear in defense of life or property is legal in Alaska as long as the hide and skull are turned in to ADF&G and a report justifying the killing is filed. Our reconnaissance of the dump revealed much odiferous, organic waste and abundant bear scat with garbage and plastic bags in it. The dump was occasionally burned by superficially throwing diesel over the area and lighting it. However, this is a surface burn only and does not eliminate the garbage or the attractive odor that brings bears into the dump to forage.

※

As most of the fish runs decline in the fall, bears begin to move away from low-elevation salmon streams and up into mide-levation avalanche slopes and subalpine meadows, where they feed on berries prior to establishing their winter dens. We radio-tracked our marked bears every week and were able to determine, usually within a week's time, when they entered their dens. Denning usually begins in October.[43] Bears are large and require substantial amounts of nutritious food. The winter season

FIG. 2.62. Open-pit garbage dump at the Corner Bay logging camp on eastern Chichagof Island. This site was irregularly burned by dumping diesel fuel on the surface. It did not incinerate the garbage, and bears were continually attracted to this camp. As many as ten bears used this site during our study, and a number of bears were killed in this area in defense of life or property.

in Alaska, and in most of North America, simply does not produce adequate nutritional resources to maintain an active bear's metabolism. Thus, bears have adapted to this period of nutritional stress by hibernating.

For many years, some biologists did not consider the bears' winter dormancy to be true hibernation, in part because their body temperature does not drop significantly and they are easily aroused. However, more recent research confirms that bears do hibernate.[44] In Alaska some females may remain in their dens for six to seven months. During this time, they do not eat, drink, urinate, or defecate. Pregnant females give birth in January or February. They then begin lactating and suckling their newborn cubs throughout the rest of the denning period, without water or food, until they leave the den, generally in mid-May. Although bears' body temperature only drops about 10 degrees Fahrenheit while they hibernate, their heart rate declines to about six to nine beats per minute and their respiration rate goes down to about one to two breaths per minute. This results in as much as a 75 percent decline in the rate of metabolism. Bears are also able to recycle their nitrogenous waste into amino acids.

While most bears are snuggled into their winter dens by early November, some bears may remain active if there is an abundant food resource available. For example, several of our radio-collared male bears in the Kadashan drainage remained active, feeding on a late run of coho salmon well into December.

FOREST SERVICE PLANS TO LOG KADASHAN

By January 1984, the Forest Service was moving ahead with their plans to build a road into the Kadashan watershed in preparation for logging this drainage. On January 20, the Southeast Alaska Conservation Council (SEACC, a longtime regional environmental organization) and community of Tenakee Springs filed suit to stop the Forest Service from constructing the Kadashan road. In a local newspaper article describing the suit, a Forest Service spokesman stated there was no evidence logging or roads are harmful to any resources.

That there would be disagreement and conflict over a major land management decision like road construction and logging in the Kadashan is not surprising. However, it was of great concern to those of us working for ADF&G that Forest Service employees would publicly deny the potential of resource impacts from road construction and clear-cutting in Kadashan.

On January 26, 1984, I sent ADF&G Game Division director Lew Pamplin a memo regarding public information on deer-forest research in reference to public statements by the Forest Service. That memo stated in part:

Responsible resource managers must acknowledge the overwhelming evidence that logging will reduce deer numbers over the long term in southeast Alaska. To do otherwise is a serious breach of the public trust. Needless to say, I am disappointed the U.S. Forest Service in Alaska fails to publicly acknowledge the facts (in fact they obscure the truth through use of the media). The result encourages public confusion and distrust of resource agencies. I believe the Department has an obligation to the public to actively present the facts clearly and honestly.

Later that spring, I was contacted by SEACC attorney Steve Kallick and asked if I would submit an affidavit describing potential impacts to brown bears from road construction and logging in the Kadashan watershed. I gave this some thought and talked with my ADF&G supervisor, Don McKnight. We decided that as long as I described the current situation and stuck to the facts, we had a responsibility to share our information with the public who pay our bills. On April 13, 1984, I provided a legal affidavit to the SEACC attorney while my supervisor was present in my office. Key excerpts follow.

It is my conclusion, based on preliminary research results showing the distribution of radio-tagged bears, that the proposed Kadashan road route will directly intersect the home range of a great number of brown bear . . . and the main feeding areas along the Kadashan River.

There is a historically demonstrated incompatibility between brown bears and humans. . . . Based on this incompatibility, it is probable that the construction and use of the Kadashan road in its proposed location would substantially increase the number of bear/human conflicts.

Increased human use of the Kadashan Basin will result in the killing of bears in three categories of taking: legal harvest, illegal harvest, and accidental harvest (i.e., in defense of life or property [DLP]) . . . only legal harvest can be effectively controlled. Illegal harvest is only partially understood and difficult to control. Accidental harvest (DLP) is virtually uncontrollable when humans are present. These latter two categories of harvest are likely to increase during and after road construction despite mitigation attempts.

In my affidavit, I also stated that the Kadashan watershed served as an undeveloped control area for ADF&G's current Chichagof bear study. Retired bear biologist Jack Lentfer, my former supervisor, also prepared an affidavit for this case in which he stated: "I am unaware of any data or studies relating to brown bears which would support any conclusion other than that the proposed Kadashan road will impact the bear population of the Kadashan watershed."

During the first week of May 1984, construction work began on the Kadashan road project. On May 8, the road was approximately half a mile out of the Corner Bay Camp. On May 10, I was asked to attend a meeting in the commissioner's office with my supervisor Don McKnight, director Lew Pamplin, deputy commissioner Denny Kelso, and commissioner Don Collinsworth. Apparently, the regional forester had talked with Governor Bill Sheffield about my affidavit on the Kadashan road, and it was rumored that the governor wanted me fired. Clearly, the timber industry and Forest Service leadership were putting pressure on the State of Alaska to keep their biologists in line. At the same time, Matt Kirchhoff and I had been preparing a department slide program about wildlife and forestry in Southeast Alaska. The commissioner also identified this as a problem area and strongly told us to completely rewrite the slide program and minimize references to clear-cutting.

Fortunately, my immediate supervisor, the director, and deputy commissioner were all very supportive of our work. At one point in the heated discussion, deputy commissioner Kelso calmly but firmly pointed out that my affidavit on the Kadashan road was true and factual, and the department should be willing to stand behind that. I will always remember his strong support with sincere gratitude.

As state researchers, our bottom line was that we carefully scrutinized our research methodology and results and worked hard to always tell the truth and represent our data in a fair and objective way. I believe it is better to use understatement than exaggeration in describing management implications of our research because our scientific integrity is our most valuable asset. As a wildlife researcher working on a public trust resource, I strongly believed that the public should have access to the implications that resource management actions are likely to have on their fish and wildlife resources. Our job is to conduct the research and prepare scientific reports and publish our findings. But how many people have access to or regularly read *Forest Science* or the *Journal of Wildlife Management*? I believed we also have an obligation to make the results of that research available to the general public in a venue that is more accessible than an esoteric scientific publication. Unfortunately, that perspective was not shared by the timber industry, the regional forester, or the governor, and there was an effort to pressure ADF&G to avoid discussing the management implications of industrial-scale logging on Alaska's fish and wildlife populations.

EXCERPTS FROM THE FIELD

While the unrelenting politics of the Tongass endured, LaVern and I continued our fieldwork collecting data on our radio-collared brown bears. This was the perfect salve for reducing the stress of dealing with the increasingly controversial Tongass policy issues that were seeping down to our level. Looking back over my field notes, I can still recall some of the highlights and excitement of our work on Admiralty and Chichagof during the 1980s.

6-21-84. Bear capture work on north Admiralty study area.

1800: We departed Juneau airfield in Hughes 500 helicopter with TEMSCO chief pilot Bob Englebrecht, LaVern, and artist Skip Wallen [then working on a bronze brown bear sculpture for the city of Juneau]. Lynn Bennett was scouting bears for us in the Helio. We landed on an alpine ridge in upper Greens Creek at about 3,500 feet elevation. This was a beautiful evening, crystal clear and 68 degrees. A few alpine flowers had started blooming and along the top of the ridge there was a distinctive bear trail with 12-inch-deep oval depressions imbedded in the tundra. This evening in Admiralty's high alpine was spectacular. What a privilege to work here.

Lynn located #99 in a steep valley in upper King Salmon drainage. We searched for a long time before we finally flushed her and her two yearling cubs out of a dense thicket of mountain hemlock. She was very aggressive. Her cubs ran up hill while she stayed below and charged the chopper. I was leaning out of chopper and pulled my feet up as she rushed downhill within three feet of the skid. Finally, LaVern got a shot on her—it was high and forward. We followed her for twenty minutes. She eventually went down in a mountain hemlock thicket. The helicopter dropped us off and we scrambled down to her. She still had head movement but we decided to pull her downhill out of the hemlocks. As soon as we pulled her down, she got up and swung her head over at LaVern's leg. Everyone jumped back and headed up hill. I had my .44 out of my shoulder holster but she settled down again. We injected her again with a very light dose of M99 and after she went down more solidly the four of us pulled her up a steep 20-foot incline and finished working on her and replaced the old collar with a fresh one. Perhaps we were on edge this evening because one of our colleagues working on brown bears in the Susitna drainage of southcentral Alaska had recently been bitten when the immobilizing drug failed to work properly.

Throughout the rest of the summer of 1984, we used the Helio to work in both study areas at least once a week, capturing bears and monitoring their movements and habitat use. One unique feature of Chichagof's Kadashan watershed is its highly productive salmon runs that include pink, chum, and coho salmon plus steelhead trout. The Kadashan River was considered among the top producers of pink and chum salmon in Southeast. Much later, in 2007, when I was working with Audubon Alaska, my colleague Dave Albert, with The Nature Conservancy, and I estimated that the Kadashan watershed ranked number two for coho and pink salmon habitat and number three for chum salmon habitat out of eighty-three watersheds within the eastern portion of Chichagof Island. Kadashan also ranked number one in this province for brown bear

FIG. 2.63. The Kadashan fish weir near the old Kadashan research cabin. The aluminum tubes block fish passage. When a gate is open, individual fish of different species can be counted to determine salmon escapement that season. Nine salmon can be seen in the bottom center.

habitat. Because of Kadashan's importance as a regional salmon producer, the department of Fish and Game had established a salmon weir on the river (Fig. 2.63). A weir is a fence across the river made up of individual aluminum pickets about an inch in diameter. The technicians running the weir open a gate and let the fish run through at certain times of the day. That way they can count and record the number of salmon of each species that move up the river to spawn. This allows the Department to closely monitor the number of salmon escaping the marine fisheries and entering their natal streams to spawn. They then adjust their fishery management accordingly.

Now that my family owned a boat, I had the opportunity to bring them with me into the field during some of our longer excursions. This was a significant plus to me and an enormous benefit to our whole family. Our intensive field season was conducted mostly from May through October, and we worked long days and well into the evening hours. Throughout my career, I saw many instances where long absences because of extended fieldwork contributed to family stress. Having the family with me on our boat allowed me to share time in these exceptional places with Mary Beth, Erik, and Sarah. These trips not only provided them with an extraordinary outing, it also gave them some ownership and understanding of the wildlife research that dominated my working life. Notes from one of my field trips to Kadashan are highlighted below.

7-10: 1230: Anchored *Orca II* off Kadashan River delta, headed up river in skiff, met LaVern at the Kadashan weir site and started setting out leg-hold snares for bears.

7-11: More capture work at weir site. I ran our skiff with Mary Beth and the kids up river to the cabin at the weir where they would spend several days while LaVern and I operated the snares. We identified six different bears at the weir. LaVern and I set out more snares up river from the weir.

While we were all at the Kadashan cabin running our bear snares at the weir, we had one particularly memorable family experience. Early one morning, while Mary Beth, LaVern, and I were making breakfast in the cabin and getting ready to check our snares, two-year-old Sarah, who was standing on the table, excitedly said, "Bear ready, Daddy!" Looking out the cabin window, she had seen a brown bear walking along the riverbank next to the fish weir. We went outside, and sure enough there was a bear in one of our leg-hold snares just above the riverbank. We soon immobilized and processed the captured bear and fitted it with a radio collar. Not only did young Sarah confidently tip us off about the captured bear, but both kids got to watch the entire process and even touch an immobilized brown bear.

The family boat cruise is an example of the kinds of experiences Mary Beth and I tried to integrate into our family life. These were experiences that money simply cannot buy, and we will all treasure such remarkable family odysseys for the rest of our lives. In reflection, I wonder if these kinds of experiences didn't have an enduring influence on both kids, as each chose a professional path leading to graduate degrees in the ecological sciences and professional careers in Alaska (Fig. 2.64). Today, Erik is a fisheries scientist at the University of Alaska Fairbanks, and Sarah is a seabird ecologist at the Alaska Science Center of USGS in Anchorage.

FIG. 2.64. Mary Beth and the kids commuting from our home in Smuggler's Cove to the end of Fritz Cove Road where we parked our car. We were living off the grid in a classic Alaska setting.

Throughout bears' active period following their winter hibernation, we tried to locate each radio-collared bear at least once a week. This work was similar to our deer telemetry surveys from 1978 through 1982, but our bear research also involved study areas on two different islands, surveys concentrated from May through October, and a larger number of radio-collared animals—up to thirty-five at one time. Most of our flights were two to three hours in duration.

Once bears emerged from their dens, they were distributed from sea level tidal flats up through forested hillsides to alpine ridges over 3,500 feet in elevation. At the start of a survey flight, we would fly high (2,000–3,000 feet) over the study site with both wing-mounted antennas scanning for signals. Typically, I would fly the aircraft and identify habitat attributes while LaVern would run the telemetry receiver—switching from one antenna to another to locate the strongest direction of the radio signal—and plot the animal's location on a topographic map and record habitat data. Once a signal was picked up, we would descend, eventually flying over the signal at about 500 feet above the surface and pinpoint the location to within about an acre. Once located, the appropriate data would be recorded on a form for later entry into a computer database: topographic features (elevation, slope exposure, and steepness), habitat type (estuarine grass flats, avalanche slope, upland and riparian old growth, clear-cut, subalpine, alpine), soil drainage, timber volume, distance to coast, roads, and salmon streams. We actually observed the radio-collared bears more frequently than we had deer, particularly when the bears were fishing in salmon streams or grazing on tidal flats or in subalpine meadows.

In the summer of 1984, I was checked out on a Piper PA-18 Super Cub aircraft and began using this plane that was on lease to the state. The Super Cub is a light, 150-horsepower two-place aircraft capable of slow flight and off-airport landings like beaches and gravel bars along rivers and streams. The pilot sits in the front seat, and the passenger behind in a single back seat. These planes have been used for years as wildlife survey aircraft in part because they offer very good visibility. They are also less expensive to fly than the larger, four-place Helio Courier. I still had the option of using the larger Helio when we needed to fly fast or haul larger loads and more passengers. However, from the summer of 1984 until 1989, most of my research flying was conducted in the Super Cub (Figs. 2.65, 2.66).

In the 1980s, nearly all radio telemetry locations in Alaska were collected from small, fixed-wing aircraft. Later, the advent of global positioning system (GPS) telemetry revolutionized this work because satellite location data could be gathered around the clock on an hourly (or more frequent) basis regardless of weather conditions. However, this new technology was not yet available for our bear research, and we had some questions that weekly locations were unable to answer. For example, we had observed that a subset of Admiralty bears did not appear to use low-elevation salmon streams during the summer and fall, but remained in interior portions of the island.[45] To address issues that needed a more intensive sampling protocol, we periodically flew telemetry surveys on a subsample of radio-collared bears once every six hours. For example, we would

FIG. 2.65. Flying the Super Cub locating radio-collared brown bears. LaVern is in the back seat running the radio and recording data.

FIG. 2.66. With the Super Cub on a beach on Admiralty Island. This was an outstanding plane to use because it flew slow and had excellent visibility. The large tires allowed us to land on off-airport sites like this beach or gravel bars. Note the two antennas under each wing. We used these to determine which direction had the strongest signal from our radio-collared animals, and then we could locate the animals within an area about the size of an acre.

sometimes depart the Juneau Airfield at about 0500, and then fly around noon, at 1800, and again just before dark, at about 2200. This was exhausting work, but it allowed us to locate the same bears throughout a single day. During most of these intensive telemetry surveys, it was rare to see individual bear movements of more than a mile. These data helped confirm that our sample of interior bears did not, in fact, use salmon streams during the spawning season. These data also gave us insights into the daily activity patterns and habitat use of individual bears.

Another intensive sampling activity included both air and ground observations of bears using the Greens Creek delta on Admiralty Island. We were interested in determining how they were responding to intensive development activities associated with the Greens Creek Mine development, including road construction and helicopter and fixed-wing aircraft overflights. I captured one memorable event from this work in my field notes.

7-28-84: Hawk Inlet, Admiralty Island. Field trip on *Orca II* to continue observations of bears at Greens Creek Delta. Observing bears all day at Greens Cr. Delta from tree blind or base of tree stand. [Fig. 2.67]

1920: At tree stand at Greens Creek Delta. Fog, mist, rain. No bears visible. Tide falling, many salmon in streams.

1954: Bear #79 (subadult female) appeared at upper forested bend of Greens Creek fishing ten yards from cover.

1959: #79 running down creek after schools of pink and chum salmon (very inefficient technique).

2000: #79 caught a fish by jumping on it with front paws, then bit into it and carried it to the bank where she began eating it, 50 yards from cover.

2002: Finished eating fish, running downstream continuing to fish.

2005: Caught fish, moved to bank to eat it, 15 yards from cover.

2010: Disappeared from view.

2015: Caught another fish; continued fishing, running up and down stream. I have left tree stand and have walked down stream along the bank to watch #79 continue to fish.

FIG. 2.67. Greens Creek River Delta in Hawk Inlet on northern Admiralty Island. Greens Creek is on the left and Zinc Creek is on the right. The small island of trees in the center is where I was watching bears from a tree blind. The upper right of this stringer of trees is where I encountered the young female bear that tried to move me out of her space. You can see the big log I was standing on just above and to the right of the trees on the left side of Zinc Creek. There is actually a bear in Greens Creek in the center of the image, just below the tree island. We used the beach to the left of the stringer of trees to land the Super Cub.

2040: #79 finished eating another fish and then began fishing again moving upstream towards my location on the bank in shoulder high beach rye (or dunegrass).

2042: #79 is headed in my direction. I moved upstream along the bank and then climbed up on an old fish trap log, about five feet in diameter, situated on the stream bank along the edge of Zinc Creek.

2045: #79 is headed right up the creek towards my location. She now has certainly picked up my scent as she is directly downwind of me. She shows no response to my scent, however. Now she is walking up the bank near where I am standing on the log. I am beginning to feel a little insecure standing here alone—with bears, there is always safety in numbers. Now she is in the tall beach rye somewhat out of sight but within about 40 feet of my location. I am not greatly concerned because she is a young bear with no offspring and should not be aggressive. She is moving my way about 30 feet away now.

2047: I decide to talk to her calmly and let her know I am here—as if she didn't know; perhaps I am deluding myself. I am standing on the big log five feet off the ground. I talk to her in a very loud confident voice. "OK bear I'm here. You can go back to the stream now." She completely ignores my now very loud voice. I continue talking in a controlled but loud tone. Finally, she stands upright on her hind legs and looks in my direction, then drops back down into the tall beach rye. She seems to be chewing something. It almost seems that she may have a fish in the deep grass but I didn't see her bring one up the bank with her. I do not believe she is popping her jaws (an aggressive display) but rather chewing something. She seems not to acknowledge my presence at all but is ignoring me entirely or perhaps quietly and methodically challenging my presence in her space. Although I am doing my best to hold my ground—the basic rule of thumb when dealing with an approaching bear—I am now definitely feeling insecure and would much rather be somewhere else. I realize that this young bear is not behaving toward me in an entirely benign manner. Although she doesn't display the typical aggressive behavior of a bear defending a food cache or a mother defending cubs, she is clearly asserting her dominance over me and doing her best to rid herself of my delightful presence. I now believe I need to back off. OK, I've decided not to rigidly hold my ground. But where the hell do I go. I don't want to get into the deep grass and lose sight of her. That does not seem like a smart option. Therefore, I back off to the end of my log.

2050 (times inexact): Now #79 climbs up on an adjacent log parallel to mine and begins to walk right toward me. Damn! Finally, I draw out my handgun [.44 Smith & Wesson]. I do this reluctantly because the last thing I want to do is to kill a bear and I really don't have much faith in the adequacy of a handgun.

2051: This situation is now entirely out of proportion to what I would have predicted with this bear less than six minutes ago. The bear continues walking slowly in my direction in spite of the fact that I am loudly explaining to her that she should go somewhere else. It has become clearly obvious that I have her attention but not her agreement. I now pull back the hammer on my .44. I think to myself, "This is not good."

2052: She has now approached me to within less than 20 feet. I cannot retreat anymore without jumping down off the log into the deep grass or jumping down the bank into the stream. Finally, I aim my gun at the log well ahead of her and squeeze the trigger. KABOOM! She stops her forward motion but, beyond that, shows very little reaction to the explosive noise. We stand facing one another for a few moments (ten, twenty, thirty seconds?) without further movement or sound. She then, very slowly begins to turn to her left off the log and moves toward the bank perpendicular to my position. With great dignity and deliberation, she slowly walks down the steep bank into the stream and very casually walks up Zinc Creek and away from me. I am most happy to concede her dignity to her as the tension dissolves and we both travel along our separate paths, each of us unharmed but perhaps wiser.

2055: When she reaches the junction of Zinc and Greens creeks, I get off my log and head up to my tree stand and climb up to check her current location.

2100: #79 is midway up Greens creek walking along the creek as if she were fishing. But I believe she is moving away from a bad situation while maintaining her self respect. I call Mary Beth (who is on *Orca II* with our kids) on my portable VHF marine radio and ask her to bring the skiff in to pick me up on the beach. She and the kids had heard the single shot and were worried. I briefly explain that there is no problem now and that I'm looking forward to spending the night on the boat.

2130: Back on the boat, I take time to relax, drink a beer, and reflect. This was an unexpected situation and #79 reacted like a "camp" or "garbage" bear rather than a wild bear. She showed absolutely no fear of me and though not outright aggressive, she caused me significant anxiety. Certainly, this situation would have resulted in a dead bear had she displayed this behavior to most people carrying a firearm. There is no question that I had invaded her space. Had I stayed in the tree stand, this would not have happened. Her response was simply not to give me any ground. All in all, I think I acted reasonably in resolving the situation after it developed into a standoff.

Years later, I learned that this bear's behavior of seeming to ignore me was typical of young subadult bears' behavior toward humans. And fifteen years later, a colleague and I held our ground to within about five feet against a similar young female on the Katmai Coast. However, there were two of us, and I believe that made a big difference in the final outcome—which was in our favor as the bear finally backed off. But only two months after my Kadashan encounter, we learned that brown bear #79 was killed by a hunter in the Hawk Inlet area.

⚜

By 1985, we were well into our bear investigation and working with a good sample of radio-collared bears in both study areas. We had developed a reasonable understanding of the seasonal patterns of habitat use and were also gaining new insights into the potential effects of resource development activities on bears and their habitat. During this time, the politics associated with forest management of the Tongass also continued.

4-17-85. Juneau: Today is my birthday, 38 years, hard to believe. I don't feel older and am generally very satisfied with my lot in life. I like my job— except, of course, for the burdensome bureaucracy and politics. But then the rough edges make you appreciate the very good parts of life: wonderful wife, mate, friend, and partner; great kids with untapped potential; good friends and colleagues, superb place to live; and a great boat. I am very thankful for the opportunity to live in and experience this extraordinary environment of Southeast Alaska. It rains too damn much but few places on Earth are so wild and beautiful. To really get out in the country here in Southeast you must be confident in yourself and take the responsibility of your life in your own two hands. I like that.

THE WILDLIFE SOCIETY WEIGHS IN ON OLD GROWTH

In 1985, on my birthday, I met with the Alaska Chapter of The Wildlife Society's position statement committee to consider the finished draft of our position statement on old-growth forest management. Founded in 1937, The Wildlife Society is a nonprofit scientific and educational association dedicated to excellence in wildlife stewardship through science and education. I have been an active member since I was a graduate student in the early 1970s at the University of Washington, and I served as Alaska Chapter president in 1986. The position statement on "Old-Growth Forest Management in Coastal Alaska" was formally adopted in June 1985. Key elements of that statement follow:

Old-growth forests are a rare, and rapidly diminishing resource throughout North America. . . . The coastal forests of southeast and southcentral Alaska represent the last major expanse of old growth remaining in the United States . . .

Approximately 4 percent of the Tongass (635,000 acres) consists of high-volume, old-growth stands with over 30,000 board feet of timber per acre. These stands, commonly found at low elevations and along broad valley bottoms, are high-quality habitat for certain wildlife species; they are also commercially important timberland ...

About two million acres of the Tongass, and an undetermined amount of state and private lands are planned for harvest over the next 100 years. Cutting as scheduled will concentrate on high-volume old growth, with over half of the forest's highest volume class (greater than 50,000 board feet per acre) scheduled for harvest over the next 40 years.

Old-growth forest provides important habitat for many species of fish and wildlife throughout southeast and southcentral Alaska. Research over the last 15 years in the Pacific Northwest, British Columbia, and Alaska presents strong evidence that cutting old growth adversely affects black-tailed deer populations, and may impact other species such as marten, river otter, brown bear, mountain goat, moose, bald eagle, blue grouse, several species of cavity-dwelling birds, and some small mammals ...

The old-growth rain forests of coastal Alaska represent a unique ecosystem of national significance, deserving of careful and farsighted planning. Adequate and representative old-growth habitat must be maintained to meet present and future demands for wildlife, fisheries, and recreation. Toward that goal, the Alaska Chapter of The Wildlife Society makes the following recommendations on old-growth forest management in coastal Alaska.

» Management of the Tongass National Forest should comply with the National Forest Management Act ...
» The Forest Service and the Department of Fish and Game should develop an education program to inform the public about the long-term consequences for wildlife and fish resulting from harvesting old-growth forests in coastal Alaska.
» The disproportionate harvest of high-volume, old-growth classes should cease ...
» A cooperative process should be developed by the appropriate resource agencies to identify specific old-growth stands with exceptional fish and wildlife values and specify management direction, including the option of no harvest, to protect those values ...
» The Forest Service and the Department of Natural Resources should assess all effects associated with the development and use of road systems on wildlife and fish ...

The Wildlife Society position statement articulated some of the key issues for Alaska wildlife biologists at that time, and many continued to be of concern for the next three decades, including the high-grading (disproportionately targeting) of the most productive old-growth stands.

During this time, I had been appointed to The Wildlife Society's North American Grizzly Bear Technical Committee, charged with preparing a technical paper on grizzly bear management and conservation. Our first meeting was held in Montana in association with a grizzly bear habitat conference.

5–6-85: Juneau. Return from Missoula Grizzly Habitat Conference and also TWS Grizzly Bear Technical committee of which I am a member. Last day of the conference considered cumulative effects on grizzly bear habitat. I think I will also look at a broader approach than purely habitat since the effects of disturbance and human-caused mortality are major factors to be considered in dealing with brown-grizzly populations.

In the rest of the U.S., grizzly bears exist in a precarious balance between resource development, human recreation, and the maintenance of true wilderness country. I am convinced that we are just about 25 to 30 years behind some of the same kinds of problems here in Alaska. I hope we are smart enough and far-sighted enough to collect the kind of information necessary to prevent us from placing the brown-grizzly bear on the brink throughout its range in North America. The bear has one of the lowest reproductive rates of any large mammal and when populations are reduced beyond a certain threshold it becomes very difficult to ensure their continued existence. This is the problem today in the rest of the U.S. and portions of Canada. It is far easier to plan for wise management of this species in the long term (and cheaper too) than to develop a recovery program which is precarious at best.

MORE BEAR FIELDWORK

Back in Juneau, I continued splitting time between the office and fieldwork on both Admiralty and Chichagof Islands. The continual fieldwork was interesting and satisfying. Although I have highlighted some of the more exciting experiences, our work was mostly routine, with long days fighting typical maritime weather obstacles that always made our work more challenging than we wanted. But the occasional bluebird day always helped us to forget the more typical gray overcast and rain.

6-27-85: Juneau. A beautiful day. LaVern and I flew all 25 Admiralty bears in three and a half hours. Bears are widely distributed from sea level to over 3,000 feet. . . . Bears are very plastic in their habitat requirements. I think that the effects of logging on brown bears will turn out to be quite straightforward. Bears will likely do OK in young clear-cuts but will find no forage resources whatsoever in dense second-growth stands which in Alaska are largely devoid of understory vegetation. If second growth represents a significant portion of the managed forest (75 percent of the timber rotation), then carrying capacity [the relative numbers of animals the habitat can support] will be reduced. Probably the most significant effect of logging will be the development of roads and the greatly increased human access into formerly undeveloped country. This will bring more people into contact with bears. Historically, large numbers of people have proven incompatible with maintaining productive brown-grizzly bear populations. Bear populations will likely decline in direct proportion to the number of bear-human conflicts that result from increasing human activity in bear country. I suspect the future is not bright for the brown-grizzly bear throughout much of their original range in North America. Alaska is the last stronghold of this species. What would North America and Alaska be like without the great bear? I believe it would be a country missing part of its character and spirit. I hope that day never comes. How many bears do we need? What value are they really? When the majority of people ask those questions, the future of the bear is greatly imperiled and perhaps so is an important part of our American heritage and spirit.

⚜

Frequently, in my day-to-day work, I would encounter situations that gave me insights into bear–human interactions. It is often remarked—and I have done so myself—that brown/grizzly bears and humans are incompatible. In hindsight, considering many later experiences working in close proximity to brown bears, I believe the "incompatibility" theory needs clarification. It may be more accurate to say that humans are incompatible with brown bears, and not necessarily the converse. We know that bears are generalists in their habitat use, and bears often show up around human activity centers, particularly when attracted by human foods and garbage. The end result is not that bears can't accommodate people, but that most people—without adequate education and behavioral modification—cannot accommodate bears. People's fear of being attacked or killed when in close proximity to bears is rational, but for the bears it is usually terminal.

8-15-85. Hawk Inlet, Admiralty Island. LaVern and I conducted ground reconnaissance and snaring on lower Greens and Zinc creeks. There were many fish in both streams this year so bear sign was well dispersed. On lower Zinc Cr. above the meadow we saw two young bears near the stream. They disappeared once they discovered we were in the area. We set out nine snares along Zinc Cr. Further up Zinc, we walked up on #56 and her two cubs at about 30 yards while they were fishing. The cubs ran off followed by their mother. However, as she crossed the stream, she put her ears back and head down and false charged us for about five yards. Then she crossed the stream and ran into the forest behind her cubs. This was close quarters and much too close for comfort, a real adrenaline pumper to say the least. LaVern and I both had our rifles at the ready. We had a similar incident in this same area with a single bear that ran within about ten yards of us but did not attack us and we didn't fire on it.

I am sure most people would have fired in similar circumstances and there are clearly times when that would be justified. Fortunately, this female only bluff charged us and I have no idea what the single bear was doing. These examples are good reasons why people should avoid these high-density bear areas at this time of the year—this is particularly the case in areas with dense vegetation where it is possible to get very close and surprise a bear. In most of our experiences, however, we have avoided serious confrontations with bears even though we spent many days and hours in high-density bear habitat.

With the exception of a mother protecting cubs or a bear on a food cache, however, most brown bears—except those conditioned to human food and garbage—appear to go out of their way to avoid encounters with humans. A growing concern on the Tongass now is that with increased human access into bear habitat—especially by means of new roads—many more people will come in contact with more bears, and bear–human conflicts will undoubtedly increase.

THE WILDLIFE SOCIETY WEIGHS IN ON GRIZZLY BEARS

On October 21, 1985, I attended The Wildlife Society council meeting in Bozeman, Montana, where the Grizzly Bear Technical Committee presented our technical report for the council's review. The council voted unanimously to approve our report[46] and position statement on the management and conservation of brown bears. Key elements from the position statement follow.

Conservation of brown bears, which includes the grizzly bear and the Alaska brown bear in North America, has become an increasingly controversial issue as conflicts between this species and human beings continue to increase . . .

Mortality of brown bears from conflicts with humans and intensive development and activity within brown bear habitat threaten populations of this species . . .

Brown bears are jeopardized when increasingly intensive human activities are carried out in their habitats and people come in close contact with bears. Non-hunting mortality is from conflicts involving perceived or real threats to life and property. People that live, work and recreate in brown bear habitat often do not keep their living areas sanitized of garbage and food stored properly.

Intensive forest development in brown bear habitat, which is most frequently undeveloped land, generally improves human access and increases both disturbance and direct man-caused mortality of bears.

The policy of The Wildlife Society in regard to conservation of brown bears is to:

» Recognize that, because many human activities are incompatible with this species, retention of self-sustaining populations of brown bears represents a major challenge in wildlife conservation . . .
» Encourage all efforts that reduce conflicts between humans and brown bears, including public information programs, and closures to human use of areas that are important habitats . . .
» Encourage all efforts that reduce nonhunting mortality, including those related to defense of life and property . . .
» Encourage the incorporation of brown bear needs into comprehensive planning for forestry, mining, agriculture and other human activities . . .
» Discourage roads and motorized vehicle access in important brown bear habitat.

TONGASS TIMBER POLITICS ON THE NATIONAL STAGE

By the mid-1980s, management of the Tongass National Forest was becoming increasingly controversial at the national level. Articles appeared in *Reader's Digest*, *Sports Illustrated*, *Audubon*, and *National Geographic*. There was growing discussion within the environmental community, both at the regional and national levels, regarding management of the Tongass Forest. Much of that concern was focused on the Alaska National Interest Lands Conservation Act's (ANILCA) Section 705, which mandated a timber harvest level of four and a half billion board feet per decade and provided funding of at least $40 million per year to maintain the timber supply. This timber mandate and annual funding—outside the normal congressional appropriation process—was unlike that of any other national forest. Many conservation organizations and some members of Congress perceived the Tongass situation to be a significant federal subsidy to build roads and harvest old-growth forest at taxpayers' expense. Additionally, many conservationists and professional wildlife biologists were concerned about the impact of logging old growth on fish and wildlife resources. Little did I know when I started my wildlife research in Southeast that I would get caught up in a political tug-of-war among state and federal resource agencies, the Forest Service, environmental organizations, local communities, and the timber industry.

During the winter of 1986, we continued monitoring our radio-collared bears while they were in their dens. I also worked on data analysis and was preparing a paper on the denning ecology of Southeast brown bears for presentation at the Seventh International Conference on Bear Research and Management in Williamsburg, Virginia, in late February.

CONGRESSIONAL BRIEFING

Just before I left for the bear conference, the ADF&G commissioner received a letter from Congressman John Seiberling (D-Ohio) asking if I could go to Washington, DC, after the conference and provide a briefing to his subcommittee staff on public lands regarding Tongass wildlife issues. The commissioner approved the request. Excerpts from my journal follow.

Following the bear conference, where I presented a denning paper on Alaska brown bears, and after arriving in DC, I met with the Governor's special assistant John Katz and went over my presentation to the congressional subcommittee staff. Mr. Katz was very interested, asked intelligent questions, and appeared to generally be pleased with the outline of my presentation. He said as long as I stuck to the biology and the facts, he would have no problem with anything I said. This may have been the most important part of my trip to Washington just to provide him with an assessment of the forest-wildlife issue. I truly believe he understands that there are irreconcilable problems between large-scale timber harvesting and wildlife habitat in southeast Alaska. In the afternoon, I went to brief the subcommittee staff with Eric Laschever, John Katz's assistant. We met with Teddy Rowe, Stan Sloss, and Russ Shea. They were very interested and attentive throughout the presentation and asked good questions. The first question Chief of Staff Rowe asked when I finished was: could I come back to Washington and testify before the subcommittee. I deferred to Eric who said he would check with the Governor's Office.

The next day, I briefed Senator Stevens' and Congressman Young's staffs. They, of course, were coming from the other side of the issue and were not pleased with what they heard from me. I felt that they initially tried to intimidate me but I gave them the same exact briefing that I provided the subcommittee staff. Basically, I told the truth and answered all of their questions. [Fig. 2.68]

US HOUSE TONGASS HEARINGS

I was comfortable with the meetings I had in DC with the House subcommittee staff, and I focused my presentations and discussion on the biological issues with which I was familiar and avoided getting into economics and societal values. Of course, we all have our personal biases, but I felt my job was to describe the results of our research and discuss the likely wildlife trade-offs that could be reasonably predicted given a particular management approach. Later that spring, however, I quickly realized that there was much more to come.

FIG. 2.68. In Washington, DC, when I testified before the US House Subcommittee on Public Lands during oversight hearings on the Tongass National Forest in 1986.

4-30-86: Juneau: I learned today that Seiberling's chief of staff Teddy Roe would like me to present the same slide show I presented to him previously at a Congressional Hearing on management of the Tongass National Forest. However, I also learned that the State of Alaska had said I was unavailable. Apparently, there had been pressure applied from the timber industry and Alaska Congressional Delegation to keep me from going back to the Washington hearings to testify on wildlife issues.

I had been told recently that the attorney representing Alaska Pulp Company and the Alaska Loggers' Association had openly stated that "the state should put a muzzle on John Schoen." That such pressure could force a public agency to keep a scientist from providing decision makers and the public the results of his science, really pissed me off and, at this point, I'm considering taking personal leave and testifying on behalf of The Wildlife Society.

Tongass political intrigue continued through the spring of 1986 and made it difficult to concentrate on bear research—and also caused me more than a little stress. On May 18, I summarized in my field journal the events leading up to and through the House Subcommittee Hearings on Tongass management.

In late April, my boss, regional supervisor Sterling Eide, had a meeting with the directors of Habitat and Game divisions. Norm Cohen of Habitat asked that I attend and show the slide program I had previously presented to the subcommittee staff in DC.

There were rumors right up to the last as to who would go to the hearings and represent the State of Alaska. There was considerable debate back in Juneau. Apparently, the directors of the departments of National Resources and Commerce and Economic Development also wanted to go and the timber industry clearly did not want me to go. Sterling made numerous calls to the Commissioner's Office to find out what was going on.

Finally, on Monday the week of the hearings, I was told that I would not be going to Washington. I heard from DC that Congressman Seiberling had made two requests to the State and heard the first time that I was unavailable and couldn't get away. The second time, he was told that the State did not have the money to send me. Of course, this was not the case. I decided that if some of those people had put so much pressure on the state to prevent me from presenting my research information, then I had a personal responsibility to go on my own. I contacted the executive committee of the Alaska Chapter of The Wildlife Society and received their strong support that I should attend the hearings and represent the Alaska Chapter [at which time I was serving as Chapter President]. At that point, I took out a personal loan for $1,000 and purchased my airline ticket.

Two days before I left, I received a call from deputy commissioner Denny Kelso. Kelso said that he had supported me and thought I should testify. . . . He also emphasized that there would be people there who would argue my credibility and would try to get me out of the "line up." He said he was worried about losing me from providing future input into this issue. . . . He said he was always surprised how aggressive the opponents can get. He was clearly (and legitimately) concerned institutionally about how significant a role I could play in the future if I went to the hearings on behalf of The Wildlife Society.

The next day, Game Division director Lew Pamplin called to reiterate some of the same cautions as Kelso but he was also personally supportive of my decision, whatever it would be. Because I had so much support from my supervisors and ADF&G colleagues, I did not feel personally that my job was in immediate jeopardy. But clearly, I had received the message loud and clear that my professional integrity as a scientist may be on the line.

After carefully considering all of these warnings and the very hostile attitudes from the timber industry and Forest Service leadership, I decided that I had to testify, and that I would stick to the biology of the issue and speak the truth as I understood it. I felt strongly that someone needed to provide Congress and the public with scientific information about the biological tradeoffs of timber management in Alaska. That is not to say that logging is good or bad but rather, if you manage the forest in this way, here are the most likely results we can expect to occur for wildlife populations, and specifically to black-tailed deer. The bottom line, in my opinion, was that this issue wasn't so much about deer as it was about providing decision makers and the public with the best scientific information from which to make reasoned decisions about public resources. I departed Juneau on the morning flight Wednesday the seventh of May. The hearing began the next day.

This was my first experience testifying before a congressional committee. I was surprised that so few members of Congress were present, with many coming in and out of the hearings as they proceeded. The hearings included a series of panels that involved the State of Alaska, the Forest Service, city officials, local residents, timber industry representatives, conservationists, commercial fishermen, scientists, sportsmen, and others.

The Oversight Hearing before the House Subcommittee on Public Lands began on May 8, 1986. Key excerpts from the official record, listed chronologically, follow.[47]

Chairman Seiberling: This morning we are beginning two days of oversight hearings on the status of the Forest Service's management of the Tongass National Forest in Alaska. . . . Also, the Forest Service is now embarked on a review and possible revision of the Tongass land management plan. . . . One purpose of such a review should be to see whether we in the Congress should consider revising the present statutory framework which governs the management of this largest of all the national forests.

Comments from Alaska Congressman Don Young: I would like to remind the people in the audience . . . that I voted against Alaska lands bill, because I still think it was bad legislation for the environment. . . . I personally would prefer a smaller, more dispersed wilderness area in the southeast. Instead the national environmental groups asked for 5.4 million acres of wilderness—large blocks of wilderness . . . the timber industry got 1.7 million acres.

Conservation Panel:

Bart Koehler (SEACC): SEACC has recommended that Congress seriously consider repealing section 705(a) [of ANILCA], thus eliminating the Tongass Timber Supply Fund and references to a 4.5 billion board feet per decade supply goal.

David Cline (National Audubon Society): We are now seeking your help in stopping their (timber industry) high grading of the best of our timber in our own backyards.... In my fifteen years of conservation work in the State of Alaska, I have to say that I haven't seen anything more serious in terms of environmental damage than the expensive clearcut logging in terms of impact on high value fish and wildlife habitat...

Timber Industry Panel:

John Galea (Alaska Loggers Association): The Alaska Loggers Association has always been under the impression that when ANILCA was passed that the wilderness timber issue in Alaska was settled and that the present timber base of 1.7 million acres of the Tongass National Forest was set aside primarily for timber management in order to maintain and protect those jobs that were in existence prior to the passage of ANILCA...

This is less than 10 percent of Alaska rain forest...

Mr. Seiberling to Mr. Galea: Do you feel that high grading timber is the correct policy in the long term?

Mr. Galea: Within the 1.7 million acres that were set aside in order to maintain the timber industry, take a look at those lands. Go in there and take out the most cost-effective volume that you can at this point in time, particularly during those poor market periods.

Science and Sportsmen Panel:

John Schoen (President, Alaska Chapter of The Wildlife Society): I am representing the Alaska Chapter here today.

I have submitted our position statement on the management of old-growth forests and in that position statement, we have ten recommendations on forest management which I will not go through specifically.

Instead, today, I will... show some slides and try to answer some biological questions.

I am on annual leave [from the Department of Fish and Game].... My remarks will be confined to the biological issues, although I recognize that there are other important resource issues, job issues, and so on.

At this point, I used slides and summarized the amount of forest and non-forest land on the Tongass, pointing out that only one-third of the land base is actually classified as commercial forest land. In addition, I highlighted the fact that commercially important timber land containing high-volume (large-tree) old growth represented only 4 percent of the Tongass land base, and this has always been the focus of the timber harvest. Next, I walked the subcommittee through a description of old-growth forest in Southeast Alaska, how it differed from second growth, and why old growth was important wildlife habitat, with a special emphasis on black-tailed deer. Finally, I described the impacts of clear-cutting old growth on deer and other wildlife. The slides and graphics were very helpful in clearly illustrating the biological relationships on the Tongass, how forest management is changing wildlife habitat values, and the implications for long-term conservation.

I summarized the slide program in the following statement excerpted here from the *Congressional Record*.

We have learned in this short period [last decade] that old-growth forests are diverse, very productive habitats for fish and wildlife.

Old-growth forests are rare nationwide. Most of the old-growth forests in the lower 48 were cut before the science of wildlife biology was really developed and in fact today old-growth forests across the continent in the United States, lower 48, probably represent less than two percent of the original forest.

Old-growth forests are nonrenewable on 100-year rotations.

In southeast Alaska wildlife biologists are concerned about the selective harvest of high-volume stands. The Alaska Chapter has a strong recommendation on that. This is reducing the forest diversity and will impact wildlife populations.

Southeast Alaska is unique. The Tongass National forest is the largest national forest in the system. It has possibly the greatest amount of old-growth forest left in the country.

It is unique because it is an archipelago made up of many, many islands, and it also has some species of international worldwide significance, such as the brown bear, the bald eagle, the wolf, and others.

Finally, I think it is important in our consideration of the management of old-growth forest and the management of the Tongass Forest to recognize that our decisions and our activities will influence this forest and the users of this forest for many, many generations to come.

Jack Lentfer (representing the Territorial Sportsmen of Juneau): I have been a wildlife biologist in Alaska for 29 years and from 1977 through 1981 I was the Alaska Department of Fish and Game Southeast Alaska game division supervisor. During this time, the greatest single issue I was involved with was the effects of logging on wildlife. I have also worked in a number of locations through the state and I consider the habitat alteration from clear-cut logging in southeast Alaska one of the most serious wildlife management problems in the State today.

Questions and answers:

Mr. Seiberling: Dr. Schoen, you say in your statement that this proportion in the harvest of high-volume old growth, you show it as disproportionate already occurring in your chart. Yet the loggers who just testified say they want to sell it. Is that in effect what they are saying?

Mr. Schoen: Yes, there is a selective harvest of high-volume classes. There is no question about that. That will impact wildlife.

I think it is important to recognize what these trade-offs mean. You cannot maximize deer production and timber production on the same lands.

Conservation Panel:

Richard Nelson (anthropologist and author, Sitka): What strikes me in sitting here today is that we have heard testimony from certainly widely divergent points of view on the proper management of the Tongass National Forest, but from this whole spectrum of testimony a single issue emerges.

This is the necessity for a national forest that serves the needs of all the people, not just a single industry.

In other words, we need to seek a reasonable balance among all the needs in the Tongass. What are these needs for the Tongass?

[T]he ones we have heard the most about . . . are those commercial needs . . .

The fishing industry . . .

The guiding industry . . .

The tourism industry . . .

The timber industry also is another important commercial need for the Tongass National Forest. A viable long-term timber industry cannot exist in southeast Alaska if the timber is high graded away . . .

We also have—and this is what concerns me more—the need for personal use of resources by the residents of southeast Alaska.

The next day, Forest Service chief Max Peterson and Alaska regional forester Mike Barton presented testimony on behalf of the US Forest Service. Chief Peterson largely summarized the Forest Service's 1985 *Status of the Tongass National Forest* report. Some of the interesting exchanges between the subcommittee and the chief are excerpted below.

Mr. Seiberling: Chief, yesterday we had a remarkable presentation and slide show by Dr. John Schoen about this very problem. Are you familiar with that? Have you seen that?

Peterson: I have not seen the slide show. I have been in Alaska, and have looked at some of the work on the ground . . .

Mr. Seiberling: Dr. Schoen's slides and the facts he presented were absolutely devastating in terms of the impact of clear cutting on the habitat for the black-tail deer. He showed in a most dramatic way how in old-growth forest you have lots of open spaces and, therefore, a lot of browse for the deer and once you cut that or it is destroyed by fire, then you get a uniform growth, no understory vegetation and then you have a virtual desert as far as the deer are concerned . . .

I wonder if you could comment on that?

Mr. Peterson: I agree completely that we ought to use all the latest research. I think most of the research he referred to is ours and it is of very short duration . . .

Let me state emphatically, Mr. Chairman, that we intend our management program in southeast Alaska to include in perpetuity a viable population of black-tail deer, and we are investing a lot of money in research to see that happen.

In the meantime, we are affecting less than one-tenth of one percent of the Tongass Forest annually and we are affecting only a small part of the old growth. There will be lots of opportunity to work in new research information . . .

Mr. Chairman, anybody that hunts in Alaska knows that the best place to hunt is in areas where you have got the food that is provided in clear cuts.

[Ripples of laughter break out in the audience.]

Seiberling: The audience is reminded that demonstrations are not allowed under the rules. We had quite devastating testimony, Chief, to the contrary yesterday, and I would like you to review the record that was established.

This hearing was my first experience with big-time natural resource politics in Washington, DC. One of the surprises during these House Subcommittee hearings was that Alaska's lone congressman, Don Young, walked out during the hearings after the timber industry panel presented their testimony and just prior to the panel on which I testified with The Wildlife Society and Territorial Sportsmen. Two of the panel members were Alaskans (Jack Lentfer and me) and constituents of Congressman Young. His departure was disappointing. The undercurrent of "gotcha" questioning coming from either side of the aisle was also apparent. This was truly high-octane politics in practice and a real wake-up call to this young, idealistic scientist.

Flying home to Juneau, I felt I had accomplished my goal of clearly laying out the science of the issue so that decision makers had a better understanding of the trade-offs between industrial forestry and conservation of fish and wildlife resources. I believed that I had done my part in ensuring that Congress had access to scientific information from which to make reasoned decisions regarding management of the Tongass National Forest in the best interest of all Americans. It seemed to me that the old era focusing primarily on "getting the cut out" was coming to an end. And I was greatly relieved to be getting back to my fieldwork in Southeast and leaving the politics to lawmakers and all the lobbyists back in Washington. I knew that if I were forced to regularly participate in the policy arena, I would lose the fire in my belly that comes largely from tramping through forests, wading across salmon-filled streams, and flying wildlife surveys over the wild islands that are the focus of my Alaska fieldwork.

BROWN BEAR RESEARCH CONTINUES

BEAR DENSITY ESTIMATES

For many years, Tlingit people, wildlife biologists, and local Southeasterners knew that Admiralty Island had a high-density population of brown bears. However, no one had completed a rigorous scientific census of Admiralty's brown bears, and this was one of the major objectives of our research. We estimated the number of brown bears in the 133-square-mile North Admiralty study area using a modified capture-mark-resight technique developed by my Alaska colleague Sterling Miller. This technique used radio-collared bears as the marked population. We conducted our aerial survey flights during early evening hours in late June and early July. I flew the Super Cub at about 500 feet over the terrain, and LaVern and I counted all of the bears we observed. During this same survey, we used radiotelemetry to determine how many of the marked bears actually occurred within our study area. Using a ratio of the total number of observed bears relative to the number of marked bears, we estimated the total number of bears in the area.

We repeated the survey flight four times in the early summer of 1986 and five times in 1987.

7-9-87: Juneau, broken overcast. This evening, LaVern and I flew another mark/recapture survey on northern Admiralty Island. We began our survey in the Super Cub after 1900 hours beginning with Wheeler Mountain. This evening was our record thus far. We observed a total of 65 brown bears in two hours and seven minutes of flying time. All of our marked bears (22) were inside the geographical boundaries of our study area and we actually observed ten marked bears. We observed 44 adults and 21 juveniles on this survey. This survey—observing 65 bears in just over two hours—was in marked contrast to the bear census I participated in during May of this year in the western Arctic with Warren Ballard and Sterling Miller. In the western Arctic survey work, our high count was nine bears in about nine hours of flying multiple aircraft. The density of bears in south coastal Alaska is many times higher than in the Arctic. One of the major differences, of course, is the high abundance of nutritious food—anchored by Pacific salmon—that is available to south coastal brown bears.

We had now completed our Admiralty bear census using Miller's capture-mark-resight technique.[48] Based on our two years of surveys, we estimated that the average density within our 133-square-mile North Admiralty study area was one bear per square mile.[49] This is a phenomenal density for a brown bear population and is comparable only to densities on Kodiak Island and the

Katmai Coast on the Alaska Peninsula. Clearly, Admiralty Island supports one of the highest-density brown bear populations on Earth.

SEASONAL DISTRIBUTION AND HABITAT USE OF SOUTHEAST BROWN BEARS

Another major objective of our research was to document the seasonal values of different habitats to brown bears in Southeast. Using radiotelemetry as our primary tool, we learned that the average size of annual home ranges for radio-collared bears on Admiralty Island was 39 and 14 square miles for males and females, respectively.[50] These were comparable to the home ranges of bears on Chichagof Island. The home ranges in our study were many times smaller than brown/grizzly bears found in northern and interior portions of Alaska and elsewhere in western North America, presumably because coastal food resources are much more concentrated and abundant.

Because bears are large, inefficient at digesting low-quality forage, and dormant for nearly half the year while hibernating, they must concentrate their foraging activity on the most nutritious and plentiful foods. These include new succulent sedges and herbaceous plants, roots, berries, meat, and fish. Thus, bears must focus their seasonal food gathering in habitats that produce the greatest abundance of these high-quality foods. Bears are also intelligent, long-lived animals that learn from their mothers during an extended maternal care period of two to three years. These attributes, combined with their extraordinary sense of smell, assist them in finding and exploiting the most nutritious food resources within their annual home ranges. A seasonal road map describing the general pattern of how the average brown bear makes its living in Southeast Alaska follows.[51]

SPRING: DEN EMERGENCE THROUGH SEA-LEVEL GREEN-UP (LATE MARCH—MID-MAY)

Most brown bears in Southeast emerge from high-elevation dens during April and May. Males leave dens first, and females with newborn young emerge last. On Admiralty and Chichagof Islands, radio-collared male brown bears spent an average of 165 days in winter dens, compared with 211 days for females with newborn cubs. After leaving their dens, many bears begin moving to lower elevations. During spring, brown bears are widely scattered from sea level, where they forage on tidal sedge flats, to south-facing avalanche slopes and higher subalpine ridges. Upland old-growth forests and avalanche slopes were the habitats most extensively used by radio-collared brown bears on Admiralty and Chichagof Islands during spring (Fig. 2.69). Female brown bears were

FIG. 2.69. Chaik Bay on southwest Admiralty Island. Brown bears are widely dispersed during spring from tidal wetlands to upland old-growth forests and south-facing avalanche slopes.

more widely distributed than males, perhaps to avoid dangerous interactions with other bears. This is particularly the case for mothers and cubs, because cubs are vulnerable to infanticide from unrelated adult bears. During spring, brown bear diets on Admiralty Island are composed largely of sedges, other green vegetation, and roots. Skunk cabbage roots and horsetail are particularly important spring forage plants, while the primary animal components of the diet include deer, voles, and herring roe.

EARLY SUMMER: GREEN-UP TO INITIATION OF SALMON RUNS
(MID-MAY–MID-JULY)

By mid-May, most bears have emerged from their winter dens. Early summer is the peak of the breeding season in Southeast, and courting pairs are often observed in coastal sedge meadows and on upper subalpine and alpine ridges. During early summer, bears are widely distributed and habitat use varies greatly. By mid-June, many radio-collared bears on Admiralty and Chichagof

FIG. 2.70. A mother bear and her three yearling cubs in alpine habitat on northern Admiralty Island. This alpine ridge complex is above Greens Creek and south of Hawk Inlet. During early summer (June through mid-July) many brown bears use these productive habitats for foraging. We also observed quite a bit of mating activity. We focused our aerial surveys in this upper subalpine habitat as well as on the large river deltas. It was not uncommon for us to see several dozen bears in an hour of alpine survey flying.

Islands were observed at higher elevations, where they foraged on the new growth of succulent plants in alpine and subalpine meadows and avalanche slopes (Fig. 2.70). Old-growth forest habitat is used substantially by bears throughout this season both for feeding and traveling between coastal and alpine habitats. During early summer, brown bear diets on Admiralty Island are dominated by sedges, other green vegetation, and roots.

FIG. 2.71. Old-growth riparian habitat adjacent to salmon spawning streams provide critical late-summer habitat for brown bears in Southeast Alaska. Note the salmon carcasses along the edges of the gravel bar. These sites are dominated by Sitka spruce, devil's club, and salmonberry. Heavily used bear trails wind through the forest and along the riverbanks.

LATE SUMMER: PEAK OF SALMON SPAWNING
(MID-JULY–MID-SEPTEMBER)

By mid-July, most brown bears in Southeast have moved to low-elevation coastal salmon streams. During this period, riparian old-growth forest represented much of the habitat used by radio-collared bears on Admiralty and Chichagof Islands, and nearly two-thirds of all Admiralty Island bears were located within a 525-foot band on either side of salmon streams (Fig. 2.71).

During late summer and early fall, salmon make up a major portion of brown bears' diet, although they also eat sedges, skunk cabbage, and the berries of devil's club and blueberry. Salmon, skunk cabbage, and devil's club are all found in abundance in low-elevation riparian sites in Southeast; blueberry

shrubs are more scattered throughout the forest; and coastal sedges occur most abundantly in association with tidal wetlands. During late summer, brown bears are more concentrated than at any other time of the year, and their activities are targeted primarily on fishing for spawning salmon along low-elevation streams, lake borders, and intertidal spawning areas.

In these late summer and early fall months, bears consume large quantities of salmon to rebuild their body condition and lay on essential fat reserves that are required to successfully reproduce and survive another four to seven months in winter dens (Fig. 2.72). Brown bears can increase their body mass over the summer and fall by as much as 50 percent when salmon are abundant. On the Kenai Peninsula of Alaska, Grant Hilderbrand estimated that individual female brown bears consume 23.8 pounds of salmon per day and 2,207 pounds per season during the summer and fall.[52]

Not only do bears utilize habitats that maximize their energy intake, but they also maximize their efficiency by feeding selectively on the most nutritious parts of salmon. LaVern and I often observed bears catching salmon but only eating the brains or roe—the egg sacs of females. Later, Scott Gende conducted pioneering research quantifying bears' preferential feeding on salmon and salmon parts on Chichagof Island.[53] When streams were shallow and salmon abundant, bears selectively captured spawning salmon that were highest in energy content. In Southeast, the fat and protein content of pink and chum salmon declines each day the fish are in freshwater streams, because the fish stop eating in freshwater. Bears can visually distinguish salmon that have recently entered freshwater from older ones that have been there a while, and they select the fish with higher nutritional value, thus maximizing their energy intake. They also selectively feed on the most nutritional parts of salmon such as the eggs, skin, and brain.

The Alaska population densities of coastal brown bears, like Admiralty and Chichagof Islands, where salmon are abundant, are up to eighty times higher than those of interior or northern Alaska grizzly bears that don't have access to salmon.[54] Riparian forest habitat associated with productive salmon spawning streams is considered seasonally critical habitat and a key component for ensuring productive brown bear populations in Southeast. During late summer and fall, bears also forage extensively on berries, including devil's club, blueberry, currant, salmonberry, and twisted stalk.

Although salmon streams provide highly valuable feeding habitat in Southeast, we discovered that not all brown bears use salmon streams. On Admiralty Island, 14 percent of our radio-collared bears—all females—remained with their offspring in interior areas of the island at higher elevations.[55] Subsequent research, measuring marine-derived nitrogen from stable isotope analysis of the hair samples we collected, confirmed the assumption that salmon was not a component of the "interior" bears' diet.[56] Female brown bears that remained at higher elevations foraged on sedges, grasses, and other green vegetation, as well as voles and some deer. On Admiralty and Chichagof Islands, the distribution of radio-collared females with cubs of the year was farther from salmon streams during the spawning season than males or females without young. Presumably, the productivity of female bears that avoid feeding on salmon is lower than those eating salmon. It is likely that limited use of salmon streams by females with young cubs is a trade-off between reducing the risk of cub mortality in areas with high bear densities—like salmon spawning streams—and acquiring higher-quality food.

FALL: END OF SALMON SPAWNING TO DENNING
(MID-SEPTEMBER–MID-DECEMBER)

By mid-September, many salmon runs are in decline, herbaceous vegetation has died back, and berry production at sea level is over. Most brown bears begin to move away from coastal salmon streams during September and head toward higher elevations. Upland old growth and avalanche slopes were the preferred fall habitats for our sample of radio-collared brown bears on Admiralty and Chichagof Islands. It is important for bears to top off their fat reserves during this time in preparation for their long winter hibernation. By the end of September, most bears move into higher-elevation avalanche slopes, where they forage on berries, particularly devil's club and stink currants (Fig. 2.73).

FIG. 2.73. High-elevation avalanche slope in the northern Admiralty study area near tree line. The steep slopes to the left are covered with devil's club and currant shrubs interspersed within alder thickets. The shrubs provided a high-density berry source for bears prior to fall denning.

By early October, the first frosts and winter snowfall usually occur in the high country, and herbaceous forage is no longer available. Winter denning begins in October and November. The mean date of den entry for radio-collared bears on Admiralty and Chichagof Islands was 30 October.[57] Pregnant females are the first to enter winter dens (average date = 22 October); females with older cubs and single females den later; and males are the last to seek out winter den sites (average date = 5 November). By mid-November, about 80 percent of males and 95 percent of female brown bears have entered dens and begun their long winter dormancy. On Admiralty and Chichagof Islands, brown bears prefer den sites on moderate to steep slopes above 1,000 feet. Upland old-growth forest at higher elevations is most commonly used by denning brown bears, although alpine and subalpine slopes are also used. The most common den sites on Admiralty and Chichagof Islands were in natural rock cavities (cave denning was common on Admiralty but unusual in other parts of North America) or excavated under the root structure of large, old-growth trees or into earthen slopes.

The annual cycle of a hypothetical brown bear in Southeast Alaska is represented on an aerial photo of a coastal watershed on Admiralty Island (Fig. 2.74).

BEAR–FOREST RELATIONSHIPS ON CHICHAGOF ISLAND

Although brown bears are adaptable generalists and once ranged widely across the northern hemisphere, their behavior and habitat choices make them vulnerable to humans and forest management.[58] For example, bears' dependence on salmon streams and beach habitats brings them into contact with humans using the same productive lands. And bears are also attracted to human foods, garbage, and livestock in rural communities and industrial campsites.

One of the major objectives of our research on Chichagof Island was to assess the influence of logging and forest management on brown bear populations. Old-growth forest habitat is used extensively by brown bears in Southeast.[59] During late summer, in particular, when spawning salmon are concentrated in streams bordered by riparian forests, from 40 to 55 percent of brown bear habitat use occurs in these food-rich habitats. On Chichagof Island, where clear-cuts were abundant, clear-cut habitat was little used (less than 4 percent) throughout the year by radio-collared bears. Based on our aerial telemetry surveys (and subsequent data from Kim Titus and LaVern Beier[60]), bears generally avoided clear-cuts throughout the year. This may be in part because other habitats such as subalpine meadows, avalanche slopes, riparian forests, and estuarine grass flats likely provided higher-quality foraging habitats. However, where clear-cuts are adjacent to salmon spawning streams, some bears will continue to fish in those streams even though the surrounding forest is cut.

FIG. 2.74. The annual cycle of a Southeast brown bear (courtesy Audubon Alaska 2016, *Ecological Atlas of Southeast Alaska*).

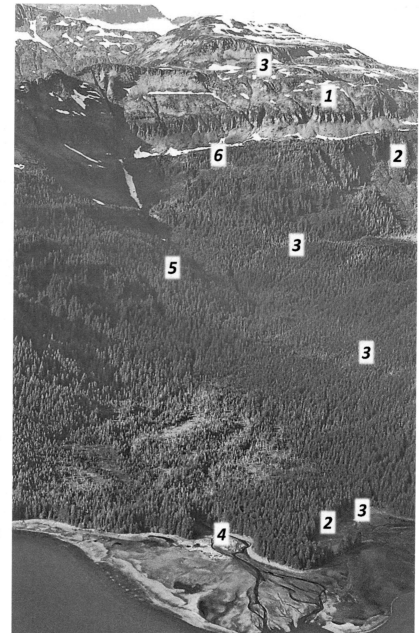

1. Den emergence: From late March through May, most bears emerge from their high-country dens. Males leave earliest, and females with newborn cubs latest.

2. Spring foraging: Bears generally move down from den areas in search of new succulent vegetations, including sedges, skunk cabbage, roots, or animal carcasses. South-facing avalanche slopes, fens, wet forests, and beaches are commonly used habitats.

3. Early summer travels: From mid-May through mid-July, many bears are actively engaged in breeding and individuals are widely distributed from sea level to alpine ridges. Some bears continue to use tidal sedge flats for grazing while others travel and graze extensively in lush alpine subalpine meadows. Upland forest and avalanche slopes are also used extensively.

4. Salmon spawning: By mid-July, most bears concentrate their activities in riparian forests and tidal estuaries in search of good fishing sites to feast on salmon. Small, shallow streams are the most efficient fishing sites, and bears spend much of their time fishing, resting within the cover of riparian forests within 500 feet of salmon streams. Dominant bears always get the best fishing sites. Sedges and berries also remain important food items at this time.

5. End of the fish runs: As most fish runs wind down by mid-September, many bears begin moving into the upper forest and onto avalanche slopes where they feed on currants and devil's club berries.

6. Fall denning: By mid-October, pregnant females begin entering their winter dens. Most dens occur on steep slopes above 1,000 feet. Dens are often excavated under the root structure of large old-growth trees. In some areas, natural rock cavities are also used. Males are the last to enter winter dens.

More recently, on north Chichagof Island, Rod Flynn and colleagues, using GPS telemetry and DNA markers, compared brown bear habitat use on heavily clear-cut Spasski Creek to Freshwater Creek where there was more intact riparian forest habitat.[61] This valuable study concluded that low-elevation riparian habitat along salmon spawning streams was important to brown bears. Females, in particular, spent more time feeding on salmon in the intact riparian habitat than in clear-cut habitat. These studies suggest that clear-cutting old-growth forest in valley bottoms with associated salmon streams will likely diminish the habitat quality of those important feeding areas for brown bears, especially females and their offspring.

There were few opportunities in our study area to evaluate bear use of second-growth forests. However, the dense stands of second-growth forests that develop within twenty to thirty years following clear-cutting offer poor foraging habitat for bears and other herbivorous wildlife. Thus, the conversion of old growth to younger forests will reduce habitat value for brown bears in Southeast.

FIG. 2.75. Bear day bed along the Kadashan River on Chichagof Island. Day beds are generally oval depressions in the earth where bears rest during the day or night. This day bed was at the base of an old-growth tree within the riparian forest.

Riparian old-growth forests with salmon spawning streams provide critical habitat for brown bears in Southeast. I remember working in both Greens Creek and Kadashan, where the bear trails wound through the large, old-growth spruce trees growing along the streams where pink and chum salmon spawn during late summer. These streams were extensively used by bears, and the bear trails, bear mark trees, and bear day beds (Fig. 2.75) under the big spruce trees were readily visible throughout this riparian habitat.

Although riparian large-tree old growth represents a small proportion of the land area in Southeast, these stands have been disproportionately harvested. For example, on southeast Chichagof Island—the region surrounding our study area, including the Kadashan and Corner Bay watersheds—Forest Service ecologist Michael Shephard and colleagues reported in 1999 that 21,564 acres of old growth had been harvested, representing a 14 percent decline of old growth in the area.[62] But that harvest also resulted in a 44 percent decline in riparian spruce (which represented only 8 percent of the entire area). In addition, they calculated that 250 miles of logging roads were constructed there, mostly in valley bottoms. Thus, the small portion of watersheds used most heavily by bears, particularly during the late summer salmon spawning season, generally are the watersheds most impacted by logging. And the construction of roads results in greater human access and more bear–human interactions, generally resulting in harmful impacts to bears.[63]

Although maintaining important seasonal habitat is essential for sustaining abundant brown bear populations, habitat alone will not ensure that bears remain an integral part of the ecosystem. Other factors include human density and human behavior and tolerance toward bears. Brown bears are large, occasionally dangerous animals, capable of inflicting serious injury or death to humans. This has shaped human attitudes toward bears and resulted in significant and often unjustified killing of bears by humans. Because brown bears have low reproductive rates, their populations are particularly vulnerable to increased mortality. Adding to this risk is the fact that population declines among brown bears are difficult to detect in a sufficiently timely way to take corrective action.

Prior to the mid-1970s, most of the hunting pressure for brown bears on northeast Chichagof occurred along the coast, where access was by small boat. At that time, fewer than five bears were killed annually. By 1988, there were over 140 miles of logging roads accessing much of the interior of this portion of the island, and the annual harvest of brown bears had quadrupled.[64] The next year ADF&G closed the season by emergency order.

In hindsight, we now know that as the inexorable wave of human settlement and resource development swept west across the continent, grizzly bear populations began a slow decline throughout their original range in the United States. Although Alaska still has abundant populations of brown/grizzly bears, those of us involved in bear research and management were encouraging resource managers to carefully consider their management plans and take extra precautions not to repeat the mistakes that occurred over the twentieth century throughout the American West. We were particularly concerned about poorly planned road networks and field camps that were proliferating throughout bear habitat in places like Southeast, as well as lack of responsible garbage management and a frontier mentality regarding human interactions with bears. My field notes during the mid-1980s reflect the day-to-day occurrences we were witnessing that suggested learning from past mistakes was not likely.

5-23-86: Juneau. I heard today that bear #88 was shot and killed at the Corner Bay logging camp last night. He had been frequenting the dump and the camp and then the bear attempted to get into a camp trailer so it was shot in defense of life or property. The dump was not cleaned up as required under the camp's Department of Environmental Conservation [DEC] permit which states that the dump will be deemed satisfactory if it does not attract bears.

7-15-86: Chichagof Island. I stopped at the dump site about twenty minutes after some camp staff had dumped and burned. The dump was smoldering but much unburned garbage remained. The dump smelled badly of garbage and fresh bear sign was abundant. The dump has not been covered since the beginning of the summer. The Forest Service camp manager discussed the dump situation with me that evening. He was in total agreement that the key to resolving the problem is putting in a fuel-fired incinerator like the one Forest Service uses at their Corner Bay facility. He said the cost of their incinerator was approximately $3,000. He felt that it would very quickly pay for itself and greatly resolve the bear problems. He acknowledged that the logging camp is completely out of compliance with their DEC permit in that they do not fill the dump and, in fact, do not have equipment at the camp for filling the dump. He said that last week they had 11 bears in the camp and that the loggers are getting uneasy about so many bears. Clearly, the "bear problem" is due largely to negligence and sloppiness of the Corner Bay logging camp.

8-19-86: Juneau. I ran into two Forest Service supervisors at the Juneau airport today and we had a chance to catch up and discuss several forest-wildlife issues. I raised the bear-dump problem at Corner Bay and suggested that the Forest Service should consider providing logging camps with incinerators as a wildlife habitat enhancement measure to mitigate bear problems and reduce DLP mortalities. They seemed shocked with the idea that the Forest Service should take responsibility for this issue. One, a forest supervisor, pursued it further and was generally quite negative about the possibility. He said it wouldn't be a proper use of government funds.

This exchange was disappointing, to say the least, and left many of us at ADF&G with a sense that the Forest Service leadership on the Tongass was motivated primarily by the unwavering goal of "getting the cut out" rather than a broader mission that included serious fish and wildlife conservation measures. With that said, however, it is important to also recognize that there were many Forest Service employees—particularly fish, wildlife, and recreation specialists—who worked very hard and had a true commitment to conservation principles and balanced management of the Tongass National Forest.

4-23-87: Juneau. I flew the Super Cub to the Cube Cove logging camp on northwest Admiralty today and looked over the situation where a bear was killed last week by employees of the logging camp. This camp is logging about 22,000 acres in the three big watersheds at Lake Kathleen, Ward Creek, and Lake Florence. The official report that was filed with Alaska's Fish and Wildlife Protection Division was that a logger had encountered a bear while felling trees between Ward Cr and Lake Kathleen. They said they were charged by the bear which they shot in defense of life. After shooting the bear, they found her spring cubs in a den which was located under a large windfall tree. The young cubs were collected and later sent to the Boise Zoo.

I landed at the Cube Cove strip and hitched a ride up the road in a truck driven by one of the camp employees. We had an interesting and cordial conversation. He said the camp manager's goal was to maximize profits and minimize expenses. There are about 60 people in the bunkhouse and about 20 households of families. Garbage is an open pit dump about four miles from camp. I told him I had heard that the loggers were charged by a bear and they had to shoot it. He laughed and shook his head. He said they used flairs to get her out of her den then shot her. This was a much different story than what was officially reported in the DLP report.

I got dropped off in the vicinity of the den and hiked up through the clear-cut. I learned later from another employee (who gave me a ride back to the plane) that the bear had denned under a windfall about three feet in diameter near the base at the root wad where she had excavated a den. He said he went back up with the loggers the second day with a rifle and shot the bear when it went for the other loggers. He said he shot it about 100 feet from the den. When I called the Camp manager to get permission to fly in to their strip and look for the den, he was very antagonistic towards the bears. He said, "The bears are a disaster. They have been a problem for humans ever since they were placed on earth."

Unfortunately, these kinds of attitudes are all too characteristic of many resource development operations in Alaska, and particularly so in most logging camps in Southeast. In contrast to the logging camp examples, the extra effort invested by the Greens Creek Mine in managing their camp appeared to be paying substantial dividends in reduced bear–human conflicts.

GREENS CREEK MINE DEVELOPMENT ON ADMIRALTY ISLAND

To assess what, if any, effects the Greens Creek Mine development would have on brown bears on northern Admiralty, we established a baseline population estimate using the aerial capture-mark-resight census technique described earlier. The density on northern Admiralty, which surrounded the mine development, was estimated in 1986–1987 to be one bear per square mile. This estimate was repeated by Kim Titus and LaVern Beier in 1993 and remained basically unchanged during that time period.[65]

We also conducted several specific projects to help us evaluate how various mining activities might influence bears in the vicinity. We monitored the denning locations of six radio-collared female bears that denned within two and a half miles of the mine site in upper Greens Creek over subsequent years. As mine activities increased (including substantial aircraft flights, mine and road construction, and blasting activity), the collared bears denned farther away from the mine site. No radio-collared males denned within the Greens Creek drainage.

In general, it did not appear that annual home ranges of adult female brown bears (with the exception of denning) were substantially influenced in the short term by mine development activities. Major road building between the mine site at upper Greens Creek and the staging area at the Hawk Inlet Cannery was well under way by 1986, and we were able to monitor twelve marked bears in the lower Greens and Zinc Creek drainage.

During late summer 1986, all radio-collared bears, except two adult males, continued to use the lower Greens Creek drainage despite intensive road construction activity, which included blasting and heavy equipment operation.[66] Intensive telemetry surveys conducted three times a day indicated, however, that the female bears remaining in the lower Greens Creek drainage did in fact shift away (at a scale of several hundred yards) from the immediate vicinity of construction activity, and then moved back near the road when activity was reduced. I believe these bears remained in the area because this was their established home range and they were attracted to the high-density food resource—spawning salmon—in lower Zinc and Greens Creeks. It appeared that the abundance of food was more important than the disturbance created by construction activity. This is somewhat analogous to a bear that is food-conditioned to human garbage and continues to use that resource in spite of aggressive actions to scare it away. I also suspect that the dense forest may have ameliorated construction disturbance by providing the bears with adequate security cover to remain in the vicinity but out of direct interaction with humans. From my field notes below, it is clear that mine workers rarely observed these bears.

7-30-86: Greens Creek Mine. LaVern and I presented a bear safety talk for Greens Cr Mine personnel. I asked the workers how many bears they thought were using lower Greens and Zinc creeks. They responded that probably six to ten bears occurred there. I told them that based on our mark-recapture study we had a density of one bear per square mile with a 25 percent sightability factor. Based on yesterday's flight where we located 10 bears in the area, we estimated about 40 bears may have been using this general area.

The construction staff was flabbergasted. I told them that they were working in an area that probably had one of the highest brown bear densities in the world. Interestingly, the bears seem to be doing their utmost to avoid people. The reason they have had few encounters is that the mine supervisors were being extremely cautious about garbage management and they use a fuel-fired incinerator to process their garbage. This is in marked contrast to the serious problems encountered at the Corner Bay logging camp on eastern Chichagof Island where the poorly maintained garbage dumps are attracting numerous bears.

During the 1987 field season, we monitored thirteen radio-collared bears in the lower Greens Creek drainage during late summer. One of the adult males that had previously used the area avoided it in 1987 when road construction activity was in full swing. Another adult male made only limited use of the construction area. The home range of an adult female we monitored from 1982 through 1988 remained relatively consistent throughout the construction period. However, on more careful examination of her movements, we observed that she shifted her late-summer intensive fishing activities several hundred yards from Zinc Creek—where major road construction was taking place—to Greens Creek, which was farther away from construction activities. As a result, several other female bears (#84 and #85) shifted their locations upstream on Greens Creek from areas they had used in previous years.

8-16-86: Greens Cr. Northern Admiralty. There definitely seems to be a separation of bears along the streams. It appears that as dominant bears move to a choice fishing area, they displace subordinate bears which move into lesser quality habitat away from the dominant individuals.

These shifts in distribution along the salmon stream are suggestive of a "musical chairs" behavior. Such subtle changes in distribution would not have been obvious without the means of radiotelemetry, which required significant effort to conduct intensive flights several times each day. It became evident that once established, bears remain quite faithful to their traditional home ranges, and in this case most of the individual bears just shifted their movements—on a fine scale of tens to hundreds of yards—away from adjacent development activity.

During our Greens Creek study, through early 1989, we had no knowledge of any bears being killed by construction workers or mine operators. We attributed this initial success to a rigidly enforced garbage policy and camp guidelines prohibiting employees from carrying firearms, littering, hunting, or recreating on site. As a result, bears were not attracted to the camp facility and interactions between bears and people were minimized. These positive results, however, only reflect short-term relationships. The ultimate test will be to compare our initial baseline bear population census to a subsequent census following mine closure. In addition, it will be important to compare salmon escapement levels of Greens and Zinc Creeks and to compare contaminant levels in those systems and in the bears and salmon using those systems. We had been collecting bear hair and blood samples to archive. These samples will provide ADF&G with a baseline to compare to subsequent samples.

MORE TONGASS TIMBER POLITICS

While we continued with our field research on Admiralty and Chichagof, Tongass political pressures continued to escalate, and the ADF&G was a prime target of those wanting to maintain the status quo in forest management. Some examples of this ongoing tension are highlighted in my field notes.

5-1-87: Juneau. We have just learned that the Commissioner is concerned about the article on old-growth forests that Matt Kirchhoff and I wrote for publication in the ADF&G magazine. Yesterday, Regional Supervisor Dave Anderson was called over to Headquarters to talk with the director and re-write the article and take out all reference to logging. ADF&G magazine editor Sheila Nickerson gave me a copy of the companion article by the Forest Service. After reading that article, we decided to withdraw our paper because taking out any reference to clear-cutting and forest management would have left the readership with only half the story. In good conscience and as a matter of professional integrity, Matt and I could not do that.

The next day, we had a meeting with the director about the article and discussed our options. I read excerpts out of the Forest Service paper indicating that with management and regulations they can assure the public that wildlife habitat and populations can be adequately maintained while also continuing to clear-cut old growth on the Tongass. In other words, they can provide all things for every interest on the same acres. The director agreed this was a problem. However, the timber lobby and legislature are pressuring the department to limit what they tell the public about the impacts of forest management on the public's wildlife resources.

I continue to believe that the public has a right to know what kinds of tradeoffs will occur as a result of resource management decisions. Regardless of my personal feeling (e.g., interest in the conservation of fish and wildlife), if the public has all the facts at hand, then accepts informed decisions affecting those resources, my job as a resource professional is completed. Although I may not agree with the final decisions, I believe it is imperative that the agency decisions should be made in an open, honest forum available for public scrutiny.

As a result of the department's concern over the old growth article in the magazine and the slide program we had spent months developing on wildlife and old-growth forests, Matt and I talked with the Alaska Chapter of The Wildlife Society and decided to completely revise the slide program and provide it to The Wildlife Society to make it available for the public. About the same time, we received an invitation from the *Natural Areas Journal* to write an article about wildlife and old-growth forests in Southeast Alaska. We accepted their invitation and revised the article we had written for the department magazine for publication as a scientific paper.[67] Although these venues would not have the same kind of in-state distribution as the ADF&G magazine or slide program, we pursued this new course in order to make recent research findings and their management implications available to a broader audience. This would meet our professional responsibilities for informing our scientific peers as well as some of the public without fanning the political flames within state government.

8-15-87: Juneau, overcast, rain. 0900: Matt and I boarded the state ferry bound for Sitka. This was a field trip for key members of Congress and their staffs involved in the Tongass issue. This field trip was organized by Congressman Mrazek from New York who had invited Matt and me to participate and show The Wildlife Society slide program on old growth and wildlife in southeast Alaska. Other participants included staff members from the Alaska Congressional Delegation, Governor Steve Cowper, Craig Lindh from the Governor's Office, ADF&G Commissioner Don Collinsworth, Deputy Commissioner Denny Kelso, Regional Forester Mike Barton, and many other Forest Service supervisors. Matt and I were on leave from the department and represented The Wildlife Society on this congressional fact-finding trip. The Forest Service had reserved the bar for the group and restricted the public from entering unless they were wearing a Forest Service button. There were state troopers at the door. We showed the slide program at 1630. This took place in the bar with about ten congressmen and their staffs present. We fielded some good questions and I believe that the audience gained a broad overview of the wildlife issues surrounding forest management on the Tongass. At the Sitka Airport, Governor Cowper cordially went out of his way to walk across the terminal and congratulate Matt and me on the slide program. I believe it was a productive and informative field trip. We had entered the lion's den and came out intact.

US SENATE TONGASS HEARINGS

In the late fall of 1987, I was again invited to participate in a congressional hearing in Washington before the Senate Subcommittee on Public Lands, National Parks and Forests of the Committee on Energy and Natural Resources. These hearings, which began on November 3, 1987, focused on Senate Bill 708 to require annual appropriations of funds to support timber management and resource conservation in the Tongass National Forest. I took annual leave from ADF&G and formally represented The Wildlife Society in my testimony before the committee. Some key excerpts from the hearing record follow.[68]

Senator Dale Bumpers of Arkansas: The purpose of the hearing today is to receive testimony on S. 708, a measure currently pending before the Public Lands, National Parks and Forests Subcommittee, which would require an annual appropriation of funds to support timber management on the Tongass National Forest in Alaska. The bill would also require the Forest Service to identify lands unsuitable for timber production on the Forest and prohibit harvesting in such areas as is the case on other national forests.

Senator Tim Wirth from Colorado: The Tongass supports one of the most magnificent stands of virgin rain forests found anywhere on earth, a resource that we all know is fast disappearing.

Many fish and wildlife species depend on that old growth forest . . .

It is also a very fragile ecosystem, for it would take 250 years or more to replace the old growth forests that are being cut down every year.

Senator Frank Murkowski from Alaska: Mr. Chairman, I think it is fair to say that if you examine the legislations closely, you will see as I do that it is very little more than an attack on a very important segment of Alaska's industry, namely, the timber industry, which is the life blood of southeastern Alaska . . .

[I]t is important to keep things in perspective. There are 17 million acres in the Tongass. The forested portion of the Tongass is 9.6 million acres. The total wilderness is 5.9 million acres . . .

Commercial suitable timberland available for harvest, which is what we are talking about, Mr. Chairman, is 1.75 million acres, less than 11 percent of the Tongass or one-tenth of 1 percent each year over a 100-year period.

Senator Ted Stevens from Alaska: In 1980, there was a compromise made. It was not my compromise. It was offered to this committee by some of the people who are here today as a fair compromise. The compromise let us double the amount of acreage that is withdrawn from the Tongass as wilderness, and we will take the appropriations for the Tongass off budget; will guarantee that there will be no less than $40 million a year for permanent improvement of the production of the Tongass . . .

Those people who think they are going to stop cutting timber by cutting the $40 million are wrong. They are cutting the future of America in an area that was set aside for perpetual timber production in the best interest of the country.

Mr. Dale Robertson, Chief, Forest Service: I believe the Forest Service is doing a quality land management job in Alaska. I do not believe there is any detrimental effect on fish and wildlife and other resources because we are managing the timber on the Tongass.

On Thursday, November 5, I testified on behalf of The Wildlife Society and explicitly stated that I was on leave from the Alaska Department of Fish and Game. I attached to my written statement a set of photographs, which I referred to during my testimony. Excerpts from that testimony follow.

Schoen: In southeast Alaska, old growth is highly variable, ranging from high-volume stands with large trees to low-volume or scrub forest.

High-volume is critical winter deer habitat, while low-volume and scrub forests are relatively poor habitat. The difference is primarily related to the stand's ability to intercept snow in the overhead canopy.

Though the Tongass is nearly 17 million acres, high-volume old growth is rare.

[O]nly one-third of the Tongass is commercial forest land. High-volume old growth makes up only 4 percent of the entire land base of the Tongass Forest . . .

It takes centuries for clear cuts to develop old-growth characteristics. When cut on 100-year rotations, old growth is non-renewable.

Using an aerial infrared photograph of clear-cuts on Mitkof Island as an example, I described the pattern of timber harvest and its relationship to winter deer habitat.

The areas cut were the highest volume stands. The adjacent areas are low-volume, or scrub forests. Though the areas clear-cut represent a relatively small percentage of the total land area, it was originally the most valuable winter deer habitat.

This selective harvest, and the fact that impacts are cumulative over time, pose significant problems for wildlife, even though only a small portion of the total Tongass will be logged in any one year.

For example, the Department of Fish and Game has predicted that under the Tongass Land Management Plan, deer populations will decline by 50 to 70 percent in over half of the watersheds scheduled for timber harvest on the Tongass over the next 100 years.

The preceding statement was based on a deer habitat model[69] that Matt Kirchhoff, Mike Thomas, and I had published in our final ADF&G deer report in 1985. Based on our radiotelemetry study of deer habitat use, we scored the winter habitat capability of various types (volume classes) of old growth, young clear-cuts, and second growth, and then calculated the change in habitat capability over the next 100 years based on scheduled timber harvests. The numbers above were clearly a wakeup call to many local residents that used venison to supplement their annual food budget.

Schoen testimony continued: The testimony (by the Chief of the Forest Service) on Tuesday that 70 percent of the deer habitat would remain after 100 years was based on a faulty definition of deer winter range. This is acknowledged by most working biologists in southeast Alaska . . .

The long-term tradeoffs associated with the scheduled harvest of old growth in southeast Alaska need to be clearly identified. The decisions made in the Tongass Land Management Plan and Alaska Lands Act need to be reevaluated in light of considerable new biological data.

Many other Southeast residents also testified at the hearings, representing a broad cross-section of interests from the timber industry to local hunters, fishers, and tourism operators as well as conservation organizations. Several additional excerpts follow and provide further insights into the diversity and strength of feelings that underpinned the Tongass debate.

Tom Beck (Mayor of Thorne Bay, representing Southeast Conference):
The timber industry cannot survive without pulp mills, and the pulp mills cannot survive without the insurance of a long-term supply of raw material. To breach the long-term contractual agreements, therefore, would in effect destabilize the industry and create a severe economic recession in southeast Alaska.

Joe Mehrkens (The Wilderness Society, retired Tongass National Forest regional economist): Based on my experience in the Tongass, I must conclude that section 705(a) of ANILCA has failed. The primary goals of this section are to make economically-marginal lands more productive, and to ensure a continued log supply to dependent industry.

[B]ased on forest service information, the taxpayers have lost on the Tongass timber program 93 cents on the dollar in 1984, 98 cents in 1985, and 99 cents in 1986.

K. J. Metcalf (retired planner Tongass Forest, representing SEACC): I want to emphasize my background of some 20 years in planning and public information with the Forest Service on the Tongass.

I was the planning team leader for the first phase of the Tongass Land Management Plan . . .

On Tuesday of this week, the chief of the Forest Service sat here and told you that in essence there are no major problems on the Tongass. No one believes that, except the Forest Service . . .

The 450 million board (feet of timber) annual supply is literally a gun at the head of the Forest Service. The Forest Service tells us that they are bound to meet that commitment, and that is why they have to go into the high-volume sensitive areas . . .

We know that our planning assumptions were wrong when we did the first Tongass plan. The 450 mandate and the 50-year contracts are not sustainable over the long term, without damage to other values . . .

[T]oday I am sickened at what I see happening on the Tongass. And I would like to publicly apologize to those people who I convinced to trust the planning process, and that I convinced them that the Tongass plan would mean multiple use on the national forest.

The excerpts above from the *Congressional Record* of the Senate hearings demonstrate the diversity and passion associated with management of the Tongass National Forest. Biologists had begun to publicly outline their concerns about forest management and some of the trade-offs between timber production and fish and wildlife habitat conservation. But there was basic denial by the Forest Service that their forest management would impact nontimber resource values and uses. And the timber industry was digging in, with strong backing from local economic development interests and unwavering support from the Alaska congressional delegation. Thus, the battle lines were drawn. The industrial-scale logging community, pulp companies, and resource development interests—particularly in Ketchikan, Sitka, and Wrangell—were on one side; smaller, rural communities, commercial fishermen, big-game guides, hunters, subsistence users, tourism operators, and regional and national environmentalists were on the other.

NATIONAL PRESS

By the late 1980s, the Tongass was becoming a high-profile national issue with considerable press in regional and national publications as well as editorials in major papers throughout the country. The *New York Times* published a scathing editorial in 1997 titled "Paying Twice to Ruin a Rain Forest."[70] Key excerpts from that article follow.

> Here's a Federal Plan so wrongheaded it's likely to provoke profanity from any fair-minded person:
>> Find a rare rain forest full of magnificent old trees.
>> Set aside millions of acres in the forest for logging, even though there's plenty of timber on the market. Since the value of the timber therefore can't possibly cover the costs of cutting roads deep into the wilderness, give a Government agency all the money it needs to bulldoze the forest.
>> To ensure that the taxpayers don't balk, make the appropriations permanent, thus averting regular review by Congress.
>> That, more or less, is the Federal program for the Tongass National Forest in Alaska, a land of pristine salmon streams and towering evergreens.
> The Carter Administration agreed to this Tongass giveaway to win votes for a division of Federal land in Alaska. Now, sensibly, many members of Congress want to undo a deal that's as reckless with Federal dollars as it is with Alaska's environment. They deserve warm support.

That *New York Times* editorial was a far cry from the 1979 ad in a local Southeast publication by the Sitka-based Alaska Lumber and Pulp Company describing "Why clearcutting in Coastal Alaska is Nature's way!"

There would be many additional Tongass hearings and congressional field trips to Southeast over the next several years, and a number of my scientific colleagues, including Matt Kirchhoff, Jack Lentfer, Dave Anderson, Tom Franklin, and Rick Reed, would provide valuable expert testimony on this issue. There was no question now that the Tongass issue had been elevated to the national level. Many members of Congress were expressing significant concerns about the management of our nation's largest national forest, and their staffs were beginning to dig into the details of the science, economics, and timber politics surrounding the issue.

FROM RESEARCH RESULTS
TO PUBLIC OUTREACH

Timber politics had considerably hampered the ADF&G efforts for public discussion of the impacts on wildlife of logging in the Tongass. We had already begun seeking other venues, such as The Wildlife Society slideshow and the article in the *Natural Areas Journal*.

In 1987, Sterling Miller, Harry Reynolds, and I published a paper, "Last Stronghold of the Grizzly," in *Natural History* magazine.[71] Later that year, I contacted the editor of *Natural History* and asked if they would be interested in a Tongass article. Not only did they say yes, but they decided to feature several articles on the Tongass as the centerpiece of their August 1988 issue.[72] The editor's article "Of Time and the Forest" began:

> The vast Tongass National Forest, shrouded in the rains and mists of southeastern Alaska, is the last primeval rain forest of North America. In the dim light that filters through the canopy of towering spruce and hemlock, the forest seems unchanging and timeless to us. For we have no clock to measure the biological time that shapes it and its creatures. Instead, we deal with the forest in political time (satisfying the short-term wishes of constituents and winning votes) or in economic time (lumbering for short-term profits). Unwittingly, in a few years we will have hacked away the heart of a forest that took millennia to grow.

> After years of fieldwork, a few scientists have barely begun to understand the 10,000-year natural history of the Tongass. They present pieces of the complex puzzle in the following pages.

> In 1909, when conservationist president Theodore Roosevelt signed the bill creating the Tongass Forest, he thought the great rain forest had been saved for future generations of Americans. Time is proving T. R. wrong.

My colleague Matt Kirchhoff wrote an essay "Silent Music" for the issue. He wrote:

> Nearly 40 percent of the Tongass is not forest at all, but rock, ice, and muskeg. Most of the remaining forested land is only marginally produc-

tive. Significantly, only a small fraction of the Tongass, perhaps half of one percent, harbors the "music" of this old-growth forest.

Today, the finest old-growth stands from the Pacific Northwest through Alaska are gone. The value of the remaining big trees is tied to their scarcity and to the important role they play in old-growth ecosystems—a role biologists are just beginning to discover. As politicians struggle with the difficult question of how to allocate the Tongass's remaining old growth, they would be wise to recall the words of Aldo Leopold, who forty years ago said: "To keep every cog and wheel is the first precaution of intelligent tinkering." With newly found appreciation of the diversity of old growth, we are beginning to understand. An old-growth forest, absent the music, would be a very quiet place indeed.

Our colleague Dr. Paul Alaback wrote the next piece, "Endless Battles, Verdant Survivors," in which he described his research into the structure and composition of old-growth forests in Southeast Alaska and how they differ from younger second-growth stands.

My studies, and those of others, suggest a consistent pattern in rain forest renewal. Frequent windthrows toss up the soil and create small forest openings. There, evergreen herbs grow rapidly and produce fruits before being shaded out again by the trees. Larger openings are at first colonized by herbs but will eventually be dominated by shrubs that seed or re-sprout. Hemlock seedlings in turn will overtake the shrubs, unless the forest canopy closes in before the hemlocks grow large enough to survive. All types of disturbance, from the fall of a single tree to the destruction of whole swaths of forest overlap in space and time and create a rich mosaic of plant species and wildlife.

In contrast, large-scale disturbances, such as clear-cutting, create huge, uniform openings that only slowly, if ever, return to the complex primeval forest. The woody plants best able to exploit these catastrophic events capture most of the light by growing dense and tall. Such growth creates a stark and barren forest floor.

Matt and I wrote "Little Deer in the Big Woods," in which we described the annual cycle of deer in Southeast and discussed the effects of logging on wildlife species closely associated with old-growth habitat.[73]

The old-growth rain forest on the Tongass is a rare and valuable resource. Although trees are renewable, old growth—which requires centuries to develop fully—is not. Responsible stewardship of the Tongass rain forest will require far-sighted planning to maintain the integrity of this complex ecosystem, including its ancient trees, black-tailed deer, grizzlies, bald eagles, salmon, and myriad other plants and animals. Management decisions made today will forever affect the opportunities of future generations to use and enjoy this unique forest.

Dr. Stan Gregory from Oregon State University prepared an insightful article, "Fish among the Trees," that outlined some of the values of old-growth forest habitat for spawning and rearing salmon in the Pacific Northwest. Chris Maser described the connection between flying squirrels, fungi, and nutrient cycling within forest ecosystems in "Buried Treasures." And Jeff Hughes from the ADF&G explained the importance of large-diameter old-growth trees to wintering birds in "Winter Hideouts."

Logging old-growth stands radically changes the habitat for birds. Cultivated second-growth trees, cut down every 100 to 120 years, would not supply the kind of snags so critical to the birds' survival, since stands less than 100 years old rarely contain trees with heartwood decay. Without the well-decayed snags, at least twelve cavity-dependent bird species would not be able to find suitable nest sites in Tongass in summer, and nearly half of the forest's permanent avian residents would not find an adequate winter habitat. The result would be a much-diminished forest.

Following publication of their Tongass report in August, *Natural History* distributed copies to every member of Congress as they deliberated on the Tongass Timber Reform Act.

In 1987, The Wildlife Society asked me to participate on a national ad hoc technical committee on old-growth forests chaired by Jack Ward Thomas (who later served as chief of the Forest Service). Our committee reviewed the current state of knowledge on old growth in the United States and developed a white paper, "Management and Conservation of Old-Growth Forests in the United States," that was published in the *Wildlife Society Bulletin* in 1988.[74] Some key findings of that paper are excerpted below.

Most old-growth forests in the United States (excluding the taiga in Alaska) have been cut or have succumbed to natural forces, leaving intact as little as 2 to 15 percent of virgin forests similar to those that existed when Europeans arrived on the continent. Most old-growth forests exist on federal land, logging continues in this remaining old growth, and more logging is scheduled. It is certain that there is an ongoing inexorable reduction of old growth, and that chances of retaining viable populations of plants and animals in a well distributed state over the long term are reduced to some degree with each additional reduction in old growth . . .

The old-growth management issue embodies the fate of complex and unique forest ecosystems of which wildlife are only part. Accordingly, it seems more appropriate to concentrate attention on the concept of a "threatened and endangered habitat or ecosystem."

Clearly, by the late 1980s the scientific community had identified the critical concerns associated with the management and conservation of old-growth forest ecosystems in the United States. But translating the science into management policy still faced substantial political resistance. Nevertheless, public attitudes were changing, and the national press and many members of Congress were asking important questions about federal stewardship of our nation's dwindling old-growth reserves.

ψ

During the summer of 1988, I carried on with my brown bear field research. However, I also devoted more time to analyzing our data and preparing reports and scientific papers summarizing our research findings. In addition to these routine tasks, the politics and management conflicts on the Tongass continued to encroach on our research efforts, requiring my time for frequent briefings and management discussions.

5-26-88: Juneau. I attended a forest diversity and fragmentation meeting at the Forest Service Ranger District which was organized by Fred Sampson. Dr. Jerry Franklin [forest ecologist for the Forest Service] made an excellent presentation on definitions of old growth and problems associated with habitat fragmentation. He discussed a new concept in forest management that aggregates disturbances in order to protect large areas of old growth including entire watersheds. I indicated that we were also suggesting the protection of complete watersheds with their natural diversity of old-growth stands. Several local Forest Service staff took objection to that, but Jerry responded that we were just ahead of our time. One of the Forest Service "old guard" climbed all over me about my watershed protection remarks during a break. He suggested I was being irresponsible suggesting such an approach which, in his view, was clearly against Forest Service regulations. I am always amazed at how much stock some career Forest Service folks place on internal Forest Service regulations rather than ecological principles.

After the meeting, I flew Jerry over northeast Chichagof Island in the Super Cub and showed him the landscape and the current forest management approach, including clear-cutting the best old-growth stands at low elevations. He was appalled and agreed that this kind of management was certainly affecting forest diversity by high-grading the best forest and leaving the lower quality stands.

Over the course of my field research in Southeast, I had many opportunities to lead a number of prominent scientists (including Jerry Franklin, David Klein, Fred Bunnell, Michael Rosenzweig, and Tom Lovejoy) on Tongass field trips. Not only were these scientists impressed with Southeast's rainforest ecosystem, but they universally recognized the potential detrimental effects that current forest practices posed to the region's fish, wildlife, and ecological integrity. These scientists also acknowledged that the ecological structure of old growth was strikingly different than the structure of younger forests following clear-cutting, and that old growth, under current 100-year timber rotations, will essentially be eliminated forever. And that, of course, was the original goal of timber management in Alaska—"to convert old, decadent virgin forest to young, vigorous timber plantations." These experiences led me to recognize the unique circumstances we were working with in the Tongass, and how important it was to increase scientific and public awareness and understanding of the conservation challenges and opportunities that remained on America's largest and wildest national forest.

MY FINAL YEARS AT ADF&G

LAST CRUISE IN THE TONGASS

The last big cruise our family took in the Tongass was in July 1988, when we loaded *Orca II* and headed west to spend more than a week in the West Chichagof–Yakobi Wilderness Area on the outer coast of Chichagof Island. One evening I headed out alone in our fourteen-foot Lund skiff from our anchorage in Soapstone Cove on north Yakobi Island. The sun was setting along the western horizon beyond Cross Sound. There were many humpback whales in the area, and I could see their spouts almost continuously. About a mile outside the cove, a large pod of Pacific white-sided dolphins—perhaps fifty or more—joined me. They played by my skiff, jumping out of the water close enough to splash me. I shut down my outboard to fully take in where I was at that moment—watching the crimson sun dipping below the Gulf of Alaska horizon while surrounded by a diverse abundance of the marine birds and mammals that thrive in this prolific ecosystem.

Later in our cruise through Lisianski Inlet, we observed a brown bear and several deer swimming across the inlet. We walked on well-used bear trails at the head of Stag Bay, and then headed down the coast to anchor at White

FIG. 2.76. My son Erik with a 150-pound halibut we caught at anchor on *Orca II* at Flynn Cove, northeast Chichagof Island.

Sulphur Springs, where we took baths in the hot springs at the Forest Service cabin. The next day, our kids were fishing for lingcod from our skiff when we saw a pod of gray whales swimming toward us. We were within forty yards of the shore and in relatively shallow water. The whales continued to swim directly toward us, so I began to tap my foot on the bottom of our aluminum skiff to be sure they knew we were there. Several of the large whales—up to forty-six feet and thirty-three tons—dove and swam right under our skiff. What an exhilarating family experience.

On our way back home to Juneau, we anchored at Flynn Cove on the north end of Chichagof Island. We had caught several Dungeness crabs, and Mary Beth was boiling them up for dinner. After anchoring, I had rigged up a halibut line and left the pole in a rod holder on the stern of the boat. Just as we started dinner, we got a strike, and the tip of the pole bent sharply toward the water. We abandoned dinner plans and spent the next forty-five minutes working that halibut. In the process, the tip of my pole broke, and it became a real rodeo to land that fish (Fig. 2.76). Based on its measurements, we estimated that it weighed approximately 150 pounds. Unforgettable experiences like these are not uncommon when one is lucky enough to explore the wilderness lands and waters of the Tongass National Forest.

A NEW OPPORTUNITY IN NORTHERN ALASKA

During the winter of 1988–1989, my professional life in Southeast took a major turn as I recorded in my journal.

December 1988: Juneau.

Game Division's Region III [northern and interior Alaska, based in Fairbanks] has re-advertised to fill their research coordinator position. I had been asked to apply for this job six months ago but said I was not interested. This time, I gave it much consideration and decided to apply. I was interviewed for the job on 16 December. I told Chris Smith and Dick Bishop that I was now interested in the job because my research had come to a reasonable transition point and I was interested in moving beyond technical research and getting involved in setting wildlife policy. I am also interested in expanding my Alaska experience into northern Alaska, both in the Arctic and boreal forest ecosystems and with some of the northern species with which to date I have had little research involvement.

Several days following my interview, I was offered the job. My God, what have I done?

WRAPPING UP MY BEAR RESEARCH

Beginning in 1989, I focused largely on completing the last significant components of my field research, summarizing more than eight years of field data, and starting to write my final report and working on several publications. My first major task was to prepare and write an invited paper for the International Conference on Bear Research and Management that was being held in Victoria, British Columbia, in February. The title of my paper was "Bear Habitat Management: A Review and Future Perspective."[75] Excerpts from the abstract of that paper follow.

Throughout the world, bears are declining in numbers and range as habitat is reduced and bear-human interactions increase. Although ursids (bears) are widely distributed and inhabit a variety of habitats, they possess a number of biological characteristics that make them particularly vulnerable to conflict with humans. . . . Because bears are wide-ranging species of landscapes, habitat relationships must be evaluated on a broader context than habitat types per se. Human activities and land uses must be factored into bear habitat relationships. Forest clearing and road building, in particular, are common problems for the conservation and management of many bear populations. An understanding of the processes of habitat fragmentation and population extinction is necessary for maintaining viable bear populations in the face of increasing habitat destruction and isolation.

MORE TONGASS POLITICS

As I was wrapping up my bear research in preparation for my departure to northern Alaska, I continued to be drawn into the escalating Tongass political discussion that was being intensely debated in the US Congress. Some memorable events are extracted below from my field notes.

4-7-89: Juneau, clear and cold.

0845: Overflight of north Tongass with Congressman George Miller from California and staff along with several key Forest Service staff. Although this was a Forest Service Charter, I was invited by Congressman Miller to participate and represent the wildlife perspective on behalf of the State of Alaska. We took off in a twin-engine float plane from the float pond at the Juneau airport.

Gary Morrison (Forest Service Supervisor for the Chatham District) sat up front with the pilot and had the only headset with a mike which was plugged into the aircraft's intercom system. Thus, we were all a captive audience to the official Forest Service narration of our flight.

Before we got underway, I asked Congressman Miller's staffer Jeff Petrich what our itinerary was. He showed me the Forest Service itinerary. It covered much of Chichagof, Icy Strait, and Lynn Canal; essentially, they planned to hit many of the wilderness proposals but avoid the areas of intensive logging. I suggested we divert the route to include Sitkoh River, Peril Strait, and northeast Chichagof. Petrich said OK and worked out the new route with the pilot.

The Forest Service narration largely glossed over the logging impacts to fish and wildlife. We landed on the water in front of Trap Bay (in Tenakee Inlet) and after Morrison was finished with his narration, including all the benefits of roads, I asked if I could address some of the wildlife concerns. Congressman Miller said, "By all means that was why you were asked to participate." I told them where we would be flying next and to especially notice the amount of high-grading of the best timberlands on the Tongass. . . . I discussed the forest habitats most valuable to deer and bears. We flew up the heavily logged Corner Bay drainage and into Kadashan. We flew down Peril Strait and over False Island, areas of heavy logging.

I caught Congressman Miller's eye as we flew over the extensive clearcutting. He gave me a look back that said it all. We landed at Elfin Cove on North Chichagof for a break then flew back down Icy Strait toward Juneau. At the break, I told Congressman Miller that I had brought my portable intercom. We hooked it up and I was on line with Congressman Miller, Petrich, and Deputy Regional Forester Sprague. I discussed high-grading, leave areas, and Native corporation selections of the best timber areas. We flew directly over northeast Chichagof and the massive logging then occurring at Point Couverden on the mainland. Finally, we flew on to Berner's Bay and then flew over the Juneau Ice Field. I pointed out how important it was to understand how percentages can be used when talking about the Tongass. Congressman Miller chuckled and said, "Yes, there is not much clear-cutting on the Juneau Ice Field is there." [Fig. 2.77]

The issue of high-grading the rare high-volume old-growth stands was always at the core of our ecological concerns. From the outset of our deer research in the late 1970s, Charlie, Matt, and I recognized that this had occurred throughout the forest and would become an increasingly serious problem for some species—deer, goshawk, marten, and others—that used and needed those specific habitat types during portions of their annual cycle. Although we continually raised this concern, it largely fell upon deaf ears at the leadership level of the Forest Service. This was made apparent during the congressional debate on the Tongass Timber Reform Act when Walt Sheridan, the Alaska Lands Act coordinator for the Alaska Region of the Forest Service, clarified the Forest Service position on high-grading in a letter to the Minority Counsel of the House Interior and Insular Affairs Committee. In that letter, Mr. Sheridan stated in part:

There is an allegation that the Forest Service is allowing the Tongass to be high-graded by allowing high volume spruce stands to be harvested at a disproportionately higher rate than their natural occurrence . . . what is alleged is that, if we continued current practices, we would run out of high volume spruce stands prior to the end of the rotation. Even if this were true, it wouldn't be high-grading. . . . It is probably obvious, but high-volume stands occur on lands with the highest potential for growing new, even higher volume, second-growth stands. Given this, the earlier in the rotation

FIG. 2.77. The Juneau ice field includes hundreds of square miles of rock and ice. Significant portions of the Tongass are nonforest lands, and only about one-third of the Tongass actually supports commercial forest lands. Using percentages of the amount of logging on the entire Tongass Forest can be highly misleading.

that the high-volume stands are harvested, the earlier in the second rotation it can be expected that a return in the form of new vigorous growth can be realized. . . . In summary, the Tongass National Forest is being managed in accordance with sound principles of forest management which, over time, will substantially increase the productivity of the forest while protecting its basic environmental integrity.

Dave Anderson, ADF&G's regional supervisor for the Wildlife Division, followed up with a letter of concern to Phil Janik, the Forest Service's director of wildlife and fisheries. Excerpts from Anderson's response follow:

Mr. Sheridan dismisses allegations of "high-grading" on the Tongass as having no basis in fact. . . . In fact, it is the Alaska Department of Fish and Game's official position that such "high-grading" has occurred and does carry serious ecological consequences for wildlife. . . . While second generation regrowth stands may produce more wood fiber/acre than the old growth before them, that argument presupposes that the entire concern is over wood-volume per se. Rather, the composition, structure, and function of high-volume old-growth stands make them important as wildlife habitat. Second-growth stands, regardless of wood volume, have extremely low wildlife habitat value. . . . At best, his letter reveals a narrow view of the forest's values to the public, and the Agency's management responsibilities.

Many of the Forest Service's wildlife biologists realized that high-grading was a problem, but unfortunately that concern rarely permeated the glass ceiling separating timber managers from wildlife and fisheries biologists. Those of us regularly working in the field, flying over timber sales, and hiking through clear-cut watersheds understood that cherry-picking the best sites might be the quickest route to maximizing profits over the short term, but would result in a significant decline in forest diversity and ecological function over the longer term. We believed that the industry would continue to target the most economically productive regions, watersheds, and stands on the Tongass until they were gone. And that pattern of timber harvest continues even today.

⚜

My next big field trip involved flying US Senator Tim Wirth, from Colorado, on an overflight of the northern Tongass (Fig. 2.78).

4-26-89: Sitka, clear.

0900: Senator Wirth met me at the airport and we climbed into the cub and departed Sitka at 0930. I climbed up to about 5,000 feet and flew over the high alpine of northern Baranof. I wanted him to see how much non-forest land there was on the Tongass. Senator Wirth immediately began asking thoughtful, penetrating questions and closely followed our route on a map. He was interested and inquisitive, and had obviously done his homework on the Tongass issue. We flew over Nakwasina Sound, Rodman Bay, Peril Strait, Sitkoh Lake, Corner Bay, and Tenakee Inlet, and then I landed the cub on the grass flats at the Kadashan River Delta. I pointed out the extensive amount of high-grading that was occurring on the forest. It is only when you actually see the physical layout of the clear-cuts, know what was cut, and see what was left, that you can appreciate how serious this issue really is in terms of reducing ecological diversity and impacting fish and wildlife dependent on those rare forest types. The bird's eye view from a small plane is ideal for understanding this issue. Senator Wirth quickly grasped the problem and he was not at all happy about what he saw.

1000: Kadashan flats. After landing on the upper beach, we took a hike into the forest edge; walking below medium to large Sitka spruce trees (four to five feet in diameter) along a well-defined bear trail. We saw much deer sign and old bear sign. Canada geese were scattered around the delta's wetlands and we heard several forest birds singing. I pointed out the variety inherent in this old-growth forest and how productive it was. Senator Wirth really enjoyed this experience and appreciated the beauty and ecological complexity of the rainforest. While walking back to the cub, he talked about global warming and the need to take a long-term global perspective on ecological-environmental issues. I was very impressed with his breadth of knowledge and his keen interest in environmental issues.

1155: I landed at the Juneau Airport and took Senator Wirth upstairs to the restaurant where he met Governor Cowper for lunch.

FIG. 2.78. With US Senator Tim Wirth (left) next to the Super Cub at the Sitka Airport prior to our flight over the northern Tongass with a landing at the Kadashan River delta, then on to the Juneau Airport.

Although there was growing national interest in the Tongass and passionate debate within Congress over how the Tongass Forest should be managed, the issue in Alaska was still largely framed as a tug-of-war between environmentalists and the Southeast business community, spearheaded by the timber industry. And the chief of the Forest Service and the Alaska regional forester continued to argue strongly for maintaining the status quo in their management of the Tongass timber program. But as hunters, fishers, and local communities began to speak out during the congressional hearings, the old economy-versus-environment argument was beginning to unravel, and more Southeastern Alaskans were beginning to speak out in favor of change. In 1989, for example, a "My Turn" column about Tongass timber reform was published in the *Juneau Empire* that stated in part:

» The high-volume timbered watersheds are also the most productive for other resources such as wildlife, fisheries and for scenic and recreational values.
» Clear-cut harvesting . . . adversely affects all of the above named resources . . .
» The Alaska timber industry has concentrated its activities in these high-volume areas, nearly exclusively . . .
» [O]ld-growth forest ecosystems are not renewable under present harvest systems and that the value of certain watersheds for other resources is far greater than for wood products.

This was not a statement from radical environmentalists. The authors were four retired federal resource agency administrators from Juneau with more than 100 years of combined experience in Southeast. These highly respected, veteran resource professionals included Don Schmiege, former director of the US Forest Service Forestry Sciences Laboratory; Sig Olson, former director of wildlife and fisheries management for the Alaska Region of the US Forest Service; Ted Merrell, former program manager for the National Marine Fisheries Service; and Jim King, former waterfowl supervisor for the US Fish and Wildlife Service. Unmistakably, we were beginning to see a growing disconnect between the official position of the Forest Service leadership and Alaska's congressional delegation and the accumulated knowledge of many Alaska scientists and fisheries and wildlife managers. As public concern grew within Southeast, the number of cosponsors of the Tongass Timber Reform legislation also increased within both houses of Congress.

HEADING NORTH

In June 1989, Mary Beth and I sold our home and the *Orca II* and loaded our kids and our car onto the Alaska ferry at Juneau's Auke Bay terminal bound for Haines. Looking back, we cherish our time in Juneau raising our family on the beach at Smuggler's Cove. From Haines, we drove up the highway to Fairbanks to begin our new life in the far north. As I sat on the aft deck and watched the coastal scenery pass, I thoughtfully considered the last twelve years of experiences studying deer, mountain goats, and brown bears in Southeast's extraordinary rainforest. I also reflected on my many adventures on Admiralty Island as I watched Eagle Peak and northern Admiralty slowly slip below the horizon as we cruised north up Lynn Canal. Admiralty Island is forever imprinted in my being; it is a place that I think of as part of my home on Earth. Still largely intact, it is one of the most ecologically productive regions of the North Pacific Temperate Rainforest. And thanks to President Carter and the Alaska National Interest Lands Conservation Act, the ecological integrity of this island is protected in perpetuity.

I still miss Southeast Alaska and our many Juneau friends, and I cherish my professional experiences working in this extraordinary coastal ecosystem. But as we headed north, I also looked forward to experiencing new and exciting challenges as we continued our Alaska odyssey. Little did I know that I would remain involved in Tongass conservation science for another thirty years.

∗

Upon arriving in Fairbanks, we were greeted by new friends and colleagues, who helped us find temporary accommodations as we began to settle into our northern home in the boreal forest. Before our baggage was completely

FIG. 2.79. With ADF&G's Beaver aircraft in the Arctic National Wildlife Refuge on our way north to conduct the photo census of the Porcupine Caribou Herd.

unpacked, I immediately embarked on a field project exploring a vast region of the state, Alaska's Arctic. My first field assignment included flying the department's de Havilland Beaver up to the North Slope where I participated in the photo census of the Porcupine caribou herd along the coastal plain of the Arctic National Wildlife Refuge (Fig. 2.79). I will never forget flying over an aggregation of 90,000 caribou with ADF&G colleagues Ken Whitten, Pat Valkenberg, and Howard Golden (Fig. 2.80). Although my new job entailed supervision of the region's wildlife research program and consisted of more administrative and budgeting tasks, I often participated in our field projects, and these were exciting days discovering the ecological complexities of interior Alaska, the Brooks Range, and the Arctic. While living and working in Fairbanks, I had many opportunities to travel throughout northern Alaska and work with wildlife scientists studying caribou, moose, grizzly and black bears, and wolves. The opportunity to pilot the department's aircraft and regularly get into the field helped keep my internal fires burning despite the added administrative burdens of my new job.

PASSAGE OF THE TONGASS TIMBER REFORM ACT

The year after we moved to Fairbanks, Congress overwhelmingly passed the Tongass Timber Reform Act (HR 987) but without support of the Alaska con-

FIG. 2.80. We photographed the large caribou aggregation on the coastal plain of the Arctic National Wildlife Refuge from ADF&G's Beaver at about 500 feet elevation in July 1989. This aggregation (which extended well beyond this image) numbered 90,000 caribou.

gressional delegation. This bill was signed into law (Public Law 101-626) by President George H. W. Bush on November 28, 1990. The act designated 280,438 acres of additional wilderness, plus 727,762 acres of land use designation II (fish and wildlife habitat areas closed to logging). The act also repealed the mandated timber harvest target of 450 million board feet per year and the annual $40 million timber subsidy. Another key measure was a requirement that the harvest of timber stands should not exceed the proportion of their occurrence on the forest. This important measure prohibited the high-grading of the rare high-volume old-growth stands. This new law was a major step toward more balanced and sustainable management of our largest national forest, and a clear recognition that fish, wildlife, recreation, subsistence use, wilderness, and ecosystem values were important to the national interest and of equal value to timber management.

One of the impressive aspects of the debate over the Timber Reform Act was how some of the environmental groups—SEACC, the National Audubon Society, The Wilderness Society, and others—incorporated science into their conservation advocacy work. I appreciated this and respected those groups for taking the extra time and care to make sure their conservation messages were accurate and defensible.

After passage of the Timber Reform Act, most fish and wildlife scientists and managers, as well as the legion of regional and national environmentalists, believed that management of the Tongass would finally make a significant course correction. But remarkably, as it turned out, this was not the case. The first significant indication that timber management still called the shots was revealed in the 1992 Tongass Forest's Record of Decision for the Kelp Bay timber sale on northeast Baranof Island.[76] According to the Forest Service analysis, only a small amount of high-volume old growth would be harvested, following the requirement of the new Timber Reform Act prohibiting high-grading the high-volume old-growth stands. In reality, however, the sale actually targeted precisely those stands for clear-cutting. The Alaska Chapter of The Wildlife Society, with technical advice from Matt Kirchhoff, appealed the record of decision to no avail. Eventually, the chapter litigated the case and, in April 1994, District Judge H. Russell Holland ruled in favor of the Alaska Chapter of The Wildlife Society and required that the Forest Service revise its methodology for complying with the anti-high-grading provisions of the new law.[77]

⚘

In the summer of 1992, after three years in Fairbanks, we moved to Anchorage, where I served as the Division of Wildlife Conservation's senior conservation biologist until I retired from ADF&G in 1996. In this new position, I had statewide oversight of several of the division's nontraditional programs, including nonhunted species, endangered species, marine mammals, and wildlife education. I continued to follow issues on the Tongass, but I was not closely involved in day-to-day Tongass research or management. Although I found my new job satisfying, it was largely an administrative position and further removed me from fieldwork. I remember experiences while participating in division leadership meetings when I would zone out from administrative discussions and think instead of "real" wildlife biology out in Alaska's wildlands. Perhaps this was a throwback to my childhood, when my mind frequently strayed from schoolwork as I contemplated that enormous maple tree outside my sixth-grade classroom on Orcas Island.

TONGASS PLAN REVISION

During the 1990s, following passage of the Tongass Timber Reform Act, management of the Tongass continued to evolve. By 1990, the Forest Service had begun working on a forest plan revision. As part of that effort, regional forester Mike Barton established an interagency committee of biologists—the Viable Population Committee (VPOP)—to develop a strategy for conserving wildlife species associated with old-growth forests in Southeast Alaska. This was, in part, a process to bring the Tongass into compliance with regulations of the National Forest Management Act of 1976 that required maintaining viable and well-distributed populations of native vertebrate species across the national forests.

The VPOP Committee was led by Forest Service biologist Lowell Suring and eight biologists from the Forest Service, Fish and Wildlife Service, and ADF&G. The Tongass is naturally fragmented, composed of many islands that have unique patterns of vertebrate species and subspecies distribution. Because of this fragmentation, maintaining viable and well-distributed vertebrate populations while harvesting large tracts of old-growth forests—important habitat for many species—was a particular challenge to resource managers.

Although I was not directly involved with the VPOP Committee, I kept abreast of this work through my ADF&G colleagues Matt Kirchhoff, Rod Flynn, and Kim Titus, who were on the team. Kim had taken over my bear research position when I left Juneau. In 1992, he and I prepared a paper, "A Plan for Maintaining Viable and Well-Distributed Brown Bear Populations in Southeast Alaska," which the VPOP team used as they developed their conservation strategy.[78] In this plan, we recommended maintaining 40,000-acre intact habitat conservation areas—complete watersheds—that are unroaded and include high-volume riparian old-growth forests and at least one salmon spawning stream. We also recommended adopting management guidelines across the forest that included maintenance of 300-foot buffers along each side of salmon streams where bears fish, as well as strict garbage management programs and a road closure program.

In 1993, the VPOP Committee completed its draft strategy for maintaining populations of wildlife in Southeast Alaska.[79] The key elements involved selecting a small subset of vertebrate species whose viability and distribution was dependent on old-growth timber stands. These included the Queen Charlotte goshawk, Alexander Archipelago wolf, brown bear, marten, northern flying squirrel, and others. To maintain sufficient habitat for these species, the group proposed a network of small, medium, and large Habitat Conservation Areas distributed across the forest. This network of reserves would include tracts of relatively undisturbed old-growth forests spaced appropriately across the landscape, including the major islands of the archipelago.

In the spring of 1994, the VPOP strategy was reviewed by an independent committee of twenty-one scientists with appropriate expertise from across North America. The review was coordinated by Ross Kiester and Carol Eckarhardt of the Forest Service's Pacific Northwest Research Station.[80] Although the peer reviewers gave the strategy high marks, they suggested that none of the planning alternatives was adequate to ensure viability of all species. One of their major concerns was to " exercise extreme caution in choosing a minimum viable population as a management target." Of course, that was not the decision of the VPOP team, but rather was a Forest Service directive. The peer reviewers made several key recommendations for inclusion in the Forest Service planning process:

» Recognize the global significance of the Tongass National Forest.
» Understand the implications of insularity and topography for natural fragmentation (i.e., consider the island character of the forest).
» Evaluate and synthesize additional landscape approaches to the Habitat Conservation Area including: inverse of the Habitat Conservation Area and large reserves. (For example, instead of having "reserves" for protecting wildlife, protect the forest for wildlife and have smaller, scattered reserves for logging.)
» Keep landscape options open: do not further fragment existing large blocks of high-volume old growth and do not differentially cut low-altitude, high-volume old growth.

The interagency VPOP Committee agreed with many of the peer reviewers' recommendations and revised and submitted their final plan to the Forest Service in 1994. Among their conclusions in the final report, they stated:

Although a relatively small percentage of the overall landscape may be affected by timber harvest, historically a much greater proportion of the high-value forest habitat has been harvested. The resulting effects of that harvesting are disproportionately concentrated in certain ecological provinces.

Central to their final recommendations was the proposal to establish a network of small, medium, and large Habitat Conservation Areas throughout the Tongass that would include tracts of relatively undisturbed old-growth forest where roads and timber harvest would be restricted.

The 1990s were a period of major transition on the Tongass. Within six years after passage of the Tongass Timber Reform Act, Southeast Alaska's two big mills closed their doors—Sitka's Alaska Pulp Corporation in 1993 and Ketchikan Pulp Company in 1997—and their long-term timber contracts with the Forest Service were canceled. This was the end of an era, brought on in part by the loss of the federal timber subsidies, noncompliance with EPA clean water regulations, declining timber markets, and public criticism of Forest Service management.

As the Forest Service continued to revise the Tongass Land Management Plan (TLMP), they theoretically were incorporating the VPOP's conservation strategy into the revision. As part of that effort, the forest planning team convened a number of risk assessment panels of experts to evaluate the plan alternatives relative to other important forest resources, including fisheries and wildlife.[81] In 1996, while still at ADF&G, I was asked to serve on the Forest Service's brown bear risk assessment panel to evaluate the relative likelihood that TLMP revision alternatives would maintain persistent and well-distributed brown bear populations throughout their historic range on the Tongass. We evaluated nine plan alternatives and the anticipated effects that each alternative would have on bear habitat over 100 years.

The brown bear panelists agreed that viable and well-distributed populations of brown bears would decline as timber harvest and road construction increased. Only one alternative—the no harvest alternative—provided high likelihood (75 percent) of maintaining abundant populations, and that alternative was unlikely to be chosen as a preferred alternative.

The panelists agreed that road management and protection of riparian habitat were two of the major issues influencing productive bear populations over time. The TLMP standards and guidelines for riparian buffers were considered inadequate for protecting brown bears. We recommended a minimum buffer width of 500 feet on either side of brown bear fishing streams. Our concern over roads was related to increased human access and the likelihood of elevating human-caused bear mortality, as well as the increased risks of roads to salmon productivity (this was a stated concern of the fisheries risk assessment panel). We favored an alternative that would provide roadless refugia of at least 40,000 acres for brown bears.

Early drafts of the plan revision raised much concern from scientists and fish and wildlife managers. Even though the big timber contracts were terminated and the mills closed, the Forest Service continued to plan for a level of timber harvest that many considered to be a significant risk to fish, wildlife, and other forest resources. In the fall of 1996, twelve members of the Peer Review Committee, based on their independent scientific review of the Tongass wildlife habitat conservation strategy, sent a joint statement of concern to the Tongass National Forest regarding the TLMP draft environmental impact statement.[82] Key excerpts from that statement follow.

» Scientific studies . . . have concluded that logging and related activities on the Tongass National Forest pose a significant risk to the viability of populations of several wildlife species associated with old growth forests.

» [T]he preferred alternative will not, in our opinion, meet the obligations of the USDA Forest Service to protect wildlife associated with old growth forests.

» One of the most important conclusions of the 1994 peer review was that, to preserve options to secure viable wildlife populations, the Forest Service must take immediate measures to protect throughout the Forest both large blocks of old growth forest and high-volume stands.

» At least until adequate research has been completed on a representative sample of fauna and flora, further logging in the remaining relatively undisturbed watersheds of the Tongass should be regarded as inconsistent with ensuring the continued viability of resident wildlife populations.

» Expanded reserves must protect the remaining large blocks of high-volume old growth on the forest.

The clear consensus among these eminent university ecologists was that the revised management plan for the Tongass National Forest did not provide an adequate conservation strategy for wildlife associated with old-growth forests. Their joint statement echoed the concerns of ADF&G fish and wildlife biologists and even many Forest Service biologists.

ADF&G RETIREMENT

In the late fall of 1996, I received an offer to lead the Alaska office of the National Audubon Society. I announced my decision to take the job in a November 1, 1996, memo to division staff at ADF&G.

> With this memo, I am announcing my retirement from ADF&G effective the first of the year. I have been offered the position of Director of the Alaska Office of the National Audubon Society . . .

> It seems like only yesterday that I began work with the Game Division in September 1976. My twenty years at Fish and Game have included many varied experiences from counting deer poop, snaring bears, flying telemetry surveys, swearing at computers, and writing reports to coping with bureaucracy, preparing budgets, dealing with politics, and always working for wildlife conservation . . . Overall, I look back on my twenty years with fondness and satisfaction. I have had the great privilege of working with an outstanding group of people. I truly cannot think of another organization where so many have worked so hard and been so dedicated to wildlife conservation . . .

> ADF&G faces many challenges as we approach a new century. Public interests in wildlife management have broadened considerably in the last twenty years and there are considerably more demands on wildlife populations and habitat. We must meet these challenges. I am convinced that there is much more common ground among all wildlife users than recent skirmishes between polarized interests suggest. I think the division's best approach for addressing this conflict is to always articulate that CONSERVATION IS JOB 1. If we focus on conservation first, we will meet our fundamental public trust responsibility and help all Alaskans recognize their significant common ground.

TONGASS RAINFOREST

SAVING ALL THE PARTS (1997–2019)

FROM A RESOURCE AGENCY
TO AN ENVIRONMENTAL ORGANIZATION

Following my retirement from ADF&G in 1996, I began work as the new executive director of the National Audubon Society's Alaska state office in downtown Anchorage. My job was to lead the Alaska office, develop policies and advocacy strategies on Alaska conservation issues, coordinate with the national office in New York, work with local Audubon chapters, and raise funds for the Alaska program. Audubon Alaska's mission was the conservation of Alaska's ecosystems—focusing on birds, other wildlife, and their habitats—for the benefit and enjoyment of current and future generations. Audubon's focus on wildlife and habitat conservation overlapped significantly with my former job at ADF&G. My biggest challenge at Audubon was the responsibility of fundraising for a nongovernmental organization. This was a significant difference from my state agency job, where annual budgets were relatively stable and did not require beating the bushes each year to find new funding just to maintain our basic program.

When I joined Audubon, the entire Alaska staff consisted of office manager Bucky Dennerlein and me. Bucky had been at Audubon for about ten years; she knew everyone in the conservation community, and was immensely helpful in smoothing my transition at Audubon. As I settled into my job free of the state bureaucracy, I soon encountered a new suite of unique bureaucratic and administrative responsibilities.

My predecessor, Dave Cline, who launched Audubon's Alaska program in 1977, had been a wildlife biologist with the US Fish and Wildlife Service, and brought a scientific approach to his conservation work. Dave was a colleague and good friend, and offered me valuable counsel as I made my transition to Audubon. He had built a strong and respected conservation program in Alaska, and my goal was to uphold and build upon Audubon's history of science-based conservation advocacy. This was one of the strengths of the National Audubon Society, and the reason the job was attractive to me. One of my first actions to enhance this underlying principle was to create an interdisciplinary science advisory group with which I regularly consulted on a variety of Alaska wildlife issues. In my two decades working for an Alaska resource agency, I had learned that agency and university scientists were some of the most knowledgeable wildlife experts in the state and were a great source of valuable information and advice.

By far the most interesting aspect of my new job was analyzing and developing Alaska conservation positions for Audubon. There is no other state in the nation with as vast an array of national interest lands and waters as those that are found in Alaska.[1] A staggering 87 percent of Alaska—366 million acres—is made up of state and federal lands. This includes 12 percent (twenty-three million acres) of all US national forest lands, 70 percent (fifty-three million acres) of national park lands, 80 percent (seventy-two million acres) of national wildlife refuges, and more than half of the nation's designated wilderness.

Each summer, Alaska's enormous and varied landscape becomes the breeding ground for many North American migratory birds, including over twenty million birds that make up eighty species of waterfowl and shorebirds. A full 20 percent of North American waterfowl and 50 percent of shorebirds are drawn to Alaska's diverse habitat. Part of that habitat includes the 33,900 miles of marine coastline of Alaska—more shoreline than all of the continental US. This vast coastline and its marine waters offer habitat for sixty-six species of seabirds that number nearly 100 million birds. These same coastal waters are home to thirty-two species of marine mammals, including some—ice seals, walrus, and polar bears—that are dependent on seasonal and permanent sea ice.

These Alaska land- and seascapes comprise functioning ecosystems with all their ecological elements, including large carnivores and the Earth's most productive salmon runs. This extraordinary environmental legacy was what Audubon and other environmental groups were committed to safeguarding for the benefit of current and future generations. In Alaska's coastal forests, we were concerned about the effects of industrial-scale logging and maintaining productive habitat for a rich diversity of fish and wildlife, including brown bears, wolves, deer, marten, bald eagles, goshawks, marbled murrelets, a variety of forest songbirds, five species of Pacific salmon, and numerous other fish and wildlife species. In Cook Inlet—surrounded by Alaska's most populated and developed area—our focus included a small, isolated beluga whale population that had dramatically declined and was being considered for listing under the Endangered Species Act (it is currently listed as endangered). And in the Arctic, we were addressing the potential impacts of large-scale oil and gas development on wildlife, including caribou, polar bears, and a variety of migratory waterfowl and shorebirds.

To be effective, Audubon needed to identify our most strategic conservation priorities. My scientific background helped me in taking this approach. Once our priorities were established, I often had to say no to taking on additional issues. This was not easy, but we simply did not have the resources or expertise to make an effective contribution on every cause. This strategy triggered numerous instances when people became disappointed or angry with us for not taking on their favorite issue.

From the outset, the most difficult part of my new job was the never-ending demands of fundraising. Shortly after I arrived at Audubon, the national leadership made the decision that state programs would be responsible for raising all of their own funding. In Alaska, with our small population and heavy reliance on resource extraction industries, the opportunities for in-state funding for conservation programs were very challenging. Audubon had about 2,200 members in five chapters within the state, but most of those members were not major donors. The majority of wealth in Alaska was connected with resource development and not supportive of environmental organizations. Our fundraising, by necessity, had to target foundations and major donors outside Alaska.

The issues, policy work, and collaboration with other conservation leaders and agency and university scientists were right up my alley. I thrived in that arena. However, after two and a half years burning the candle at both ends—sometimes waking up in the middle of the night in a cold sweat wondering how I was going to make our budget—I proposed an alternative to Audubon president John Flicker. I had been recruiting my friend and colleague Stan Senner, who was working across town as the science coordinator at the Exxon Valdez Trustee Council. The upshot was that Stan came to Audubon in the summer of 1999 as the new executive director, and I became Audubon's senior scientist.

⚜

Stanley Senner first came to Alaska in the 1970s when he was working in support of the Alaska National Interest Lands Conservation Act (Fig. 3.1). Stan was an experienced ornithologist and had completed his master's degree at the University of Alaska Fairbanks studying shorebirds on Alaska's Copper River Delta. He had worked previously as the director of the Hawk Mountain Sanctuary and for the US House of Representatives. Stan was skilled in conservation administration and the policy arena, and was also a talented fundraiser. Stan's arrival at Audubon Alaska was a good fit for both of us, and Stan and

FIG. 3.1. Stanley Senner joined the Audubon Alaska staff as the executive director in the summer of 1999.

I became an effective team, working together for ten years on issues ranging from conservation of the Arctic National Wildlife Refuge and Tongass National Forest to identification of Alaska's important bird areas and development of an Alaska WatchList of birds at risk.

*

From 1997 through June 2011, I was involved in a variety of Alaska conservation issues, including familiar ones like the Tongass. In the following pages I will recap some of the more significant Tongass issues I dealt with during that time. For a comprehensive review of the people and political aspects of Tongass conservation from the 1970s through 1999, I recommend Kathie Durbin's excellent book, *Tongass: Pulp Politics and the Fight for the Alaska Rain Forest*.[2]

During the Clinton Administration, from 1993 through 2000, significant changes were taking place within the highest levels of the US Forest Service. President Clinton appointed two Forest Service chiefs in succession, Jack Ward Thomas and Michael Dombeck, both of whom brought strong scientific backgrounds and a broader perspective of forest stewardship than the old paradigm that largely focused on timber management. However, leadership of the Tongass Forest still seemed to lag behind other national forests as timber and road building dominated forest management in Alaska due to political pressures from the timber industry and the Alaska congressional delegation.

TONGASS LAND MANAGEMENT PLAN REVISION

When I joined the Audubon staff in January 1997, the Forest Service was in the final year of its Tongass Land Management Plan revision. While at ADF&G, I had closely followed the work of Lowell Suring and colleagues who were developing the conservation strategy for maintaining viable and well-distributed populations of Tongass wildlife species. As mentioned previously, I had also been a member of the TLMP brown bear risk assessment panel. With this background and my previous years of Tongass research, I critically reviewed the revised TLMP when it was released in May 1997. I sent a memo to Audubon president John Flicker in June with the following recommendations.

> My recommendations are for National Audubon to acknowledge the progress made in the direction the plan has taken but to express our continued concern about the high level of (timber) harvest and the significant potential for "high-grading" the best wildlife habitat. With the departure of the two big pulp mills and their fifty-year contracts, we have an opportunity to establish a new direction for forest, wildlife, fisheries, and recreation management on the Tongass. We urge the administration to take a closer look at the plan and move the Tongass Forest toward a truly sustainable, multiple use form of management.

On July 3, I sent a letter to Alaska regional forester Phil Janik outlining Audubon's preliminary assessment of the new plan, and on September 24, Audubon filed a notice of appeal to the chief of the Forest Service on this newest revision of the TLMP. Although we recognized the progress the Forest Service was making in managing the nation's largest national forest, we had numerous concerns about the lack of balance in their proposed management of the Tongass and their ability to conserve fish and wildlife resources in the national interest. Key excerpts from our appeal follow.

> The revised Forest Plan and Record of Decision do not prohibit the harvest of the high-volume, old-growth stands. Although the ASQ (allowable sale quantity or maximum timber harvest level) has been reduced from original TLMP levels, inadequate provisions to prevent "high-grading" the best old-growth stands will result in the destruction of important wildlife habitat and unravel the integrity of this already impacted ecosystem. The committee of scientists (established by the Forest Service and charged with recommending steps needed to maintain viable wildlife populations on the Tongass) recommended a moratorium on the harvest of higher-volume (classes 6 and 7). <u>This is one of the most critical conservation issues on the Tongass but was totally ignored in the revised Forest Plan.</u>

> The revised Forest Plan, selected alternative, and Record of Decision fail to address fundamental issues raised by the 1996 and 1997 Brown Bear Risk Assessment Panels and represent an unacceptable risk to the brown bear population on the Tongass National Forest.

The southern islands of the Tongass, particularly Prince of Wales and Kosciusko islands, are key to maintaining a healthy and well distributed population of the Southeast Archipelago wolf. An abundance of productive old-growth habitat is essential for sustaining deer which serve as the primary prey for wolves . . . the revised Forest Plan does not contain specific, enforceable standards limiting road densities in critical habitats or closing specific roads. This is a serious flaw with the Forest Plan revision and . . . will likely result in gaps in their natural distribution.

In conclusion, I stated that there "is a significant risk that this plan will not maintain well-distributed populations of brown bears or wolves across their historic range on the Tongass National Forest."

In October 1997, I received a follow-up letter from deputy regional forester James Caplan (for regional forester Phil Janik) responding to Audubon's appeal. Regarding the timber harvest level, he emphasized this was a maximum, not a target, and stated, "I believe this level of timber harvest (maximum 267 million board feet per year) is biologically sustainable." Regarding our concern about high-grading, he wrote, "I need to bring to your attention the application of a revised timber volume class stratification used in the TLMP Revision . . . A new, more statistically defensible timber volume stratification of high, medium, and low volume classes was used in the TLMP Revision."

After years of criticism from scientists that the Forest Service was high-grading the best timber stands on the Tongass, they finally addressed this concern by redefining high-volume stands. Their new definition of high-volume old growth became much more expansive, now including hundreds of thousands of acres of forest stands with midsize trees. Caplan went on to claim, "We have not scheduled a disproportionate amount of high volume for timber harvest."

This new classification may have resolved the issue to the agency's satisfaction, but, unfortunately, scientists and wildlife and fisheries managers remained concerned. Although the level of proposed timber harvest was reduced in the second plan, the Forest Service's new management direction for the Tongass still did not incorporate the most recent science.

The widening gap between independent scientists and Tongass timber managers became apparent when, in September 1997, eleven members of the Peer Review Committee of scientists—established in 1993 by the Pacific Northwest Research Station of the Forest Service to evaluate the conservation measures being incorporated in the Tongass revision—issued a joint statement concerning the inadequacy of conservation measures in the new Forest Plan.[3] The scientists stated that the new plan relies "on an inadequate reserve system" and "ignores the adverse consequences of fragmenting habitat." They also emphasized that "large blocks of habitat must be preserved to ensure overall species viability." The Peer Review Committee also stated:

Perhaps the greatest concern is the failure to protect the Forest's remaining pristine watersheds. . . . The 1994 Peer Review concluded that, to keep important landscape options open, the Tongass should "not further fragment existing large blocks of high-volume Old Growth."

The Forest Service's management of the Tongass continued to face strong criticism from regional and national environmental organizations, sportsmen, fishermen, and many residents of small Southeast communities, as well as scientists and state fish and wildlife managers. According to the Forest Service, the 1997 plan revision received thirty-three separate appeals by organizations and individuals. In 1999, the undersecretary of agriculture issued a new record of decision for the 1997 TLMP, but that decision was vacated by the US District Court. A Sierra Club legal challenge to the 1997 TLMP, asserting that the plan should have considered making wilderness recommendations for roadless areas, resulted in the need to write a supplementary environmental impact statement by 2003. Thus, the political turmoil surrounding Tongass management continued through the turn of the century.

NATIONAL ROADLESS RULE

Anyone who has flown coast to coast across the lower 48 states on a clear day and looked out the window can't help but see the spiderweb of roads crisscrossing the continent. From Washington State to Washington, DC, there are few roadless areas of significant size remaining in the contiguous US. With an extensive road network of more than four million miles, a person can now drive to within a mile of most lands within the contiguous forty-eight states. Scientists have documented the impacts roads have on fish and wildlife populations and natural ecological systems: roads destroy and fragment habitats into smaller and more isolated patches; they directly and indirectly (e.g., increased legal hunting pressure and illegal poaching) kill wildlife and change their behavior; they introduce deleterious invasive species; they cause soil erosion and sedimentation of water bodies, which impact fish and aquatic organisms; and they facilitate resource development activities, which further impact fish and wildlife populations.[4] Today, roadless areas have become important watersheds for maintaining precious water sources, critical refugia for many species of vulnerable plants and animals, and important areas for remote recreation and spiritual renewal.

In recognition of the importance of our nation's shrinking roadless areas, Forest Service chief Mike Dombeck announced in 1998 his plans to develop a new transportation policy for national forests in the United States that would preserve the roadless character of eligible lands. Strong supporters of the administration's roadless proposal included national environmental groups and many of the nation's leading scientists. Originally, the roadless plan was designed to exempt Alaska's national forests and several forests in the Pacific Northwest because of forest plans there that had recently been completed. However, most environmental groups were strongly urging the Clinton Administration to move forward quickly on a national roadless policy; many were also seeking inclusion of Alaska's two national forests. In March 1998, I sent a letter to Dombeck stating in part: "We strongly recommend that adoption of a national roadless policy not exempt the two largest national forests in the United States . . . To leave Alaska out of such a policy simply doesn't make good sense. After all, it is in Alaska where we still have the opportunity to conserve fish and wildlife right the first time."

Over the next two years, environmental groups across the country ramped up pressure for a national roadless policy and inclusion of Alaska's national forests with strong support from scientists across the nation. In 1999, I helped draft and recruit scientists to sign on to a letter to President Clinton requesting that he include the Tongass in the national roadless policy. Three hundred and thirty scientists signed this letter, including some of the nation's most prestigious academics as well as many scientists with direct Tongass experience. Key excerpts from that letter follow.

> It has been consistently demonstrated that roadless areas are crucial to the protection of our nation's wildlife, fisheries and water resources . . . There is no scientific basis to exclude the Tongass National Forest from the Forest Service's national roadless policy . . . We encourage you Mr. President to please afford the remaining roadless areas within America's largest national forest and our nation's most substantial old-growth forest ecosystem the same level of protection and precautionary management as those in national forests throughout the rest of the United States.

In November 2000, the Forest Service proposed prohibiting new road building in roadless areas of all national forests except the Tongass. This proposal created a maelstrom of controversy, particularly among western states. The timber and mining industries, along with many western governors, attacked the proposal as limiting development opportunities and economic growth. Although there was growing public support for a roadless policy in our national forest system and the Clinton Administration was providing strong leadership for this effort, the likelihood of including the Tongass in this landmark initiative remained uncertain. National and regional environmental organizations continued to advocate aggressively for inclusion of the Tongass, and my colleague Stan Senner and I wrote numerous letters and provided input during many of the public comment periods.

On January 5, 2001, President Clinton announced the final roadless policy for national forest lands in the United States. We were extremely pleased that the Tongass was included. However, our enthusiasm was short-lived. The incoming Bush Administration, inaugurated just three weeks later, postponed the roadless rule. In October 2004, I joined over 100 other scientists on a letter to the US Forest Service Analysis Team. That letter stated in part: "There is growing consensus among the scientific community that a strong roadless conservation rule is one of the cornerstones to sustainable public lands management, biodiversity conservation, and ecosystem health of the national forests. Therefore, we request that you reinstate the 2001 Roadless Conservation Rule." For more than a decade, appeals, lawsuits, and countersuits would continue on this controversial national rule, including the Tongass exemption.

MAINTAINING THE DIVERSITY OF SOUTHEAST'S RAINFOREST

Southeast Alaska's forests still offer many opportunities for people to experience nature on its own terms, free of significant industrial or residential development. It is important to recognize that Native Alaskans have inhabited Southeast for millennia, and sustainably used the natural resources of land and sea without significantly altering the ecological function of the region. However, much of the North American continent has changed substantially over the last four centuries, with a consequent diminishment of wilderness lands and waters. Few people today have had the opportunity to walk through dense jungles of dripping devil's club, salmonberry, and stink currant shrubs beneath towering spruce trees four to eight feet in diameter; to follow massive bear footprints embedded in deep moss and saturated earth; to inhale the stench of spawned-out salmon; to listen to a cacophony of eagles, gulls, and ravens, all the while anxiously looking over their shoulders for the great bear that indisputably owns this ancient forest. Such a walk among centuries-old trees is truly an extraordinary—and primeval—experience possible in few places in the world outside of the coastal rainforest of Southeast Alaska and portions of northern British Columbia's coast. Wild rivers, teeming fish, gigantic trees, eagles, deer, wolves, bears, and a variety of forest birds are all interconnected parts that make up the heart and soul of Alaska's Tongass National Forest. But, unfortunately, some of the fundamental parts of this incomparable forest ecosystem are now unraveling from death by a thousand cuts.

Ecological systems are composed of many interconnected parts that make up the Earth's biological diversity. Biodiversity embodies much more than the variety of plant and animal species. It encompasses the genetic diversity of species and distinct populations within species. It includes a range of habitat types and ecological communities, as well as the variation within landscapes and aquatic and marine systems. Biodiversity also comprises ecological processes such as predator–prey interactions, interspecific competition, decomposition, and nutrient cycling.

Considering the size of Southeast Alaska and the amount of timber harvested to date, you may ask why the concern. As discussed earlier, the region's largest and most valuable trees have always been rare and have been the primary target of clear-cut logging over the last sixty years. Richard Carstensen, leader of the Landmark Trees Project that surveyed and inventoried the largest individual trees remaining throughout Southeast Alaska, estimated that today's top five Landmark Tree stands would not have made the top 1,000 in 1950. For over three decades, scientists and conservationists have raised concerns about declining forest diversity in Southeast Alaska and the serious risk it poses to the integrity of this rich forest ecosystem. This concern was emphasized in the scientific peer review and in Audubon's appeal of the 1997 Tongass Plan. Unfortunately, these concerns fell on deaf ears at the Forest Service.

Because of our continued concerns with high-grading, Audubon Alaska facilitated a three-day forest diversity workshop in Juneau in the fall of 2002. Our group included Matt Kirchhoff and Dave Person from ADF&G; university professors Paul Alaback and Marc Cramer; Forest Service ecologists Wini Kessler, John Caouette, and Eugene DeGayner; Jim Strittholt of the Conservation Biology Institute; and Richard Carstensen from the Landmark Trees Project. The scientists agreed that the 1997 Tongass Land Management Plan did not adequately address conservation concerns over the decline of rare, low-elevation stands of large old-growth trees. In fact, as described earlier, the revised plan actually modified the timber inventory procedure so that it became increasingly difficult to track the change in abundance of stands of large trees. Our goal was to figure out how to map and classify forest diversity and develop a conservation strategy for maintaining what remains of the rare, ecologically valuable stands of the largest trees on the Tongass.

During our workshop, we shared presentations on forest ecology, forest classification systems, historical logging patterns, and forest–wildlife relationships. Our discussions carefully defined terminology so that our interagency and interdisciplinary group could clearly communicate with one another and increase our understanding of the issue. We were keen to untangle this difficult problem that had been the root of much misunderstanding and confusion over forest management in the Tongass for decades.

Among the important consensus findings of our workshop were that some stands of old-growth forest—particularly those on alluvial fans, floodplains, and porous limestone-marble karst substrates—contain an abundance of large trees that have important conservation values for fish and wildlife, and that these stands have been disproportionately harvested throughout the forests of Southeast Alaska. While this finding was not new, it was significant because our interagency group included expert ecologists from the Forest Service. Timber managers within the Forest Service and some Forest Service leaders had consistently ignored or evaded this issue. Our group also agreed that maintaining and restoring the natural diversity of forest communities, including stands of large, old-growth trees, is essential for maintaining Southeast Alaska's biodiversity. We evaluated and recognized the value of using a new forest mapping system for forest inventory, monitoring, and planning on the Tongass. We also discussed the merits of expanding the management indicator concept beyond individual species, such as deer, bear, and salmon, to include forest community types such as large-tree old growth.

The new forest mapping system—developed by Forest Service ecologists Caouette and DeGayner—replaces the original timber volume categories with measures of tree size and density, canopy texture, soil drainage, and slope exposure. This approach provides foresters, wildlife managers, and conservationists a refined mapping system for describing the structure of areas of the forest used as habitat for many fish and wildlife species. In theory, this should help us identify, monitor, and conserve the rare stands of large, old-growth trees. These forest communities represent distinct habitat types that are rare and highly productive, and have features that are unique and important to many species of plants, animals, and fungi. Although the opportunity to maintain the natural forest diversity in some areas like Prince of Wales Island, the largest island in the Tongass, has largely been lost because of past logging, we still have the potential to identify ecologically important watersheds with large trees in other unlogged areas of the Tongass—and even portions of Prince of Wales.

One of my fundamental motivations for Tongass conservation is to maintain all the ecological parts of this still functional ecosystem so that it continues to provide productive fish and wildlife habitat and all the many ecosystem services—clean air and water, maintenance of water flow, nutrient cycling, decomposition, carbon storage, aesthetic wilderness landscapes—people value. Our challenge on the Tongass today is to preserve the full variety and complexity of Alaska's coastal rainforest in perpetuity.

FROM DEFENSIVE CONSERVATION
TO A SCIENCE-BASED STRATEGY

From the time I began working on Tongass issues in 1977, wildlife and fisheries managers, scientists, conservationists, and many local Southeast residents have been struggling with the Forest Service and timber industry over forest management plans and individual timber sales that ultimately impacted nontimber resources. After the 1997 Tongass Plan revision, I recognized that trying to address habitat conservation issues one timber sale at a time was an inefficient and unsuccessful strategy. This reactive approach to conservation was costly and conflict ridden, and often ended in endless and expensive litigation. My recent experience working with Audubon's western Arctic strategy suggested an alternative approach that could be transferable to the coastal rainforest.

In 2000, Stan and I initiated an Audubon conservation assessment of Alaska's western Arctic—essentially much of the area that overlaps the 23.5-million-acre National Petroleum Reserve-Alaska (NPR-A), the largest block of public land in the nation.[5] The goals of that project were to synthesize information on ecological, subsistence, wilderness, and economic resources of the region, and develop a science-based conservation strategy. Instead of simply fighting any development of this area, our basic concept was to develop a balanced management plan that would identify and protect the most biologically valuable habitats while accepting responsible development elsewhere in the region.

Using Audubon's western Arctic project as a template in Southeast Alaska and with initial funding secured from several foundations, Audubon Alaska joined forces with The Nature Conservancy in Alaska (TNC) to begin work in 2004 on a southeastern Alaska conservation assessment.[6] I served as Audubon's project leader and joined forces with Dave Albert, who was TNC's project leader.

I first met Dave in the early 1990s, when he was a graduate student at the University of Alaska Fairbanks and I was working as ADF&G's regional research coordinator in Fairbanks. Dave was a very bright, energetic grad student with tremendous analytical and computer skills (Fig. 3.2). After grad school, he moved to Juneau, where he worked for Interrain Pacific producing GIS (geographic information system) maps of the Tongass Forest to help conservationists evaluate the effects of timber management on fish and wildlife habitats. Soon thereafter, he began working for TNC as their landscape ecologist and GIS specialist. Although Dave was a crack computer analyst and mapping expert, he also had a solid background in biology and landscape ecology. His broad disciplinary background and analytical mind were terrific assets to our collaboration.

FIG. 3.2. David Albert (right) and I in front of my plane on the Kadashan River Delta. Dave was The Nature Conservancy's landscape ecologist, based in Juneau, and a partner in developing the Conservation Assessment of the Tongass Forest.

※

About the same time that Dave Albert and I were formulating the approach for our conservation assessment of Southeast, two former chiefs of the US Forest Service wrote a commentary that was published in the *Seattle Post-Intelligencer.*[7] Mike Dombeck and Jack Ward Thomas, with combined national forest experience of more than half a century, were the most progressive chiefs ever to lead the US Forest Service. In their opinion piece, "Declare Harvest of Old-Growth Forests Off-Limits and Move On," they stated, "[A]lthough no one knows exactly how much old growth remains, what's left is but a small fraction of what once was and will ever be again. And what remains did not survive by accident. Most remaining old-growth stands occur in rugged terrain where the economic and environmental costs are simply too high."

Dombeck and Thomas went on to say that scientists are increasingly recognizing the many and varied ecological values of old growth. "It's time to stop fighting over what little old growth remains unprotected," they said, pointing out that "a large and growing number of people want old-growth forests preserved for posterity . . . It is time to move beyond the board feet of timber debate . . . Recognizing that harvest of old growth from the national forests should come to an end is a good start."

Recall that industrial forestry became established on the Tongass in the mid-1950s with the two fifty-year timber contracts in Ketchikan and Sitka. For more than half a century, the timber industry and US Forest Service had the first shot at designing and implementing their timber harvest strategy, largely in the absence of effective conservation regulations. The timber industry's strategy was to target logging in the most productive and accessible timber stands in order to maximize profits. As a result, hundreds of thousands of acres of the most valuable trees along shorelines and valley bottoms were clear-cut in large swaths. For many years, conservationists, fishermen, hunters, and fish and wildlife managers had heard the same refrain: "But we are logging only a small percentage of the Tongass." While true, that small percentage of the Tongass was always rare across the forest, and it represented some of the most valuable fish and wildlife habitats throughout Southeast.

Half a century later, we believed that it was past time to give conservation a fair shot at future land allocation on the Tongass. Although the Dombeck-Thomas recommendation to end the logging of old growth on national forest lands had no influence on Tongass management, Dave and I, in consultation with our scientific steering committee, intended to craft a conservation strategy focused on the remaining highest-value fish and wildlife habitats. Our objective was not to stop all logging on the Tongass. Instead, as in the western Arctic, we aimed to design a science-based protected-areas strategy that would conserve the diversity and abundance of the remaining fish and wildlife habitats while allowing other sustainable development activities—including forestry—to proceed outside those critically important areas.

SOUTHEASTERN ALASKA CONSERVATION ASSESSMENT

The overarching goal of the Audubon-TNC collaboration was to conserve the biological diversity of plants, animals, and ecological processes, and maintain the ecological integrity and resilience of southeastern Alaska's temperate rainforest. The term *integrity* means wholeness or completeness while *resilience* is the ability of a system to bounce back after disturbance. These conservation goals were not focused on a human-free zone. Instead, we aimed to provide forest and wildlife managers with information and an analytical tool that would help them maintain intact and healthy habitats and fish and wildlife populations that could support a variety of human needs and sustainable economic enterprises, including fishing, hunting, tourism, wilderness recreation, and traditional subsistence uses beyond old-growth logging.

A major objective of this project included developing a GIS database of selected resource values across the region. GIS provides the means to digitally store, manipulate, and manage maps and various data layers that enable land managers to visualize and understand relationships across the landscape. In the old days, we tediously hand-colored Mylar overlays on topographic maps. But today, GIS stores and displays an abundance of ecological and geographical information—shorelines, rivers, lakes, landforms, vegetative cover types, and fish and wildlife distributions as well as human infrastructure such as land ownership, transportation corridors, and local communities. These GIS capabilities help scientists analyze and predict biological relationships and the effects of land use activities on natural resources such as fish and wildlife populations. They provide resource managers an essential tool for land use planning. We also had additional objectives for our project that included developing a process for measuring and ranking the ecological values of watersheds and developing a conservation strategy for protecting those with the highest values—the biological hot spots—throughout the region.

The GIS tools and analytical techniques we employed in our Tongass project represented a quantum leap over the simple tools used in the initial western Arctic project.[8] Because there was incomplete data on most fish and wildlife species in Southeast, we selected a suite of ecological systems and focal species that had reliable data. We then used these as surrogates to estimate overall ecological values within watersheds across Southeast and the Tongass. Our focal systems and species included estuaries; large-tree, old-growth forest communities; and key habitats for spawning and rearing salmon, brown and black bears, black-tailed deer, and marbled murrelets (a robin-size seabird that often nests in the upper limbs of old-growth trees). We assessed these attributes within each of 1,006 watersheds distributed across twenty-two biogeographic provinces, or regions, of Southeast. We also tabulated the total land area for each watershed; amount, distribution, and chronology of timber harvest; miles of roads; and acres of lands in conservation or development status. Finally, we used a computer optimization program to help us identify the most effective habitat protection strategies for conserving these resources (e.g., salmon spawning habitat, bear habitat, large-tree old growth, etc.) within each watershed and province of the forest.

This process was highly labor intensive, and we conferred regularly with our science advisors and other experts to verify that our approach and results were reasonable. We also conducted aerial reconnaissance to further verify our mapping products. I recall spending much of a day flying over Admiralty Island with Dave Albert and Richard Carstensen confirming that our computer-generated maps of large-tree stands actually identified the areas with the largest old-growth trees.

I remember one interesting but personally stressful experience in Sitka when I met with the Sitka Tribe's natural resource staff and several Forest Service biologists. We spent two and a half hours going over the database for our Tongass assessment. After I had explained our process and demonstrated how we could interactively display the various mapping layers across all of Southeast, someone asked me to look at a particular watershed near Little Port Walter on southeastern Baranof Island. Several of the Sitka staff had recently hiked into an impressive stand of very large old-growth trees in this valley. Since I had never been there and had no idea what to expect, I became anxious about what our GIS maps would show. However, as we navigated through the map layers to that particular location, sure enough, there was a small patch of large-tree old growth. The staff of the Sitka Tribe was impressed that our maps did indeed reflect their on-the-ground knowledge of the forest, and I was relieved our mapping efforts were validated by this unexpected test case.

⚜

Our Tongass conservation assessment was embraced by biologists from ADF&G, the US Fish and Wildlife Service, and many Forest Service biologists, as well as university scientists working on the forest. We anticipated that the conservation community would be particularly supportive of this science-based effort to establish clear conservation priorities for the Tongass and increase our strategic focus. However, early in the development of our Tongass project, I remember a meeting where Dave Albert and I described our objectives and methodology to a group of environmental activists associated with the Alaska Rainforest Campaign. Although most of our conservation colleagues were enthusiastic, there was a minority undercurrent of dissatisfaction about establishing conservation "priorities." To some environmentalists, all wildlands are of equal value and to focus our conservation on a subset of lands and, in their minds, "abandon" other lands was anathema.

Concern over setting conservation priorities was a recurrent theme that we faced in both the western Arctic and the Tongass. Dave and I, however, had seen how costly, and often ineffective, reactive conservation can be. In the Tongass situation, where we were dealing with hundreds of thousands of acres that could potentially be developed, it didn't make sense to fight equally hard to protect vast areas of high-elevation rock and ice or sparsely timbered muskeg bogs that were not at risk compared to the fewer remaining stands of productive old-growth that contained some of the best fish and wildlife habitat. Instead of always playing defensive conservation, our goal was to develop the database and scientific tools to safeguard the diversity and productivity of fish and wildlife habitats across the Tongass.

One of the first analyses we performed with our new Southeast database was to compare the biological values and conservation risks among each of the twenty-two biogeographic provinces of Southeast—including the nineteen provinces largely contained within the Tongass (Fig. 3.3). What we uncovered was in stark contrast to the conventional wisdom that the six and a half million acres of congressionally protected areas of the national forest provided

Biogeographic Provinces

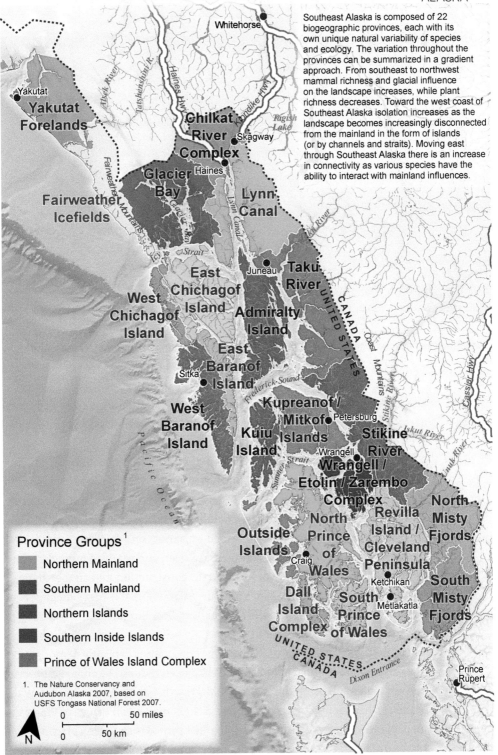

Southeast Alaska is composed of 22 biogeographic provinces, each with its own unique natural variability of species and ecology. The variation throughout the provinces can be summarized in a gradient approach. From southeast to northwest mammal richness and glacial influence on the landscape increases, while plant richness decreases. Toward the west coast of Southeast Alaska isolation increases as the landscape becomes increasingly disconnected from the mainland in the form of islands (or by channels and straits). Moving east through Southeast Alaska there is an increase in connectivity as various species have the ability to interact with mainland influences.

Province Groups[1]

- Northern Mainland
- Southern Mainland
- Northern Islands
- Southern Inside Islands
- Prince of Wales Island Complex

1. The Nature Conservancy and Audubon Alaska 2007, based on USFS Tongass National Forest 2007.

0   50 miles
0   50 km

N

FIG. 3.3. Map of the biogeographic provinces of Southeast Alaska (courtesy Audubon Alaska, 2016, *Ecological Atlas of Southeast Alaska*).

FIG. 3.4. Clear-cuts, second growth, and roads around Nakuti on north central Prince of Wales Island. Old growth is identified by the tall, shaggy forest canopy while second growth has a smooth, even canopy. Muskeg bogs are identified by the yellowish-brown open areas.

adequate conservation protection for the Tongass. Both the industry and Forest Service argued that, because only 10 percent of the productive old growth had been clear-cut on the Tongass, conservation risks were low.

Our new analyses unequivocally demonstrated that the most productive regions and watersheds were predominantly designated as timber areas, while the regions with the highest levels of protection were largely composed of the least productive timber lands.[9] Generally speaking, the regions of highest biological value—regions that contained estuaries, stands of large old-growth trees, and valuable habitat for salmon, bear, deer, and marbled murrelet—had, in the past, seen the highest levels of road construction and timber harvest. These areas included north Prince of Wales Island (Fig. 3.4), east Chichagof and Baranof Islands (Fig. 3.5), and the central islands of Etolin, Zarembo, Wrangell, Kupreanof, and Mitkof. Although north Prince of Wales originally had the highest biological values of all the regions, our analysis explicitly demonstrated that this region's original habitat values had been reduced by about 40 percent. And only about half of the *existing* old-growth habitat on Prince of Wales Island is permanently protected. Today, a flight over north Prince of Wales in a small plane—or even an Alaska Airlines jet—provides a striking view of about 300,000 acres of cutover lands with over 4,000 miles of forest roads.

FIG. 3.5. Clear-cuts and roads in the Game Creek area of northeastern Chichagof Island. Note that the old growth is now fragmented into smaller patches. Muskeg bogs are identified by the yellowish-brown open areas in the lower left and are surrounded by scrub forest.

In contrast, many of the congressionally protected lands on the Tongass (with the exception of Admiralty Island) had lower biological values than the lands that were slated for logging. These protected areas include Misty Fjords National Monument, South Prince of Wales Wilderness, West Chichagof-Yakobi Wilderness, Tracy Arm–Fords Terror Wilderness (Fig. 3.6), South Baranof Wilderness, and Stikine-LaConte Wilderness. And, of course, the other major federal land holding in Southeast is Glacier Bay National Park—2.7 million acres, representing 12 percent of Southeast—which is primarily rock and ice (Fig. 3.7). These wild, protected areas have stunning scenery and provide wonderful opportunities for wilderness recreation. However, they are not representative of Southeast's biological diversity. With the exception of Admiralty, the abundance of fish and wildlife in Southeast is significantly lower in designated wilderness areas than in lands open to industrial forestry. As so often happened across the nation—and was pointed out by Forest Service chiefs Dombeck and Thomas—it has been the less productive but scenic lands that are ultimately allocated to parks and wilderness, and this is certainly the case for Alaska's Tongass National Forest. The land allocation strategy of the Tongass Forest Land Management Plan represents a risky strategy for conserving the region's biological diversity.

FIG. 3.6. Rugged mountains and glaciers and little productive forests are typical habitat in the Tracy Arm–Fords Terror Wilderness along the mainland coast south of Juneau.

FIG. 3.7. John Hopkins Glacier below Mount Fairweather within Glacier Bay National Park and Preserve in northern Southeast Alaska. Little productive old growth occurs in this large conservation unit, which makes up about 12 percent of the land base of Southeast Alaska.

During the summer of 2005 following completion of our initial mapping work, Mary Beth and I flew our plane down the coast to Juneau, where we conducted aerial reconnaissance of many of the priority watersheds that Dave Albert and I had identified during our conservation assessment of Southeast. Our objective was to "air truth" a significant sample of these conservation priority areas to verify that our computer mapping exercise was accurate and representative. During these flights, we also photographed the watersheds and recorded observations relative to wildlife habitats, river and stream systems, estuaries, and the type and quality of old growth. These observations and photographs were to become invaluable resources in our field documentation and public outreach. Early in my career, I recall one of my first ADF&G supervisors encouraging me to take every opportunity to explore new places. He said few people will ever see some of these places, and if you have local knowledge, it will give you confidence and credibility with others who have never been there. That was sage advice and I took it to heart.

In Sitka, I teamed up with Anissa Berry-Frick—a retired commercial pilot who was then a volunteer LightHawk (environmental air force) pilot—to continue reconnaissance flights over the outer coastal islands in her floatplane. Safety considerations precluded flying my own wheeled plane over this portion of the rugged outer coast, where a forced landing would likely end up in the drink or the trees. Anissa was a very competent and seasoned float pilot, and she had a strong interest and background in Tongass conservation.

After more than a decade away from fieldwork, I was enthusiastic about the opportunity to get back into it in the Tongass. Spending time in the field has always been essential for maintaining my passion and enthusiasm for conservation. The daily routine of office work—pulling myself out of bed to fight the traffic and sit inside for eight or nine hours, especially in summer—is in glaring contrast to waking up with unbridled excitement about the day's new adventure exploring unfamiliar territory and possibly discovering new insights into how wildlife make their living in the rainforest. My passions were ignited flying over pristine valleys and alpine ridges or exploring forested game trails, untrammeled salmon streams, and fertile marine estuaries. Working outdoors in remote, stunning country while applying science to maintain the ecosystem integrity of a national treasure like the Tongass made my so-called "job" a privileged responsibility to accomplish with pride and passion.

Highlights from my field notes reflect the kinds of information I was collecting during the fieldwork with Anissa:

7-17: Sitka, overcast, fog, and rain. Anissa and I departed Sitka in her Cessna 180 on floats about 1400 and headed out Peril Straits to Cape Fanshaw and Farragut Bay on Southeast's central mainland coast. Farragut is a very special area with great diversity, an outstanding estuary, and a good rep-

FIG. 3.8. Rocky Pass looking over Big John Bay is a narrow channel separating Kuii and Kupreanof Islands in central Southeast Alaska, northeast of Petersburg. This passage makes up a very productive coastal estuary and provides valuable habitat for a diversity of fish and wildlife.

resentation of large-tree old growth. A small amount of old logging on one peninsula does not detract from this watershed's ecosystem values.

We flew Mitkof Island and observed that the Bear Creek watershed has been heavily clear-cut and roaded. This area is significantly fragmented and not now a priority for conservation. We also overflew Blind Slough. The south facing slope has been heavily clear-cut but the north facing slope is still in old growth. This is a very unique area. Although half of the watershed has been cut, I think it is worth protecting the uncut portion. It appears to me that Mitkof has received some of the heaviest high-grading on the forest, perhaps comparable to northern Prince of Wales Island. We flew over a portion of Kupreanof Island. Rocky Pass is an extraordinary area, with a complex of highly productive estuaries that should receive very high conservation priority [Fig. 3.8]. We also flew key sites on Kuiu Island. Bay of Pillars is a very high value watershed and should be protected. Saginaw Bay has been hammered with clear-cutting, and is not a priority compared to Security Bay, Kadake, or Bay of Pillars. Although Security

Bay has had extensive logging and roads on the east side, the west side is pristine and has very high value as does the head of the bay and the riparian estuary. Security should be considered as a restoration priority as well as to protect the west side and head of the bay from further impacts.

In August, I flew with Anissa again.

8-8: Ketchikan, Clear, visibility 60 mi. Today, we were joined by a National Geographic writer and photographer who are doing a story on the Tongass. We flew all day and covered much of Prince of Wales and the outer islands (Fig. 3.9). This was a very productive day of flying, photographing, and documenting some of the key watersheds identified in our conservation assessment. However, it was relatively depressing to see from the bird's-eye view the significant level of past logging that has occurred in this once most productive region of the Tongass. It is astonishing to see the level of high-grading of the very best timber by both the Forest Service and Native corporations. I would estimate conservatively that 75% of the best large-tree old growth has been logged by the timber industry. This is particularly true of the most accessible, lower elevation sites. I suspect this has had a substantial impact on ecological integrity of this area. In some cases, whole islands

FIG. 3.9. Native corporation logging around Hetta Inlet on central Prince of Wales Island.

FIG. 3.10. Native corporation logging on Dall Island, southwest of Prince of Wales Island.

have been impacted. I photographed major harvested sites at Klukwan Lake, Heceta Island, Dall Island, Long Island, and the Kasaan Peninsula [Fig. 3.10].

We flew the South Prince of Wales Wilderness area and noted that it has very low abundance of large-tree old growth and there is much muskeg and scrub forest [Fig. 3.11]. It is not surprising, based on the lower timber values there, this may have been why it was designated for wilderness protection. It was a very long day but excellent flying weather.

Back in Juneau, I once again began flying my own plane. After years of flying with ADF&G, I was familiar with this portion of northern Southeast, and there were many more opportunities for safely landing a wheeled plane.

8-10: Juneau, clear, visibility unlimited. We departed the Juneau Airport in my Cessna 180 at 0930 with Mary Beth and Dave Albert for a reconnaissance flight over eastern Chichagof Island. We flew over Spasski Cr and Port Frederick where we documented much clear-cutting. We flew up Neka River near the head of Port Frederick. This is a high value watershed but it has had some significant logging of riparian and upland large-tree

FIG. 3.11. Looking north along the west coast of the South Prince of Wales Wilderness. The productivity of the forest land on southern Prince of Wales Island is much lower than northern Prince of Wales.

FIG. 3.12. Mud Bay on northern Chichagof Island was protected as a Land Use Designation II in 1990. Mount Fairweather and Glacier Bay National Park in the background across Icy Strait.

old growth and the riparian area is now fragmented. We flew down Mud Bay. Lower Mud Bay has a very large and important estuary [Fig. 3.12]. It has moderate upland and riparian large-tree old growth and no significant timber harvest. We also flew down Idaho Inlet. This is a high value area with no industrial impacts. Both lower Mud Bay and Idaho Inlet were designated as protected areas under the Tongass Timber Reform Act in 1990. The portage area of upper Port Frederick adjacent to upper Tenakee Inlet has had significant harvest.

We surveyed the Kadashan watershed and documented it with aerial photos. It is a very large watershed and has among the highest ecological values within the east Chichagof region. There is some old second growth in the lower riparian forest and it still has the recently constructed road on the east side of the river. [Construction had been halted by court order, and then Kadashan was designated a protected watershed in 1990 under the Tongass Timber Reform Act.] We flew over Little Basket Bay watershed which is essentially a small refuge surrounded by a "sea" of clear-cuts to the north around Kook Lake and Basket Bay that are connected to the Corner Bay road system [Fig. 3.13].

※

Throughout 2006, I spent most of my time working with Dave completing the final analysis for our Tongass conservation assessment. Erin Dovichin from TNC-Alaska also worked with me as coeditor. While we were finishing up our report, there was an ongoing conversation within the environmental community about various strategies different groups were using in their Tongass conservation work. Some were focused primarily on defending the Clinton Administration's Roadless Rule, which had designated nine million acres of the Tongass off-limits to new roads and logging. Although most groups, including Audubon, strongly supported the Roadless Rule, some of us also recognized that there were a number of key watersheds across the Tongass that had previously been logged and roaded but still maintained relatively high biological values. Because some of these areas—particularly those with high salmon values—already had roads, they were not classified as roadless and would not be protected under the Roadless Rule. Another concern was that the Roadless Rule was an administrative action and didn't have the permanency of a congressional designation.

Audubon and several other groups argued forcefully that we should also have a place-based conservation strategy. Our basic premise was that all roadless areas were not of equal value. While they deserved protection, we felt it was also important to restore logged and roaded watersheds that still had high biological values. For example, a substantial roadless section of the mainland

FIG. 3.13. Kook Lake and Basket Bay on eastern Chichagof have been heavily clear-cut and are connected to the Corner Bay road system. Note the older second-growth stand between the head of Basket Bay and Kook Lake. More recent clear-cuts are scattered to the right and behind the lake.

coast, including the Juneau icefield, simply didn't have the same biological productivity and diversity as some of the partially roaded areas on north Prince of Wales, north Kuiu, or east Chichagof Islands.

Melanie Smith at Audubon Alaska used our GIS database to compare the biological values of the Audubon-TNC conservation and restoration priority watersheds to the values of all the roadless watersheds. It is important to recognize that there was significant overlap between these two sets of watersheds. For example, many of the roadless watersheds also had high ecological values while some (e.g., many along the mainland coast) were primarily composed of nonforest or scrub forest. Melanie's analysis explicitly demonstrated that we could conserve more biological value (e.g., salmon, bear, deer habitat) through a combination of roadless protection and place-based protection that targeted watersheds with the highest habitat values. Unfortunately, this difference in strategy—protecting only roadless areas versus protecting a combination of roadless plus some high-value roaded areas—resulted in tension among individual members and groups within the environmental community. This difference was never completely resolved, and it caused confusion and uncertainty within the funding community, Native organizations, municipalities, and the timber industry regarding the goals of the environmental community.

TONGASS FUTURES ROUNDTABLE

Early in 2006, The Nature Conservancy asked me if I would be interested in serving on a panel of diverse stakeholders—the Tongass Futures Roundtable—to discuss opportunities for finding a resolution to long-term conflicts over forest management on the Tongass National Forest. The overarching goal was to work together to achieve a balance of healthy and diverse communities, strong local economies, and responsible use of resources—including timber—while maintaining the natural values and ecological integrity of the forest. The Tongass Futures Roundtable was initiated by groups and individuals who saw the need to change the paradigm, where nearly every policy initiative involving the forest was subject to conflict, controversy, appeals, and litigation. The organizers were initially inspired by a similar multiparty process—the Great Bear Rainforest—that was taking place along the northern British Columbia coast. Although the British Columbia process shared a similar forestry conflict, the agreement between the First Nations and the BC government was politically different than the Tongass situation.

The roundtable's organizing groups included several large environmental foundations, The Nature Conservancy, the National Forest Foundation, and the US Forest Service. I agreed to participate because I thought this would be an opportunity to use science and our conservation assessment to help inform the group's decision-making. While I was a formal member of this group, my colleague Dave Albert served as support staff from TNC. The roundtable's broad goals were to address land management, quality of life, and a sustainable economy. Specifically, the roundtable was charged with supporting an agreement for a twenty-four-to-thirty-six-month supply of "bridge timber" that would allow time for a consensus process to craft recommendations to the ongoing Tongass Plan amendment. From the outset, one of the roundtable's major challenges was that it really didn't have a formal decision-making authority beyond seeking consensus.

The inaugural meeting was held in Woodinville, Washington, from May 17 to 19, 2006. Twenty-seven initial members represented a broad group of stakeholders, including the Forest Service, timber industry, environmental groups, fishing and tourism industries, Native Alaskans, Native corporations, environmental foundations, and municipalities. In addition, the chief of the Forest Service and commissioner of the Alaska Department of Natural Resources attended. This was a big deal, and no one knew what was going to happen, but nearly everyone felt a high level of stress when we began. During our introductions, we shared some of our personal Tongass history, values, goals, and concerns.

Brian Rogers, of Information Insights, facilitated. Brian was a former Alaska State Representative who went on to become chancellor of the University of Alaska Fairbanks. He emphasized that the first meeting would have an unstructured agenda, and the focus would be to determine whether or not dialogue among these diverse stakeholders would even be possible. The first ground rule was to check your numbers—annual timber harvest levels, acres protected, etc.—at the door. I recall one of the environmental attorneys saying, "I'm cracking up. How will this end in anything but chaos?" There were several breakout groups of seven to eight people who convened for an hour of discussion, and then reported back to the group with a summary of their issues, values, and concerns. Brian was a real pro at bringing disparate groups together for problem-solving. He emphasized that he would not push toward a solution but rather focus on whether we could pursue constructive dialogue or just continue the fight.

This was a very interesting prospect. I had never actually sat down and calmly discussed these issues with the owner of a timber mill or the mayor of a local community dependent on the timber industry. Most of my dialogue with local communities, the timber industry, and the Forest Service had been in meeting settings where I explained our research results and the management implications for fish and wildlife populations. These were often stressful, conflict-laden experiences. This new approach was quite different, and I figured it was worth an investment of my time and energy. I had recently been involved with two other stakeholder groups—the Kenai Brown Bear Stakeholder Group and the Western Arctic Caribou Working Group—and both of these experiences were personally fulfilling and contributed toward crafting more effective conservation strategies while also building support among local, but diverse, user groups.

The following themes were among those discussed at the first roundtable meeting:

» We need to maintain community opportunities and healthy communities; this requires economic development.
» How can we maintain a national treasure and also supply timber to local businesses?
» Fighting and litigation don't solve a lot; we need to find a better way to do things.

- » Southeast has a rich cultural heritage. How can we maintain this?
- » The Tongass is special and magical, but so are eating and jobs.
- » TLMP is a busted model.
- » We're in a bottleneck having to move from old-growth to second-growth harvest.
- » We need to get economical timber available on the Tongass now.
- » We need to address Native land selections.
- » Old growth is important for fish, wildlife, and recreation; clear-cutting old growth reduces those values.
- » We need to maintain the natural range of forest diversity across the Tongass.
- » We need to manage for timber and conservation at the watershed scale.

In my personal statement, I described how the Tongass and northern British Columbia make up the most significant portion of the world's temperate rainforest. The best opportunity we had for maintaining a representation of intact rainforest with all its ecological parts was on the Tongass. My professional goal was to maintain the ecological integrity of Southeast Alaska so people could use its resources sustainably for generations. This would require adjustments to the forest plan amendment, including the protection of intact watersheds.

A wide range of values and issues was discussed during the initial meeting. These varied from a desire to bring back an integrated industry that could log over 360 million board feet of old growth annually on the Tongass to a complete cessation of old-growth logging and protection of all roadless acres. After this initial meeting, it did not appear that we were moving any closer to a consensus resolution of the timber wars on the Tongass. At the end of the meeting, however, all parties agreed to meet again to continue our dialogue.

Following the roundtable meeting, members of the Alaska Rainforest Campaign discussed various options for effectively participating in the roundtable. In our discussions with the broader membership, the environmental community was consistently asked by the Forest Service, timber industry, and some of the small community representatives what specifically we wanted. But many ARC members hesitated to clearly articulate the specifics of our conservation goals. Several of the groups—including Audubon Alaska, Alaska Wilderness League, TNC, and Trout Unlimited—suggested that we use the results of our new conservation assessment to identify conservation priority watersheds. However, the Natural Resources Defense Council (NRDC) and several other groups strongly recommended against identifying any priority areas on a map. Instead, they considered the optimal approach to be a united position in support of protecting all roadless areas on the Tongass. This lack of clarity on what the environmentalists wanted from the Tongass caused confusion and frustration among many other member groups.

I learned a lot at this initial meeting and gained a better understanding of the hopes and dreams of people who lived on the forest and with whom I had never talked. Fundamentally, I was hopeful that this dialogue might be productive and help us find a reasonable compromise that could sustain local communities while also conserving key watersheds with the most valuable fish and wildlife habitats at greatest risk.

⚜

Over the five years that I participated on the Tongass Futures Roundtable, there were thirty to thirty-five active participants; the membership changed some over the course of our meetings. Some of the meetings also included interested local, regional, and national observers. The timber industry was represented by the Alaska Forest Association, Viking Lumber, Sealaska Corporation, the State Division of Forestry, and several other timber industry leaders. The industry interest, in general, was focused on maintaining a consistent long-term supply of old-growth timber to meet industry demand. Although there was some diversity of opinion on how much timber was needed, the Alaska Forest Association advocated strongly for an integrated industry (several mills producing a variety of products) and a substantial increase in timber supply to 360 million board feet a year—many times more than the current harvest level of about thirty-five to forty million board feet per year. The timber industry at that time included one large mill—although much smaller than the two in Ketchikan and Sitka that flourished under the fifty-year contracts—and several smaller operations that acquired timber primarily from national forest or state lands. The State of Alaska had some forest lands scattered throughout Southeast that provided a relatively small level of timber for local operators. The Sealaska Corporation also logged Native corporation lands throughout Southeast, but much of their timber inventory—which was primarily exported—had already been harvested.

Local community representation included Craig, Coffman Cove, Juneau, Petersburg, Wrangell, and the Southeast Conference. The Southeast Conference was a support group of municipalities that supported activities to promote strong economies, healthy communities, and a quality environment in Southeast Alaska. Some of these communities, like Craig and Coffman Cove on Prince of Wales Island, were closely tied to the timber industry, while Juneau and Petersburg were not as directly linked economically with timber. All the communities voiced strong interest in maintaining a healthy economy throughout Southeast. Some of the smaller communities had experienced substantial economic impacts following the long-term decline in the timber industry and closure of the big mills. The frustration of these community leaders was often close to the surface during our meetings. I recall one instance when the mayor of Craig dramatically walked out of a roundtable meeting in disgust when he thought environmentalists were trying to shut down the timber industry. On another occasion, the Coffman Cove representative introduced her grandchildren to the roundtable and remarked that without growth of the timber industry, they might have to move away from Coffman Cove and the school would be at risk of closing. Clearly, these experiences with local people living in the forest and depending on a stable timber supply got our attention and empathy.

The roundtable also included a variety of other forest users and interests, including commercial fishing, tourism, Native Alaskans, state resource agencies, several foundations that provided financial support for this effort, and national, regional, and local environmental groups.[10] Several other organizations and individuals consistently attended all roundtable meetings as observers.

Within the environmental groups, opinions regarding the future of the timber industry on the Tongass ranged from trying to find a reasonable balance between timber and conservation to ending all logging on national forest lands, particularly an immediate end to all old-growth logging. Just as there were a lot of differences in the priorities and ideologies within the environmental community, there were substantial differences within other stakeholder groups regarding Tongass Forest management. Owen Graham of the Alaska Forest Association had little interest in compromising his demands for restoring an integrated timber industry with access to a much larger annual allowable harvest than was currently sold on the Tongass. Chris Maisch, Alaska Department of Natural Resources' state forester, also advocated for the timber industry but worked tirelessly trying to find solutions for meeting current timber demands while minimizing impacts to fish and wildlife resources. Within the Native community, there were also varied opinions regarding the role of timber in the Southeast economy and how to balance timber harvest with maintaining habitat for fish and wildlife species important for Native subsistence users. The Sealaska Corporation often had a different perspective than Native village residents with their particular interests and needs associated with protection of habitat that supported their fishing and hunting activities.

NATIONAL GEOGRAPHIC CRUISE

In the spring of 2006, I received a call from Doug Chadwick, a wildlife biologist and science journalist working on assignment for *National Geographic*. I had met Doug years earlier and greatly respected his natural history writing. Doug was researching a story on the Tongass and asked me if I would accompany him for a few days as he traveled around Southeast. After a considerable discussion about various options for getting on the ground and really seeing the Tongass, we decided to charter a Nordic Tug out of Juneau. *National Geographic* would pay for a bare boat charter of a thirty-two-foot Nordic Tug, which I would skipper, and Mary Beth would serve as our cook and deckhand. Doug also brought his friend John Swallow on our cruise. We met in Juneau on August 5, stocked the boat with groceries and personal gear, then departed the next day in overcast, rainy weather to circumnavigate Admiralty Island with side excursions along the mainland coast and Kupreanof, Baranof, and Chichagof Islands. This cruise was designed to provide Doug with a good overview of the rainforest ecology as well as some of the conservation issues associated with industrial logging of the nation's largest national forest. As an important side benefit, this also allowed me to get my feet on the ground in some of the conservation priority watersheds I had not visited but which Dave and I had identified in our conservation assessment. Here are some excerpts from my field notes describing our route and variety of experiences.

8-7: 1300: Anchored at head of Gambier Bay, S Admiralty Is. overcast and rain.

2000: After dinner, we headed out again in the skiff to the north arm of Gambier Bay. We saw several brown bears to the east of the big flat and a couple on the flat. The light was becoming dusky. We observed many gulls and harbor seals at the head of the bay working over the incoming schools of salmon. Gambier Bay is an incredibly rich watershed and ranks number one out of sixty in overall ecological values for our Admiralty watershed analysis [Fig. 3.14]. The weather while we were here was marginal and we didn't hike into the most productive portion of the river. Nevertheless, the richness and productivity of this watershed were still impressive.

8-8: Gambier Bay, Admiralty Island, overcast, fog, and heavy rain, SE wind ten knots.

0745: Departed Gambier.

1100: Abeam Pt Hobart. As we headed up into Port Houghton, we observed many pairs of marbled murrelets sitting on the water. Port Houghton is a spectacular drainage. The area to the north along the mouth has been clear-cut and connects with Hobart Bay which has been extensively logged by Native corporations. Port Houghton Salt Chuck is ranked as the number three watershed out of fifty-seven in the Taku Mainland province. I have never been here on the ground before but flew over last summer and photographed it from the air [Fig. 3.15].

FIG. 3.14. Gambier Bay on southern Admiralty Island is the highest-ranking watershed in terms of overall ecological values on the Admiralty. Gambier and most of Admiralty was protected in 1980 by the Alaska National Interest Lands Conservation Act.

FIG. 3.15. Port Houghton looking east over the head of the inlet into the Salt Chuck on the western edge of the coastal mountains west of the British Columbia border. The Port Houghton Salt Chuck is second highest in terms of its overall ecological values out of fifty-seven watersheds in the Taku Mainland Province.

1245: Anchored at the head of Port Houghton, overcast with rain. The four of us climbed into our fourteen-foot skiff and headed up the saltwater passage into the salt chuck. (This is almost like a lake with a constricted saltwater river that ebbs and floods with the change of tides.) We headed in just before high tide and the tide was running swiftly into the salt chuck. We observed a Steller sea lion in the passage and many harbor seals. Eagles lined the trees and gulls were in profusion as large schools of salmon were running into the chuck on their journey to spawn in the freshwater rivers and creeks that empty into the salt chuck.

Inside the chuck, we observed a minimum of seventy harbor seals hauled out along the shore of the small island in the middle of the chuck. There were also at least fifteen eagles in the trees on the island. I estimated in excess of seventy-five eagles and one hundred harbor seals in the chuck as well as several Steller sea lions. We observed one sea lion vigorously shaking a freshly caught salmon at the water's surface. We also observed a black bear fishing in the river at the head of the chuck. We saw red-throated loons, mergansers, Thayer's gull, Bonaparte gulls, pacific wrens, and spotted sandpipers in the chuck which is biologically diverse and productive. There were many commercial crab pots along the shore of the chuck . . . This watershed, which was ranked in our analysis as a conservation priority, should be protected as a biologically productive, intact ecosystem.

8-9: 0900: Eight miles west of the Five Fingers Light, we shut down for two hours to watch humpback whales lunge feeding. Approximately fifty to one hundred whales—and possibly twice that many—were spread out across Frederick Sound. I photographed whales feeding and breaching [Fig. 3.16]. We also observed red-necked phalaropes feeding on the surface in association with whales. Many humpback whales were blowing and trumpeting. This was an incredible opportunity to observe and photograph whales.

8-10: 1145: Anchored the tug in Saook Bay, north Baranof Is.

1200: We ran the skiff up near the delta at the head of the bay and anchored it off shore. We hiked up the delta with Doug, John, and Mary Beth across bear trails and toward an "island" of large trees. We observed old logging along the shoreline and along both sides of the delta. We hiked throughout a large-tree old-growth stand with several six to seven-foot diameter Sitka spruce trees and a few big hemlocks [Fig. 3.17]. This was a very beautiful stand of old growth and I captured multiple images. Many pinks and chums were working their way upstream as eagles, ravens, and gulls were

FIG. 3.16. Breaching humpback whale in Frederick Sound between south Admiralty and north Kuiu Islands. This whale was part of a major feeding aggregation of perhaps a hundred or more whales I observed on a cruise with *National Geographic* writer Doug Chadwick.

concentrated in the area. We observed abundant bear sign along the stream banks and throughout the adjacent forest. Our assessment identified Saook Bay as the top ranked watershed on eastern Baranof Island and our tromping through the flood plain forest confirmed our earlier computer analysis. Saook Bay is a high value site even though there has been some limited old-growth logging at the head of the bay near the estuary.

8-12: Long Bay, Tenakee Inlet, overcast, rain, calm.

0730: I counted 168 bald eagles (biased toward white-headed adults) along the head of Long Bay and on the estuary grass flats. I estimated there were probably well over 200 eagles in the bay. Both pink and chum salmon were running in the river at the head of the bay. I observed one single brown bear

FIG. 3.17. Mary Beth admiring a large-tree old-growth stand in Saook Bay on northeastern Baranof Island. Some individual trees were over six feet in diameter and many centuries old. This riparian area was adjacent to a salmon stream and was full of bear trails. Large-tree old growth stands are rare on the Tongass.

on the tidal flats at the head of the bay as well as two family groups of bears (female and two cubs) near the creek. After breakfast, Doug and I had a long discussion about Tongass Forest management issues.

One of the key issues we talked about was how little large-tree, old-growth forest remains on the Tongass. Doug wanted to see such a stand that was still in the Forest Service's timber base and potentially subject to logging. I got out my laptop computer and searched our GIS database in Tenakee Inlet and found a suitable site in Crab Bay.

8-13: 1130: Anchored at the head of the north arm of Crab Bay just east of a small patch of 50- to 60-year-old second growth. We went ashore and hiked up the hillside looking for a large-tree stand that is in the Forest Service timber base and outside of the 500-foot beach-fringe buffer. This was a beautiful forest with large spruce and hemlock. Much early hand logging (prior to 1940s) had occurred along the lower beach fringe of this forest and we could still see stumps with spring board notches where the early loggers stood to hand saw these trees. This stand still retained its old-growth character, however, in spite of a select harvest of individual trees 50 to 80 years ago. This old harvest is not discernable from the air or water, however, but is clearly detectable on the ground. The contrast between clear-cutting all the trees versus taking only a few individuals is ecologically very different as the individual selection harvest still retained old-growth character. We hiked up the forested slope above the beach-fringe buffer and found a very large old-growth spruce at about 500 feet elevation. I estimated that the tree was somewhere between eight and ten feet in diameter. I later passed on this photo to Richard Carstensen of the Landmark Trees project and he thought it was likely one of the largest trees left in Alaska.

Doug Chadwick's "The Truth About Tongass" appeared in the July 2007 issue of *National Geographic*.[11] He concluded his article with these observations:

With so much of the American frontier in the rearview mirror, we begin to see more clearly that no forest has ever been just a repository of trees. Each is at once a vibrant structure, a community, the live scaffolding within which creation continues to unfold. That is the ultimate natural resource growing out there between Alaska's snow-bright summits and the sea.

WATERSHED CONSERVATION STRATEGY

In 2007, Audubon Alaska and The Nature Conservancy of Alaska published our 544-page report, *A Conservation Assessment and Resource Synthesis for the Coastal Forests and Mountains Ecoregion in Southeastern Alaska and the Tongass National Forest*.[12] The ten-chapter report, with contributions from twenty-two authors, includes a conservation assessment of Southeast, summarizing original and current conditions of selected resources; a resource synthesis describing the current state of knowledge of habitats and species, as well as perspectives on human use of the region; and conceptual recommendations for a Tongass conservation strategy. In 2016, Audubon Alaska significantly updated and revised that assessment into the *Ecological Atlas of Southeast Alaska*.[13]

One of the major recommendations of our proposed conservation strategy was to conserve the most ecologically valuable intact watersheds remaining on the Tongass. For over half a century, the timber industry had the first shot at the forest. Now it was time to focus on conservation. The 1997 Tongass Land Management Plan was predicated on a conservation strategy that would presumably maintain viable and well-distributed populations of wildlife species across the forest. Although that strategy was a notable improvement over the former Tongass plan, which had minimal conservation measures for fish and wildlife, it still had significant limitations, such as high timber harvest targets and inadequate measures to prevent high-grading, described earlier. In areas that were to be managed for timber harvest, the TLMP strategy largely focused on protecting habitat patches (e.g., old growth reserves and riparian and beach fringe buffers) *within* individual watersheds. We posited that this "within watershed" approach would ultimately reduce old-growth habitat and habitat diversity, increase habitat fragmentation by creating smaller, more isolated habitat patches, and expand road density.

Numerous ecological studies have suggested that conservation actions should take place at the scale of entire watersheds, and some key Tongass wildlife species (e.g., salmon, bears, wolves) are strongly linked to ecological processes at the watershed scale. By conserving entire watersheds—from ridgetop to ridgetop and headwaters to estuary—habitat diversity can be maintained more effectively, particularly for the relatively rare large-tree old-growth communities. In addition, such an approach will minimize habitat fragmentation, reduce impacts from roads, and maintain watershed integrity. Watershed conservation is particularly appropriate in the Tongass because the forest is naturally fragmented by its archipelago of islands separated by large water bodies and coastal ice fields. Further, many islands have unique floral and faunal distributions. Thus, our analysis and proposed conservation strategy strongly recommended that the Forest Service strengthen their Tongass conservation strategy by protecting additional intact watersheds with the highest ecological values. This complementary approach to the TLMP strategy would be particularly beneficial for maintaining salmon productivity and conserving wide-ranging species like wolves and bears. These recommendations paralleled comments by the scientific peer review committee that evaluated the Forest Service's Tongass conservation strategy: "Perhaps of greatest concern is the failure to protect the Forest's remaining pristine watersheds."

Once Dave and I had completed the GIS mapping layers for the Tongass and the rest of Southeast and identified the most ecologically valuable watersheds in the region, we used our optimization program to rank the watersheds within each province of the Tongass (such as Admiralty Island, East Chichagof, North Prince of Wales). We did this for both intact watersheds and watersheds that had historically been logged and roaded. This was important because the areas logged first were, in fact, the most productive forest lands on the Tongass. With this information in hand, we designed a conservation strategy for the entire Tongass. This strategy—Conservation Area Design—included watersheds where conservation was the priority and those where restoration was the priority.

Just as the timber industry originally targeted the highest-value timber regions for logging, we were now targeting the remaining watersheds with the highest fish and wildlife values for conservation. Although we were half a century behind in this fundamental conservation effort, we still had an opportunity to maintain some semblance of natural biological diversity across the Tongass—an opportunity that has been foreclosed in all other national forests in the contiguous United States. An initial map (Fig. 3.18) of the Conservation Area Design was presented in our conservation assessment report. That map served as the template for further iterations that followed over the course of the next few years.

※

As I sit here in front of my computer in 2018, I admit to hitting the proverbial wall as I try to recap my work from 2007 through my retirement from Audubon in May 2011. Those years were the most difficult and stressful period of my professional career in Alaska. Early in my career, regular fieldwork and a strong connection to wildlife ecology kept my personal fires glowing. Even midway through my career, as my fieldwork diminished, I still had the opportunity to directly apply my ecological expertise to conservation. But by 2007, the bulk of my work had dramatically shifted away from biology to what seemed like never-ending meetings focused on defensive conservation efforts with limited long-term conservation gains. A notable exception to this was the Roadless Rule, but this was still in limbo in the courts.

During this challenging period, the focus of the conservation community was becoming increasingly fragmented. Although we all shared a similar long-term vision, the strategies for reaching our ultimate conservation goals were scattered and out of sync. A few groups and individuals were even beginning to question their colleagues' conservation ethics. At the same time, some of us—through the Tongass Roundtable—were engaged with Forest Service administrators, the timber industry, and local communities in an effort to identify common ground and potential compromise solutions for resolving decades of bitter conflict over Tongass management.

In this new phase of work, it became progressively clear that some stakeholders—across the spectrum from industry to environmentalists—had little desire to use science in decision-making, much less to actually consider some level of compromise toward developing a durable solution to the decades-old Tongass war. Because the roundtable operated on consensus, a single stakeholder could derail any potential compromise. As a result of these growing tensions, my stress increased, my patience deteriorated, and it became ever more apparent that we were all on a treadmill just trying to hold our ground. In

A Conservation Area Design for Southeast Alaska

Audubon
The Nature Conservancy
Protecting nature. Preserving life.
ALASKA

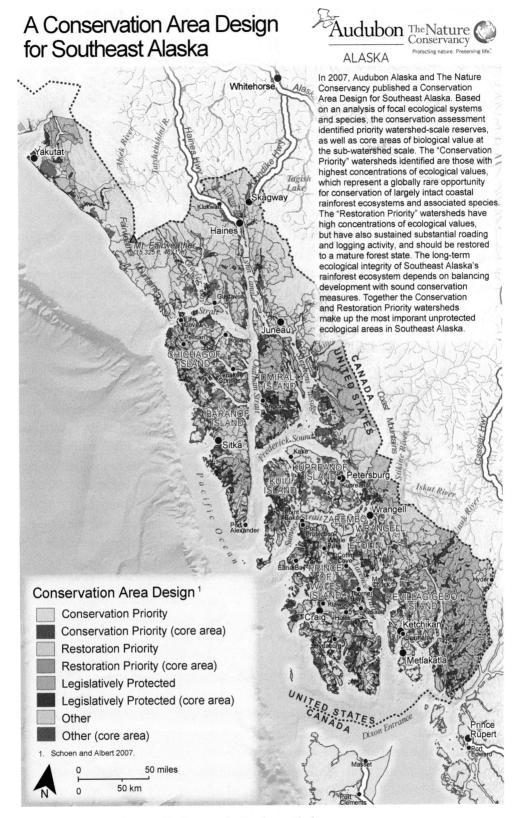

In 2007, Audubon Alaska and The Nature Conservancy published a Conservation Area Design for Southeast Alaska. Based on an analysis of focal ecological systems and species, the conservation assessment identified priority watershed-scale reserves, as well as core areas of biological value at the sub-watershed scale. The "Conservation Priority" watersheds identified are those with highest concentrations of ecological values, which represent a globally rare opportunity for conservation of largely intact coastal rainforest ecosystems and associated species. The "Restoration Priority" watersheds have high concentrations of ecological values, but have also sustained substantial roading and logging activity, and should be restored to a mature forest state. The long-term ecological integrity of Southeast Alaska's rainforest ecosystem depends on balancing development with sound conservation measures. Together the Conservation and Restoration Priority watersheds make up the most imporant unprotected ecological areas in Southeast Alaska.

Conservation Area Design [1]

- Conservation Priority
- Conservation Priority (core area)
- Restoration Priority
- Restoration Priority (core area)
- Legislatively Protected
- Legislatively Protected (core area)
- Other
- Other (core area)

1. Schoen and Albert 2007.

0   50 miles
0   50 km

N

FIG. 3.18. A Conservation Area Design map for Southeast Alaska
(courtesy Audubon Alaska, 2016, *Ecological Atlas of Southeast Alaska*).

addition to these challenges, my close friend and colleague Stan Senner moved from Audubon to the Ocean Conservancy in the fall of 2009. When Stan left, I reluctantly agreed to fill in as acting executive director of Audubon Alaska until Nils Warnock was hired in June 2010. I then worked part-time from home for the next year as a senior science advisor to Audubon. The following summary briefly recaps some of the key Tongass issues I participated in during this time.

2008 TONGASS LAND MANAGEMENT PLAN

The Tongass National Forest released the record of decision for their revision of the 1997 Tongass Land Management Plan in January 2008.[14] Although the roundtable had been unable to come to a consensus on specific Tongass Plan recommendations, Audubon provided the Forest Service with our scoping comments and a copy of the Audubon-TNC 2007 *Conservation Assessment and Conservation Strategy* that provided specific conservation measures for protecting fish and wildlife values.

The revised plan used an adaptive management approach that established three phases for new logging and road building based on increasing levels of timber demand. On the plus side, phase 1 of the new plan deferred new logging and road building in some of the most valuable fish and wildlife watersheds on the Tongass. For example, only 400,000 acres of our conservation priority watersheds—11 percent of 3.4 million acres—were open for timber harvesting.

On the minus side, the upper limit of timber harvest under the amended plan—2.67 billion board feet per decade—was unchanged from the 1997 TLMP. In the long term, implementation of this plan would place at risk many of the most important fish and wildlife values that people care about, including subsistence use, hunting and fishing, recreation, and tourism.

On May 15, 2008, Audubon Alaska appealed the new Tongass Plan to the chief of the Forest Service, Abigail Kimbell. Key excerpts from that appeal follow.

Audubon Appeal: Conclusions and Requested Relief

A major focus of Audubon's appeal is the significant loss of large-tree old growth (SD67) habitat, especially in certain biogeographic provinces. This forest type represents a rare and unique ecological community with high habitat values for fish and wildlife. The loss and fragmentation of this forest type is not compatible with the goal of maintaining habitat diversity well distributed across the Tongass . . . The ROD (Record of Decision) and FEIS (Final EIS) still fail to quantify the cumulative effects of high-grading on the long-term ecological integrity of the Tongass.

... As a result of logging in conservation priority watersheds and sub-watershed core areas, Audubon contends that the Amended Plan is an unacceptable risk for maintaining ecosystem integrity, habitat diversity, and abundant populations of fish and wildlife well distributed across the Tongass.

To reduce significant conservation risks to the Tongass Forest, Audubon seeks relief through the following modifications to the Amended Plan:

» Establish clear biogeographic province goals for maintaining the natural range of environmental variability across the Tongass, including protection of rare habitats and forest types (e.g., large tree floodplain and karst forest and cedar stands), and establish thresholds of habitat diversity (e.g., a minimum of 50%) and watershed intactness below which timber harvest and road construction will not occur.
» Protect Conservation Priority Watersheds throughout each biogeographic province of the Tongass . . .
» Protect old growth within the Core Areas of ecological values within Integrated Management Watersheds throughout each biogeographic province of the Tongass.
» Adjust the ASQ (allowable timber harvest) based on a more realistic assessment of market demand and timber supply and to minimize the disproportionate harvest of rare forest types, including large-tree stands, karst forest, and cedar trees.

In retrospect, phase 1 of the new forest plan bought us some time to protect some of the most ecologically valuable intact watersheds remaining on the Tongass. However, the plan did not provide a long-term conservation strategy for maintaining the natural diversity of habitats nor the ecological integrity of the forest. Much work remained to ensure that this rainforest ecosystem was sustainably managed to support the diversity and abundance of the region's fish and wildlife populations in the long-term best interest of the American public.

2008 TONGASS SCIENCE CRUISE

In the spring of 2007, Stan received a call from the David and Lucile Packard Foundation about the potential for a special grant for science-based work on the Tongass. We discussed this opportunity and decided that one of our key needs was to broaden our science outreach and engage scientists from outside

Alaska in the Tongass issue. Over the next two months, we put together a proposal to host a Tongass scientists' cruise in northern Southeast, and then convene a Tongass science conference in Juneau the following year. Our Packard grant was approved, and the next spring, Dave Albert and I, along with Matt Kirchhoff from ADF&G, hosted seven scientists on a six-day cruise aboard the seventy-foot vessel *Sundance* in mid-May 2008 (Fig. 3.19).

Our primary goals were to discuss strategies for conserving biodiversity and ecological integrity of Southeast Alaska and the Tongass National Forest, as well as seek peer review of the Audubon-TNC conservation assessment. We also used this group of scientists as a steering committee to design the agenda for the Tongass Science Conference.

The invited scientists included seven academics and researchers with expertise in ecological science and natural resource policy: Paul Alaback, University of Montana; Joe Cook, University of New Mexico; Andy MacKinnon, British Columbia Ministry of Forests; Martin Nie, University of Montana; Barry Noon, Colorado State University; Gordon Orians, University of Washington; and David Secord, Wilburforce Foundation and University of Washington. Each scientist was sent a copy of our conservation assessment and conservation strategy, the record of decision for the 2008 Tongass Land Management Plan, and a variety of other information.

I have included selected excerpts from my field journal to capture the flavor and extent of our experiences and discussions during this stimulating scientific exploration through the coastal waters, islands, and forests of the northern Tongass.

5-19-08: Juneau, scattered overcast: When the scientists arrived in Juneau, they were briefed by state and federal agency experts about the Tongass forest and wildlife ecology and management.... We flew over the Mendenhall Glacier then headed to north Admiralty, and across Chatham Strait to northeastern Chichagof. We crossed over Spasski Bay, Hoonah, Game Creek (where we observed extensive Native corporation logging). Then we viewed the patchwork of clear-cuts on Forest Service lands at Freshwater Bay, Pavlof Harbor, and across Tenakee Inlet to Corner Bay. We next overflew Kadashan, Crab Bay, and Saltry Bay, which are mostly unlogged, and then landed on the water at Tenakee Springs.

We ... boarded the Sundance, owned and operated by Will Petrich and his wife Melanie. After stowing our gear, we headed up Tenakee Inlet to Long Bay observing humpback whales, eagles, ravens, marbled murrelets, pigeon guillemots, and harbor seals. We anchored at the head of Long Bay at 1830.... During our first evening aboard looking out across our anchorage at old-growth spruce and hemlock trees crowding the shoreline, we shared enthusiastic discussions about what we learned from our flight and

FIG. 3.19. The research vessel *Sundance* in Tenakee Inlet. We used this boat for our Tongass science cruise from northeastern Chichagof Island to Juneau.

today's expert presentations covering a wide array of Tongass conservation and management issues.

The aerial overview during our flight to Tenakee provided everyone with an excellent opportunity to see and understand the inherent patchiness of the forest, how much of the landscape is dominated by high-elevation subalpine and alpine habitats, and how limited the low-elevation productive forest lands are. Compared to the forests farther south in the Pacific Northwest, those on the Tongass are naturally much more scattered and fragmented. Both Paul and Joe were intimately familiar with the Tongass from their previous research. Paul had focused many years of his research on the forest ecology of Southeast, while Joe is recognized as the world's expert on the island biogeography of mammals of this coastal region. Their local knowledge, along with the interdisciplinary expertise of our other invited scientists, led to great discussions throughout our cruise as we dissected each day's activities and considered and vigorously debated various strategies for conserving the ecological integrity of the Tongass.

5-20: Long Bay, Tenakee Inlet, broken overcast.

0900: We began hiking along the beach at the edge of the forest toward grass flats at the head of the bay where we entered the flood plain forest. We observed many small salmon fry in the intertidal area near the estuary. As we hiked along the shoreline, Dave Secord shared much of his knowledge of marine invertebrate ecology. We saw deer grazing along wetlands and much evidence of recent deer sign. We also observed fresh bear tracks and scat as well as their recent excavations for the succulent roots of skunk cabbage. It took our group a great deal of time to move a small distance as we shared ideas and information from a multidisciplinary perspective which included forest ecology, ornithology, mammalogy, lichenology, wildlife biology, and marine biology. Zack, the first mate, exclaimed that he had never seen a group move so slowly and espouse so much information.

Under the forest canopy of old growth, Paul Alaback and Andy MacKinnon described the structure of this forest and how it differs from younger forests and those further to the south in British Columbia and Washington. Andy and Paul are coauthors of the excellent field guide *Plants of Coastal British Columbia including Washington, Oregon, and Alaska*, edited by Pojar and Mackinnon.

1715: Anchored at the head of Crab Bay where we observed many marbled murrelets on the water as we cruised into bay [Fig. 3.20]. We all went ashore to look for the big spruce tree that I had located two years earlier with Doug Chadwick during our *National Geographic* cruise. I did not have a GPS coordinate for this location so we were on a wild spruce chase and I received more and more friendly criticism the further up the slope we walked in search of this tree. I told them that I thought it was one of the biggest trees in Alaska. This was an incredible forested slope with many large spruce and hemlocks scattered across the lower hillside.

1800: Whew! I found the big spruce. I had my tripod and camera, so this time I got good images including a group photo of our science crew [Fig. 3.21]. Matt ran a tape around the base of the tree and it measured 9.45 feet in diameter. This would make it one of the ten biggest trees currently known to exist in Alaska based on the Landmark Trees Project described earlier. Matt also estimated the height at 190 feet. There was an old notch at the base suggesting that someone had considered cutting this with a springboard during the early hand logging era.

1930: Back on the *Sundance* our happy crew was ready for cocktails and dinner.

5-21: Crab Bay, Tenakee Inlet, broken overcast breaks of sun.

1300: We cruised a short distance to anchor off the Kadashan River estuary. This watershed ranked number one out of seventy-three watersheds for overall biological values in the East Chichagof Province. Zack ferried three skiff loads of us up the lower river on the rising tide. While at Kadashan, we observed six different brown bears including one grazing on sedges right in front of our team . . . and some fine riparian large-tree spruce-hemlock stands.

This excursion was particularly satisfying for me because of all the research I had conducted on deer and bears in the Kadashan watershed when I worked for ADF&G. Those experiences gave me a special fondness for this extraordinary place.

FIG. 3.20. A marbled murrelet in breeding plumage on the water in Southeast Alaska. These small seabirds often nest on the large limbs of old-growth trees. Southeast Alaska has the world's highest-density breeding population of marbled murrelets.

FIG. 3.21. Large, old-growth Sitka spruce tree in Crab Bay with our team of scientists. This tree measured nine and a half feet in diameter. Top row from left to right: Andy MacKinnon, Martin Nie, Paul Alaback, Gordon Orians, Joe Cook, Matt Kirchhoff; bottom: Dave Secord, Barry Noon, John Schoen, Dave Albert.

Kadashan is a large watershed for Southeast, encompassing nearly 35,000 acres. It is nearly pristine, having had some minor logging years ago, and then, of course, it had the short-lived road construction that was stopped by court order in the early 1980s. The river has abundant runs of pink, chum, and coho salmon plus steelhead trout. The brown bear population is highly productive. On an early summer evening, I have watched more than a dozen brown bears grazing on the sedge flats of this very large estuary along with hundreds of Canada geese and other birds. In midsummer, hiking up bear trails under the rich riparian forest canopy with scattered giant spruce trees, it is not unusual to see hundreds of salmon carcasses that brown bears have fed on. But these carcasses are also used by scores of mammals, birds, and insects. And the marine-derived nutrients that are soaked up in the soil are an important fertilizer for many riparian plants. On this occasion, we had the opportunity to share our knowledge and experience with this expert group of scientists and watch them absorb their own experiences, which I'm sure will be long remembered and cherished.

1930: We headed to the Tenakee Springs community hall where the local community graciously provided a dessert reception for our group. Dave and I outlined our project and after introductions, we had a round robin discussion that everyone entered into including our guest scientists. The majority of the community is concerned about future logging and want to maintain the environmental quality of the inlet that provides high value to their lifestyle. All in all, this was a very cordial and valuable interchange.

5-22: 1230: Anchored in Whitestone Harbor. Lunch on board and then ashore to meet Rich Jennings of the Forest Service's Hoonah Ranger District. We headed up the road through Spasski and Hoonah Totem Corp lands and Sealaska Corp lands. This area has been logged extensively by the Native corporations and the overland trip was a real eye-opener for our group. In some cases, there was logging right across the streambanks and clear-cuts hundreds of acres in size. We traveled through the corporation lands and then got back into Forest Service lands in upper Game Creek. We stopped at an old one-hundred-year-old wind forest (initiated by a major wind event) that the FS is planning to do selective or partial harvest to remove 30 to 40 percent of the basal area. Rich asked what we thought and Andy jumped right in with some specific suggestions and comments based on his forestry experience in British Columbia. It was interesting, in that I don't think the Forest Service expected us to have this level of forestry knowledge. It broke the ice and we had a good discussion.

We traveled further up the road to a recent selective harvest site operated by Wes Tyler of Icy Bay Lumber Company based in Hoonah. This was a very interesting site in that there was variable retention while individual trees were selectively harvested. The old-growth structure of the stand was maintained and there was little slash but a number of trees had been removed from the stand. Everyone in our group was impressed and enthusiastic about this kind of harvest since it more closely mimics the natural disturbance regime and maintains the old-growth character of the stand. We suspect that there may be the need later to do a pre-commercial thin if a second layer of dense hemlock comes into the stand. We asked Rich what proportion of logging on northeastern Chichagof is done like this and he said 100 percent. If we could move the Forest Service into this kind of old-growth harvest, it would be a significant conservation gain compared to clear-cutting and a movement toward a more ecologically sensitive management of the Tongass.

1830: We departed Hoonah and headed up Port Frederick for Neka Bay. Port Frederick has had substantial corporation logging. Dinner on board and then intense Tongass discussions well into the evening.

5-23: Neka Bay, Port Frederick. Clear, warm. Our crew explored the shoreline and forest on their own during the morning.

1400: Lunch and then we cruised up to the head of Port Frederick near the Portage. The rest of the afternoon was spent in extensive and lively discussions about Tongass management and conservation and we also began discussing the structure of the Tongass Science Conference to be held next February. Gordon Orians suggested restricting the conference to a few focal papers with extensive discussions. Everyone agreed with this approach and we began crafting what the conference structure should be and identified some of the key speakers.

5-24: Head of Port Frederick–Portage. Clear, warm.

1200: Depart Port Frederick bound for Juneau. Long, rigorous discussions first to finish our work on the framework and agenda for the science conference, and then a discussion of the Audubon-TNC conservation assessment. The team of visiting scientists, facilitated by Dave Secord, then crafted a set of consensus findings for the cruise and review of the Conservation Assessment.

1700: In Stephens Passage heading into Auke Bay, we encountered a pod of humpback whales including several breaching whales within 200 to 300 yards of our vessel. It was a stunning day without a cloud in the sky. Our discussions were completed and everyone was celebrating a very successful cruise!

One of the interesting discussions from our science cruise was how important the land-sea interface is within the Tongass. This region of the temperate rainforest is one of the most productive marine ecosystems of the North Pacific. Here we have glacier-fed rivers entering the Gulf of Alaska and dumping tons of nutrients into that system. And the annual migration of salmon moving upstream to spawn transfers literally tons of marine-derived nutrients into aquatic and riparian ecosystems. There are nearly 14,000 miles of anadromous fish habitat in Southeast Alaska, and the Alexander Archipelago ranks among the largest and most complex estuarine systems on Earth. It is not surprising, then, to consider that Southeast Alaska has one of the most productive salmon habitats in the Pacific. Further, Southeast Alaska has the highest-density nesting populations of marbled murrelets and bald eagles on Earth, as well as one of the highest-density brown bear populations.

What follows are key excerpts from the consensus finding and peer review of our visiting scientists.

Trip Summary and Scientific Consensus: Tongass Science Cruise,
19–24 May 2008

Distinctiveness of the Tongass and Recent Historic Change in Tongass Land Use

The Tongass is one of the largest coastal temperate rainforest ecosystems in the world, certainly the largest when considered in combination with British Columbia's Great Bear Rainforest immediately to the south. It is unique among US national forests in being by far the largest in area, but also in that it spreads across a large island archipelago, with the endemism and genetic distinctiveness typical of island ecosystems worldwide.

The Tongass features intact food webs with all trophic positions, including large predators, filled. The forest is naturally fragmented by a globally significant marine ecosystem, whose fjords produce a high prevalence of land-sea interface . . .

Despite undeveloped watersheds and roadless places, substantial change on the Tongass in the last century may limit future management options . . . Age-class distribution (of the forest) has changed, and there has been disproportionate harvest of old growth, especially non-random removal of the biggest trees in highly productive high-volume stands. Some 5,000 miles of roads now fragment the landscape, exemplifying the shifting historical baseline that forms our view of the past, present, and future of the Tongass...

Scientific Issues Raised, Key Findings and Preliminary Recommendations
We support the basic concept, methods, and analytical approach of the Audubon-TNC Conservation Assessment, Resource Synthesis, and Conservation Area Design. We find the document to be excellent overall. It is by far the best available integrated planning tool for Southeast Alaska...

TONGASS SCIENCE WORKSHOP

In mid-February 2009, over forty scientists from across the United States and British Columbia met in Juneau to participate in a two-day science workshop convened by Audubon Alaska and The Nature Conservancy. The workshop enabled us to bring to Southeast Alaska internationally recognized scientists with expertise in forest ecology and conservation biology. Our purpose was to discuss current scientific understanding of temperate rainforest ecology and how to integrate concepts of conservation biology into forest management strategies on the Tongass National Forest.

The workshop featured discussion of eight preselected focal topics. Dr. Gordon Orians, professor emeritus at University of Washington, masterfully moderated the workshop. A member of the National Academy of Sciences, Gordon was an ecology professor whom I greatly respected when I did my graduate work at Washington.

Our invited authors agreed to complete their papers four to six weeks prior to the workshop. These papers were sent to all forty-two of the invited participants several weeks prior to the workshop. At the beginning of each session, authors briefly summarized their papers. This was followed by brief remarks from two reviewers. All participants then discussed each topic in detail during two-hour sessions. Unlike traditional conferences where discussion is limited or nonexistent, this approach provided a unique opportunity for focused discussion and creative problem-solving.

Dr. Joe Cook from the University of New Mexico kicked off the workshop with a paper he coauthored with Stephen McDonald on the island biogeography of the Alexander Archipelago. Island species are particularly vulnerable to extinction, so an understanding of island biogeography is of fundamental importance for land management decisions and conserving biological diversity.

Dr. Bruce Marcot from the Forest Service's Pacific Northwest Research Station provided a review and critique of key concepts in conservation biology useful for conserving old-growth ecosystems in Southeast Alaska.

Dr. Paul Alaback from the University of Montana described natural disturbance patterns of Southeast Alaska's old-growth rainforests and the importance of maintaining the complex structural and functional patterns found in old growth for maintaining the region's biological diversity.

Dr. William Beese, from Western Forest Products in British Columbia, described the company's experience with variable retention harvesting in BC forests as a technique for maintaining greater habitat diversity. In this approach, unlike clear-cutting, mature trees are maintained within harvest units.

On the second day of the workshop, Drs. Rick Edwards and Dave D'Amore from the Forest Sciences Lab in Juneau kicked off a discussion of riparian ecology on the Tongass. We learned that the total freshwater discharge in Southeast Alaska was comparable to that of the Mississippi River. The complex interactions between marine, estuary, aquatic, and terrestrial systems are key elements that make Southeast Alaska such a highly productive ecosystem.

Dr. Dave Person from Alaska Fish and Game discussed the problems created for wildlife by converting productive old-growth forest habitat to sterile second growth. He also described the ecology of roads in Southeast Alaska and their impacts on wildlife.

Dr. Ken Lertzman and Andy MacKinnon from Simon Fraser University and the British Columbia Forest Service, respectively, evaluated the effectiveness of using intact watersheds for conserving forest ecosystems. Watersheds work well for maintaining natural habitat diversity and ecosystem integrity.

Dr. Lisa Crone from the Forest Service in Sitka provided an overview of past, present, and future commercial uses of the Tongass. Her paper generated substantial discussion of the influence of global market forces on Southeast Alaska's timber economy.

Following two days of intense interdisciplinary discussions, we offered a one-day public conference that summarized each of the focal topics, and over 200 Southeast locals attended. In addition to our previous presenters, we invited three keynote speakers to address particular perspectives on the Tongass. Byron Mallott from the First Alaskans Institute offered an Alaska Native point of view, Dr. Terry Chapin from the University of Alaska Fairbanks addressed climate change in relationship to the Tongass, and Dr. Jerry Franklin from University of Washington presented a global perspective on the conservation and management of old-growth forests.

The science workshop stimulated a valuable exchange of ideas regarding the ecology and conservation of temperate rainforests. The public conference attendees appreciated the opportunity to gain additional insights into some of the new science that will inform management decisions for our nation's largest national forest. Following the conference, Gordon and I met with the invited speakers and decided to publish the papers in a book. We contacted several publishers and got an invitation from the University of Washington Press to submit a manuscript. Gordon and I agreed to coedit the book, and soon began working with the authors to develop a draft manuscript.

COLLABORATIVE CONSERVATION EFFORTS

During this period (2008–2011), the Tongass Conservation Collaborative had formed.[15] It was not an official organization nor a complete representation of environmental groups working on the Tongass, but rather a coalition of willing players, both in-state and national, who had some relationship with the Tongass Roundtable process. The collaborative was developing a conservation framework based largely on the Audubon-TNC Conservation Area Design, with additional recommendations from others within the roundtable. Our overarching goal was to develop a pragmatic, enduring conservation strategy for the Tongass, including a blueprint for a stand-alone conservation bill that could be introduced in Congress.

This was a place-based strategy that differed from the previous Alaska Rainforest Conservation Act and the Roadless Rule in that it was strongly science-based and designated specific conservation and restoration management prescriptions on a watershed scale. Conservation areas would be established to manage old-growth forest ecosystems within intact watersheds across the Tongass. Restoration areas would be established to restore old-growth stand structure and fish and wildlife habitat, particularly riparian salmon habitat, in previously impacted watersheds within the Tongass. Through hours of meeting and mapping work over many years, we were intent on creating a strategy that could be embraced by a coalition of local, regional, and national environmental organizations.

Our April 2009 draft of this conservation framework included the following major provisions:

Fish and wildlife management areas: Establish a network of protected watersheds across the Tongass, comprising approximately 2.5 million acres, to protect, conserve, and restore watersheds of ecological importance in their natural condition. These watersheds would not be available for commercial development, timber harvesting, or new road construction. Examples of Fish and Wildlife conservation areas included Port Houghton on the mainland coast; Lake Eva, on the northern ABC Islands; Rocky Pass between Kuiu and Kupreanof Islands; and Honker Divide on Prince of Wales Island (Fig. 3.22).

FIG. 3.22. Honker Divide on north-central Prince of Wales Island is one of the few intact old-growth landscapes on this portion of the island. It provides valuable habitat for Sitka black-tailed deer and gray wolves and is an example of a Fish and Wildlife Conservation Priority Area.

Rainforest restoration areas: Establish a system of restoration watersheds within the Tongass, comprising approximately 1.8 million acres, to restore natural old-growth stand structure and stream function over the short and long term. Examples included watersheds on northern Kuiu, northern Prince of Wales, and southeastern Chichagof (Fig. 3.23).

Wilderness: Add approximately 1.2 million acres of land in the Tongass to existing Wilderness Areas designated in the Wilderness Act of 1964. Examples included Bay of Pillars on Kuiu Island and portions of the Mansfield Peninsula on Admiralty Island.

FIG. 3.23. Port Protection on northern Prince of Wales Island was identified as a Rain Forest Restoration Area.

Mount Edgecumbe National Monument: Establish a Mount Edgecumbe National Volcanic Monument, containing approximately 116,000 acres, to preserve and protect for present and future generations Mount Edgecumbe's remarkable geologic landforms and to provide for the conservation of its ecological, botanical, scientific, scenic, recreational, cultural, and fish and wildlife resources.

CRUISING COASTAL ALASKA

In 2009, Mary Beth and I had the opportunity to purchase a thirty-six-foot diesel trawler, the *Alaskan Star*, in Sitka (Fig. 3.24). It had been twenty years since we sold our boat in Juneau, and we were very excited about expanding our cruising experience from Southeast up into Prince William Sound and the Kenai Fjords. The last few years had been particularly stressful for me, and I needed a break. Cruising the coast of northern Southeast Alaska and crossing the Gulf

FIG. 3.24. Mary Beth and me on *Alaskan Star* anchored in Young's Bay on northeastern Admiralty Island. This was part of our shakedown cruise for our new boat before we headed north up the gulf coast to Prince William Sound.

of Alaska to Prince William Sound was a great opportunity for recharging my batteries and reconnecting with this wild coastal rainforest.

On June 20, Mary Beth and I flew to Sitka and outfitted our new boat for a shakedown cruise in northern Southeast before we headed out into the gulf for the long trip north up the coast to Prince William Sound. Our boat had a displacement hull and was very seaworthy. The cruising speed was only seven and a half knots, but it was fuel-efficient, burning, just a gallon and a half of diesel an hour. We spent a week cruising north through Peril Strait between Baranof and Chichagof Islands, then headed into Port Frederick on northeastern Chichagof Island. I had explored this same area during the science cruise earlier in the spring. We were delighted to be back on the water in the Tongass, where we enjoyed hiking in old-growth forests and taking in the abundance and diversity of forest and marine wildlife, including humpback whales and brown bears. Our first week on the boat was enjoyable but also immensely valuable—we discovered issues with our navigation software, steering gear, and anchor windlass that we were able to diagnose and correct before they could pose a challenging problem.

As part of our shakedown cruise, before heading north into the Gulf of Alaska, we also planned to spend time in Glacier Bay National Park to assist Matt Kirchhoff and his research team, who were conducting Kittlitz's murrelet studies in the bay. He had asked me to join him there for nine days to provide logistical support for his crew and help with their research, including photographing both Kittlitz's and marbled murrelets. We were provided a research permit to operate our boat in the national park waters, and were joined by two other boats that were also helping Matt with his research.

Glacier Bay National Park is quite a contrast to much of the Tongass Forest. The bay is a highly dynamic landscape with active glaciation and limited old-growth rainforest. When Captain George Vancouver traveled through Icy Strait in 1794, he passed by Glacier Bay, which was still covered with glacial ice. Glacier Bay has experienced one of the most rapid glacial retreats in the world. By 1879, when John Muir explored this region, the ice had retreated about thirty miles into the bay. Since then, the ice has continued to retreat to over sixty-five miles from the mouth of the bay. As we entered Glacier Bay in *Alaskan Star*, only seven glaciers still reached tidewater. Johns Hopkins Glacier is fed by heavy snowfall in the Fairweather Range, the highest coastal range in North America rising steeply from sea level to over 15,000 feet. Marine storms dump significant snowfall in these mountains, feeding the rivers of ice that flow down to saltwater. A few excerpts from my field notes of our Glacier Bay cruise follow.

7–4: Reid Inlet, Glacier Bay. Clear, high thin overcast, calm, 48 degrees.

1400: I went ashore and photographed a black oystercatcher pair feeding chicks blue mussels at the edge of tide [Fig. 3.25]. They inserted their bills between the mussel valves and then extracted meat and brought it to the downy chicks to eat. I also watched a peregrine falcon putting a stoop on Arctic terns on the point and observed a jaeger chasing terns. Terns dive-bombed me when I walked near their nesting area at upper beach. Yellow and red paintbrush were in full bloom along with beach pea and buttercups.

FIG. 3.25. An adult black oystercatcher feeding its chick blue mussels in the intertidal area of Reid Inlet, Glacier Bay National Park.

1620: Picked up some of the research crew and took them to Lamplugh Glacier where we surveyed and photographed Kittlitz's murrelets. We counted at least 300 Kittlitz's in the Lamplugh area associated with floating ice and the tideline between the glacial silt and clear water. Many murrelets had fish in their bills. Clearly, the area around Lamplugh Glacier is a hot spot for murrelets and nearly all are Kittlitz's murrelets [Fig. 3.26].

FIG. 3.26. Kittlitz's murrelet taking flight out of glacial waters of Reid Inlet in Glacier Bay National Park. These birds are commonly associated with tidewater glaciers and may be impacted by climate change.

It is interesting to note that in 1977, following our move to Juneau, Mary Beth and I joined my parents on their sailboat for a weeklong cruise from Juneau into Glacier Bay. One of our anchorages was in Reid Inlet, where we had a beautiful view of the Reid Glacier, which was still a tidewater glacier. When we anchored *Alaskan Star* in front of the Reid Glacier in July 2009, the glacier was stranded on dry land, coming in contact with saltwater only at high tide. Alaska is clearly on the front lines of climate change. Over the last half century, the average temperatures in the state have increased about twice the rate of the continental US. In my forty years of flying and boating in Alaska, I have witnessed the dramatic retreat of many glaciers in Southeast and southcentral Alaska.

7-7: Wachusett Inlet, Glacier Bay National Park, clear and unusually warm.

0630: I woke up in my bunk to deep exhalations. I thought it might be a porpoise. I walked out on deck stark naked to take a pee and I saw a brown bear foraging along the beach at low tide seventy-five yards from the boat. I dove down below to get my pants and my camera. When I came up and started photographing the bear, I heard another big exhalation and turned to see a large humpback whale asleep in the water less than 50 yards from the boat. What's a photographer to do [Figs. 3.27, 3.28]?

7-8: Glacier Bay.

1505: Anchored North Sandy Cove. We went ashore and hiked the intertidal meadows of both North and South Sandy coves. North Sandy is a much

FIG. 3.27. To our stern, a humpback whale asleep fifty yards from our boat anchored in Wachusett Inlet in Glacier Bay.

FIG. 3.28. Off our bow, a brown bear foraging along the intertidal beach for marine invertebrates. We were anchored between these two beautiful creatures enjoying the morning sun in Glacier Bay.

more protected anchorage. It is interesting that the plant growth in this area is much more advanced than further up the bay near the glaciers. There is obviously glacial rebound here as there is a young stand of spruce on the edge of the intertidal zone along with alders. This forest is transitioning into a spruce-hemlock forest from an alder, cottonwood, willow forest. Up bay there is just cottonwood, alder, and willow. Here we observed moose, bear, and wolf tracks on the beach and evidence of willow browsing and moose scat on the beach along with fresh bear scat. Salmon berries are almost ripe and cow parsnip is in flower.

1730: Back on the boat for a halibut dinner with chilled wine. What could be finer?

1900: Great dinner and calm anchorage, incredibly serene and beautiful. Tide is falling and gray beach shells are concentrated with the orange of the Fucus seaweed at mid-tide line. A smoky overcast (from northern forest fires in Canada) and an orange ball of sun high above the horizon. The distant blue mountains looking west across the bay are crisscrossed with white lines and patches of last year's heavy snowfall. Mary Beth just passed me a home baked cookie as I type up my notes while keeping vigil for that elusive bear that is, without doubt, lurking behind the forest edge. Life simply doesn't get better than this.

2000: Wolves are howling and yipping along the northeast shoreline. We can't see them but they vocalize for about five minutes.

2040: A big black bear is walking along the northeast shoreline visible from our anchorage. Looks like it is overturning rocks looking for marine invertebrates in the intertidal area. The sun, like a glowing red ball, is sliding down to the western horizon. And later the moon rose from the eastern horizon with a dull red glow.

☘

After our Glacier Bay research cruise, Mary Beth and I ran the boat back to Juneau, where we met our son Erik and his wife Jenny. They would spend a few days with us on the boat, and then Mary Beth and Jenny would fly home and Erik and two friends, John Wright and Mike Hanscam, would help me run the boat up the Gulf of Alaska to Whittier in Prince William Sound. This would be a big trip—approximately 530 miles as the albatross flies—across open ocean waters, and we would have several days of nonstop running through the night to complete our passage between protected anchorages in Yakutat, Icy Bay, and Prince William Sound.

Our short cruise with Erik and Jenny was fun and relaxing. By this time, we had learned a great deal about the boat and how it handled. On July 23, we departed Auke Bay and headed to Funter Bay on Admiralty Island. We cruised by our old Juneau home nestled in the forest above high tide in Smuggler's Cove. Off the Kitten Islands near Funter Bay on northwest Admiralty, we watched a dozen humpback whales breaching and lunge-feeding. One whale breached within fifty to one hundred feet off *Alaskan Star*'s stern while Jenny was on the aft deck fishing for salmon. What a way to start our trip. Jenny and Erik caught several silver salmon, then we headed in to anchor in Funter Bay for the evening. Our anchorage was right in the northern portion of my brown bear study area, and I could look up at Robert Barron Mountain and reminisce about capturing bears in the alpine fifteen years ago when I worked for the Alaska Department of Fish and Game.

The next morning, we picked up our crab pot and were pleased to have secured dinner with several legal-size Dungeness crabs. We departed our anchorage and headed across Chatham Strait to Point Couverden, where Jenny caught a very nice 110-pound halibut (Fig. 3.29). That evening, we enjoyed a crab, salmon, and halibut dinner with an unobstructed view of rainforest and mountains. Southeast Alaska is, without question, a rich and productive ecosystem, and we were beneficiaries of its natural bounty.

On July 26, we put Mary Beth, Jenny, and some halibut on the flight home, changed the oil on *Alaskan Star*, and welcomed John and Mike to our crew. Early that evening, we departed Auke Bay and headed to Swanson Harbor on the tip of the Chilkat Peninsula, where we anchored for the evening. The next morning, we got up bright and early and headed out Icy Strait for Cross Sound and our voyage up the coast to Prince William Sound. A few excerpts from my journal recount our Gulf of Alaska cruise.

FIG. 3.29. My son Erik and daughter-in-law Jenny cleaning Jenny's halibut on the beach at Point Couverden on the northern mainland between Admiralty Island and Glacier Bay.

7-27: Swanson Harbor, overcast and calm.

0540: Depart Swanson Harbor heading out to Cross Sound.

0920: Abeam Pt. Gustavous, Ebb tide, overcast, westerly winds at six knots, sea one foot. Observing many birds including black-legged kittiwakes, marbled and a few Kittlitz's murrelets, fork-tailed storm petrels, Bonaparte and glaucous-winged gulls, and tufted puffins.

1110: Entering mouth of North Inian Pass, ten-foot seas and fog. We are running out of Cross Sound on an ebb tide against an incoming wind and it is building up quite a short, steep sea that sometimes has waves from trough to crest close to fifteen feet. It is a very uncomfortable ride with a cross swell at times. A couple of folks getting seasick. We are now basically in dense fog running under our chart plotter, GPS, and radar.

1230: Rounding Cape Spencer, big seas and fog; once we were out of Cross Sound the short-coupled, steep swells began to moderate. After we were in the open ocean of the Gulf of Alaska, our ride was much more comfortable and everyone felt better. The boat handled the seas fine.

7-28: Gulf of Alaska abeam Fairweather Range.

0045: Abeam Lituya Bay, overcast, fog, dark, SW winds about five knots and seas are three feet. Running under GPS and radar.

1130: Fog breaking up, Mt. St Elias and Fairweather in view. Spectacular clear day, six knot wind with light chop and easy swell.

1225: Three to four Dall porpoise are surfing off our bow. All the coastal mountains are visible and spectacular. Kittiwakes, gulls and a few northern fulmars, fork-tailed storm petrels, and shearwaters have been soaring over the waves around our boat.

1515: Tied up at Yakutat City Dock, clear and sixty-four degrees.

7-29: Yakutat. Fog, wind SW five to ten knots.

0600: Depart Yakutat Dock in dense fog; all crew up. We are running in a thick ocean fog. We can see blue sky above but visibility on the water is less than a quarter of a mile.

1500: Abeam Pt Biou Spit, Icy Bay, wind ten knots, fog. Once we turned into Icy Bay we had a more comfortable ride with the swell astern. As we came into the Bay the fog lifted and we had spectacular views of Mount St. Elias, glaciers, and the adjacent mountains. We contacted the U.S. Fish & Wildlife Service vessel *Curlew* and talked with daughter Sarah who is doing murrelet research in the bay [Fig. 3.30].

FIG. 3.30. My daughter Sarah at work with the Fish and Wildlife Service capturing murrelets in Icy Bay located along the Gulf Coast between Yakutat and Cordova.

1650: We anchored up near the *Curlew* in clear weather. Sarah and the murrelet research crew came aboard and we chatted for an hour with old friends and colleagues: Sarah stayed on board for dinner with Alaskan Star's crew. It's a great treat to have both my kids on board our new boat here in Icy Bay.

7-30: Icy Bay, fog.

0455: Anchor up and headed out the bay. We snagged a couple of small bergy bits (chunks of ice) for our coolers on the way out the bay.

0635: Course set to Kayak Is at 231 degrees magnetic. We cruised up the coast in fog, four-foot ocean swell, and a SW wind at five knots.

1500: Abeam Cape Suckling 17 nautical miles to our starboard, wind West at six knots, six-foot seas, and fog. We observed many northern fulmars and a few red-necked phalaropes, and black-footed albatross around the boat.

1820: Abeam Cape St Elias at southwest end of Kayak Is where Vitus Bering made landfall in Alaska in 1741. We established a course to Hinchinbrook Entrance which was run in darkness and fog. We charted this just to the east of the shipping lane.

7-31: 0445: Cape Hinchinbrook Light visible, four to five-foot swell is running with light wind. It has been a hard, long watch in these conditions. Dawn light in the sky improves visibility and steering is easier.

0700:   Dropped hook in Rocky Bay on Montague Is in Prince William Sound. We made it! We ate a big breakfast of scrambled eggs and sausage and enjoyed the morning.

0930:   Anchor up and we headed up bay to Smith Island for some fishing. Prince William Sound is flat calm, overcast and good visibility.

1145:   Anchored off Smith Island and fished for halibut. Tufted and horned puffins around us in the water. Also, a pair of ancient murrelets and two humpback whales are feeding near the east point of the island near our anchorage. Erik caught a 155# halibut. It was quite a chore to land.

The next day, we arrived at the Whittier Harbor. We had two big days when we were under way offshore all day, through the night, and into the next morning. Making an offshore run like this in a single-engine boat always keeps the skipper alert with an ear open for unusual sounds or changes in the tone of the engine. I have to say that once we reached the protected waters of Prince William Sound, my heightened senses and level of stress declined like the moderation of a day breeze at sunset.

This was an amazing trip but hard work—not the kind of trip you take without a lot of preparation and planning. However, I have now operated my own vessels up the entire North Pacific Coast from Washington State to Alaska's Kenai Peninsula—*Orca II* from the San Juan Island up through the inland passage to Juneau, and then *Alaskan Star* from Sitka up the Gulf of Alaska to Prince William Sound, Kenai Fjords, and on to Homer. This is an incredible stretch of coastline, beautiful but unforgiving. It has been a great pleasure and given me a sense of pride to have navigated this entire stretch of rainforest coast in my own boats.

While cruising the Inside Passage in British Columbia and Alaska's southern coast from Southeast to the Kenai Peninsula, I have observed interesting similarities and contrasts. There is no doubt that, historically, the southern British Columbia coast and Vancouver Island had tremendous forests of giant spruce, hemlock, and cedar. Today, however, much of the most productive coastal BC old growth has been logged and, in some areas like Vancouver Island, the older second growth is being cut again (Fig. 3.31). A flight up the coast on a clear day provides a vivid image of the magnitude of this past timber harvest. Farther up the BC coast, many of the northern islands—particularly the outer islands—support only scrubby muskeg forests of little commercial value, while many of the northern mainland V-shaped valleys have had substantial logging in the lower floodplains. In some respects, Prince William Sound is a smaller microcosm of Southeast Alaska. Both regions encompass

FIG. 3.31. Aerial view of central Vancouver Island showing the patchwork of clear-cuts and second-growth forests and the network of logging roads that now dominate this coastal rainforest. The most productive old growth on Vancouver Island was logged many decades ago.

temperate rainforests of western hemlock and Sitka spruce. However, the quality and extent of the rainforest declines substantially in a gradient from BC up through Southeast, and then northwest across the Gulf of Alaska. In Prince William Sound, the tree line is much lower—often less than 500 feet—and the diameter of the biggest old-growth spruce and hemlock (three to four feet) is much smaller than what is found at the southern edge of Alaska's Panhandle at the Canadian border, where twelve-foot-diameter spruce used to occur and the tree line extended to 2,000 feet or more. Muskeg bogs and scrub forest are also more common in Prince William Sound than in Southeast (Fig. 3.32). The abundance and diversity of land mammals also declines as you move northwest beyond Southeast. For example, the natural range of the Sitka black-tailed deer terminated at Lynn Canal along the northern mainland of Southeast. Deer were later introduced into Yakutat, Prince William Sound, and Kodiak Island. From what I've observed, the terrestrial productivity in Prince William Sound, particularly the Kenai Fjords, appears to be significantly lower than what I have documented throughout the Tongass Forest in Southeast. This is reflected in

FIG. 3.32. Barnes Cove in Drier Bay on Knight Island in western Prince William Sound. The tree line in Prince William Sound is lower and the forests are much less productive than in Southeast Alaska.

more limited extent of old-growth rainforest caused in part by the more recent active glaciation in western Prince William Sound and especially the Kenai Fjords (Fig. 3.33).

After this cruise, I felt refreshed once again, and my passion for conservation was rekindled. It has always been important for me to get out in the field, tromp through forests, hike along beaches, and connect with wildlife and wildlands. I strongly believe that a personal engagement with nature helps people understand why conservation of the natural world is essential to our future.

FIG. 3.33. Northwestern Fjord in Kenai Fjords National Park on the east coast of the Kenai Peninsula. This area still has many tidewater glaciers and much of the habitat has only recently been deglaciated. Thus, the extent of productive forest habitat is very limited.

MY LAST ROUNDTABLE AND FAREWELL TO AUDUBON

In May 2010, I attended my last roundtable meeting in the village of Kake. For the last year, I had been serving as the acting executive director of Audubon Alaska and had many competing demands on my time. I also realized that it was unlikely I could effect any constructive change in Tongass management through my continued roundtable participation, which was filled with personal stress and frustration. Eric Myers, Audubon's policy director, joined me at the Kake roundtable, and graciously agreed to step in to represent Audubon in future roundtable discussions.

The most significant event at that Kake meeting was Alaska regional forester Beth Pendleton's announcement of the decision to "transition" from clear-cutting old-growth forests to logging second-growth stands. She quoted from secretary of agriculture Tom Vilsack's letter to the roundtable, calling for "transitioning quickly away from timber harvesting in roadless areas and old-growth forests" through the development of a "transition framework" for the Tongass National Forest. The Forest Service said this new transition would help communities and the timber industry move from an old-growth timber-based economy to a more diversified economy, providing jobs in renewable energy, forest restoration, second-growth timber, tourism, subsistence, fisheries, and mariculture industries. The announcement was met with enthusiasm from many roundtable members, but those representing the timber industry were disappointed and argued that there was not enough second-growth timber on the Tongass for a quick transition out of old growth.

In June 2010, Nils Warnock joined the staff of Audubon Alaska as its new executive director. Nils was eminently qualified for this position, having come from the Point Reyes Bird Observatory. He has a PhD in ornithology, is an international expert on shorebird ecology, and had previously conducted shorebird research in Alaska. On top of that, he is a remarkably nice guy and has a knack for getting people to work together on behalf of conservation.

Nils's arrival was a great relief to me. I agreed to continue working for Audubon on a part-time (20 percent) basis out of my home as senior science advisor. In this new capacity, I continued to share my expertise and advice with Audubon staff on a variety of issues, but my primary focus was on the Tongass and western Arctic. Most of my time during that year was working with Gordon Orians editing and writing portions of our North Pacific rainforest book. In addition, I was collaborating with my colleague Dave Albert on a paper on historical logging patterns in Southeast Alaska in review by the journal *Conservation Biology*.

I retired from Audubon in June 2011. I have excerpted below comments from my last message for the *Audubon Alaska Newsletter*.

I will be leaving Audubon after nearly 15 years to explore new opportunities and challenges. I first began work with Audubon in January of 1997 following 20+ years with the Alaska Department of Fish and Game.... Mary Beth and I plan to remain in Alaska and I will continue my life-long interest in wildlife conservation, wildlife photography, and exploring Alaska's wild lands and waters.

I plan to stay engaged in several key Alaska conservation issues, including Tongass, but at my own pace. My Audubon colleagues have my cell phone number and I will be available for quick discussions if I can help.

Audubon Alaska has a unique leadership role in Alaska conservation. We have a proven track record for pragmatic, science-based conservation work that has garnered broad respect from friends and adversaries alike. I am proud of that record that was first established by Dave Cline and expanded upon by Stan and myself. I have much confidence that our conservation legacy will continue to flourish under Nils Warnock's capable leadership . . . and dedication of Audubon Alaska's staff. We have a unique opportunity and *responsibility* in Alaska to protect ecosystems on a landscape/seascape scale with all their ecological parts. There are few places in the world where that opportunity still exists.

⚘

One afternoon, the first week after my retirement, Mary Beth and I were on our boat, *Alaskan Star*, heading up Kachemak Bay out of Homer, when my cell phone rang. I was at the helm enjoying a beautiful day looking out at snowcapped mountains and glaciers, watching sea otters and seabirds scattered across the deep blue rippled bay as we cruised along at a leisurely seven knots. I reluctantly answered my phone. It was an attorney who had caused me more than a little stress and anxiety during those days of endless meetings of the Tongass Roundtable and other environmental debates over what course of action organizations should take to conserve the Tongass. We had a short and cordial discussion. After putting my phone away, I felt a surge of relief. I was free. Now I could focus my energy on making science-based contributions to Tongass conservation without the pressure, stress, and unproductive debate that had occupied the last few years of my work. I still cared passionately about rainforest conservation on the Tongass, but I was unburdened from the interminable and ineffective internal deliberation that had characterized the last few years. The next chapter of my life had the freedom and flexibility of a kittiwake soaring over a tidal eddy, and that invigorating feeling rekindled my spirit.

⚘

Prior to my retirement from Audubon, I had begun to collaborate with Tim Bristol and Mark Kaelke, both with Trout Unlimited (TU) in Juneau, on their effort to identify key salmon watersheds on the Tongass National Forest. It was becoming increasingly clear that passing a comprehensive Tongass conservation bill was unlikely. This was in part due to the conservation community's inability to achieve consensus on a conservation strategy as well as the challenge of working with a dysfunctional Congress. Thus, we began looking at a more modest effort focused on salmon. Nearly all Alaskans share common ground in conserving salmon.

Salmon fisheries are important economic drivers throughout Southeast Alaska and provide over 10 percent of regional employment and contributed nearly $1 billion to the regional economy. According to TU, salmon harvested from the Tongass represented about 70 percent of all wild salmon harvested in our nation's national forests, and more than 25 percent of Alaska's total salmon harvest.[16]

Trout Unlimited put together a proposal—referred to as the Tongass 77—that derived in large part from the Audubon and Nature Conservancy's *Conservation Assessment of the Tongass National Forest*. This study evaluated and ranked habitat values for several focal species, including all five species of Pacific salmon that spawn in Southeast's 17,000 miles of free-flowing streams and rivers. Most fisheries biologists suggest that salmon conservation and management should take place at the scale of entire watersheds. Based on our analysis and ranking of Tongass watersheds, and the evaluation of Southeast fisheries experts and local fishermen, we identified the highest-value unprotected salmon watersheds and assigned them conservation priority. Preserving these watersheds—which encompass 1.9 million acres—would provide the foundation for long-term conservation of salmon and trout populations on the Tongass and help maintain the ecological integrity and resilience of the Tongass for its fisheries and wildlife values as pressures increase from future resource development and climate change.

⚘

In 2013, I saw the completion of two major projects I had continued to work on following my retirement from Audubon. The University of Washington Press published *North Pacific Temperate Rainforests: Ecology and Conservation,*[17] and the journal *Conservation Biology* published "Use of Historical Logging Patterns to Identify Disproportionately Logged Ecosystems within Temperate Rainforests of Southeastern Alaska."[18]

North Pacific Temperate Rainforests, which I coedited with Gordon Orians, evolved from our 2009 Tongass Science Workshop. It offered a multidisciplinary overview of key conservation and management issues pertaining to the rainforests of coastal Alaska and British Columbia. The twenty-two authors have a range of expertise from biogeography and hydrology to forest ecology and economics. Here is a brief summary of some key conclusions and recommendations from the book:

> » Indigenous people have lived in this region and used its natural resources for thousands of years and should be involved in discussions regarding land use decision-making.
> » Because connectivity in this coastal rainforest is naturally limited by water barriers and nonforest habitat, considerable endemism occurs in island populations. Overlaying this natural pattern is a network of logging roads and timber harvest units that further fragment the land-

scape. Greater attention to connectivity and endemism is necessary for strengthening conservation of this region.

» A rigorous taxonomic inventory, using modern genetic techniques, is essential for developing a comprehensive conservation strategy for the region.

» Introduction of nonnative species to islands should be prohibited.

» Because clear-cutting fundamentally alters the structure and composition of old-growth forests, transition from harvesting old growth to second growth is desirable. Where old-growth harvest occurs, it should be designed to emulate natural disturbance patterns.

» Intact watersheds are areas of the landscape with strong internal and external connections among ecosystem processes. Therefore, these watersheds have a greater likelihood of maintaining long-term ecological integrity and resilience. Because primary watersheds with their terminus in saltwater are likely to be key in capturing ecological and genetic diversity and trophic-level interactions among terrestrial and marine ecosystems, these watersheds are important conservation and restoration targets for this rainforest ecosystem.

» The remaining undeveloped and minimally developed watersheds within the coastal North Pacific temperate rainforest should be inventoried and evaluated for their geographic and ecological characteristics and conservation values. We recommend a moratorium on future development in such watersheds.

» Ecological restoration is a goal for this rainforest and should focus on riparian and upland restoration that restores the composition, structure, and function of the original forest habitat. Riparian and in-stream restoration should receive high priority.

» More emphasis should be placed on interdisciplinary and transboundary collaboration and coordination of long-term ecological research and monitoring programs and climate change. Understanding effects of climate change will also help us determine what to monitor so as to predict and understand potential negative trends affecting habitats, species, and ecosystem functionality.

In our *Conservation Biology* paper, Dave Albert and I retrospectively reviewed past logging patterns to document how logging has changed the structure of the rainforest, at the landscape scale, throughout Southeast. Although we had addressed this issue in our conservation assessment, some timber managers were still unwilling to acknowledge that high-grading was a significant issue on the Tongass. In this peer-reviewed scientific paper, we clearly demonstrated the extent of ecological changes that have occurred throughout Southeast and the Tongass. The abstract from that paper follows.

The forests of southeastern Alaska remain largely intact and contain a substantial proportion of the Earth's remaining old-growth temperate rainforest. Nonetheless, industrial-scale logging has occurred since the 1950s within a relatively narrow range of forest types that has never been quantified at a regional scale. We analyzed historical patterns of logging from 1954 through 2004 and compared the relative rates of change among forest types, landform associations, and biogeographic provinces. We found a consistent pattern of disproportionate logging at multiple scales, including large-tree stands and landscapes with contiguous productive old-growth forests. The biggest rates of change were among landform associations and biogeographic provinces that originally contained the largest concentrations of productive old growth. Although only 11.9% of productive old-growth forests have been logged region wide, large-tree stands have been reduced by at least 28.1%, karst forests by 37% and landscapes with the highest volume of contiguous old growth by 66.5%. Within some island biogeographic provinces, loss of rare forest types may place local viability of species dependent on old growth at risk of extirpation. Examination of historical patterns of change among ecological forest types can facilitate planning for conservation of biodiversity and sustainable use of forest resources.

One of the remarkable findings that came out of this study was the impact of high-grading on Prince of Wales Island. Northern Prince of Wales was historically the most productive timber-producing region in all of Alaska. Based on our research, we determined that the amount of contiguous high-volume old-growth forest on northern Prince of Wales Island had been reduced by 93.8 percent from 1954 to 2004. Today, stands of large-tree old growth have been significantly reduced in area, and the distance between these stands has been significantly increased compared to their original distribution. This habitat fragmentation will have a substantial impact on those species that rely on this old-growth forest habitat. We have already seen declines in deer populations where whole watersheds have been converted from old growth to second growth. Further, the population of the endemic Southeast Archipelago wolf, which preys largely on deer, has also declined. The significant change in ecological structure of the forest in this area will likely impact other species as well, including the Prince of Wales flying squirrel and Queen Charlotte goshawk (Fig. 3.34).

FIG. 3.34. Northern goshawks are affiliated with old-growth forest habitat. The Queen Charlotte goshawk is an endemic subspecies that occurs throughout the Tongass Forest and the islands of Haida Gwaii on the northern coast of British Columbia.

SCIENTISTS WEIGH IN ON THE TONGASS

In the spring of 2014, I worked closely with a group of scientists to craft a letter to President Obama recommending a national policy prohibiting the logging of old growth on national forest lands. Remarkably, the Tongass is the only national forest where old-growth logging is still a standard management practice. On June 25, seventy-eight scientists from across North America—including former US Forest Service chiefs Jack Ward Thomas and Mike Dombeck—sent our letter to the President of the United States. Key excerpts follow.

> We are seeking your support for a National Old-Growth Conservation Policy that would preserve existing old-growth forests within the United States. The remaining old-growth forests, from the redwoods of California, to the Douglas-fir forests of Washington, to the spruce-hemlock rainforests of southeast Alaska, provide the nation with many irreplaceable ecological benefits. These include clean water for millions of Americans, outdoor recreation, and key habitat for salmon and other important wildlife species. Because old-growth forests store vast quantities of carbon, protecting these remaining forests from logging could also play a role in reducing the effects of global climate change. . . .

> The most important ecological characteristics of old growth take centuries to develop and, hence, are never achieved in managed forests with typical harvest rotations of 50–120 years. . . .

Currently, only about 5–10% of the original old-growth forests that existed prior to European settlement remain in the United States (excluding Alaska's taiga) and most of that occurs in the Pacific Northwest and southeast Alaska. . . . The largest extent of remaining old-growth forest is found in southeast Alaska. But even there, more than half of the largest trees have been logged, and pressure continues to cut the best of what's left. The diversity and productivity of forest communities, along with the myriad of ecosystem benefits that they provide to people, have been significantly reduced.

We, the undersigned scientists, respectfully request that you direct the Secretary of Agriculture and Chief of the U.S. Forest Service to utilize their authority to craft a National Old Growth Conservation Policy that fully protects the remaining old-growth forests on national forests throughout the United States and also encourages the restoration of representative stands of mature forests where old growth has been depleted.

This letter was signed by many of the nation's eminent scientists from a broad range of academic institutions. It also included a number of former Forest Service scientists, some with specific expertise on the Tongass. As I communicated with many of these scientists, I heard a common refrain: "I can't believe the Forest Service is still clear-cutting old growth." Although our letter requested a national policy on old growth, we all recognized that the primary issue was to bring the Tongass into compliance with recent scientific understanding and modern management approaches. Unfortunately, there was no action from the Forest Service.

Later that same year, we took another shot at seeking an administrative policy to end old-growth logging on the Tongass. Working closely with several colleagues, we drafted a joint letter from seven scientific societies to secretary of agriculture Tom Vilsack seeking a transition out of logging old growth on the Tongass. Attaining signatures on a letter from seven large organizations representing thousands of scientists is not a simple task. However, we did reach consensus, and a letter was sent to the secretary on January 20, 2015, from the Alaska Chapter of the American Fisheries Society, American Ornithologists' Union, American Society of Mammalogists, Ecological Society of America, Pacific Seabird Group, Society for Conservation Biology, and The Wildlife Society. Excerpts from that letter follow.

As the nation's premiere scientific societies engaged in studies of fish, wildlife, ecology, and conservation, we are writing to express our full support for an accelerated transition away from clear-cut logging of old-growth forests on the Tongass National Forest. . . .

Because it takes centuries for forests to develop fully, the ecological characteristics of old-growth habitats, once clear-cut, are essentially lost forever. The Tongass is the only national forest in the United States where clear-cut logging of old growth still occurs. . . .

The Tongass National Forest has the greatest abundance of old growth remaining in the nation. Managing for its old-growth forests, carbon stores, and fish and wildlife populations, would provide an example to the world of the administration's commitment to climate change remediation as well as assure that the Tongass region will continue to provide robust natural resources for future generations. For these reasons, we request that you (1) provide additional guidance to the Forest Service to end clear-cut logging of old-growth forests during the forest plan amendment process, and (2) ensure that the timber industries' transition to second growth is completed as rapidly as possible, ideally within the next three years.

These seven scientific societies cumulatively represented a membership of over 30,000 North American scientists and natural resource managers. We received no response from the secretary or the Forest Service, nor did the Forest Service accelerate their promised transition out of old-growth clear-cutting on the Tongass National Forest.

TONGASS LAND MANAGEMENT PLAN AMENDMENT

Throughout most of 2015 and into 2016, the Forest Service was actively involved in amending the Tongass Land Management Plan (TLMP). I reviewed this plan closely and evaluated how well it addressed fish and wildlife conservation issues. In my career, I had reviewed every plan the Forest Service had prepared since their first Forest Plan in 1979, making this my fourth TLMP review. Without question, the Tongass National Forest has come a long way over the last thirty-eight years, when it was logging 450 million board feet annually under fifty-year timber contracts, with limited emphasis on fish and wildlife conservation. I appreciate that fact but recognize that, in many respects, forest management evolved slowly on the Tongass and required much pushing by nontimber interests. Today, although the Tongass has much more emphasis on recreation and fish and wildlife conservation, I do not believe it has kept pace with the progress that has been made on other national forests in the lower 48 states. My review and comments on the new Tongass Plan were predicated on new science on forest ecology and the growing public desire to manage America's national forests for the broader public interests beyond a focus on timber production. Excerpts from my February 20, 2016, TLMP comment letter to forest supervisor Earl Stewart follow.

The Earth's old-growth forests are today exceedingly rare. In the United States, perhaps as little as 5–10% of our original forests still remain and most of that occurs on the Tongass National Forest. The ecological structure and function of old growth requires many centuries to develop. Thus, when clear-cut on short (less than two–three century) harvest schedules, the many ecological, economic, and societal values old-growth forests support will be permanently lost. . . .

Today, the Tongass is the only national forest in the United States that is still clearcutting old growth. And the scientific support for ending this unsustainable silvicultural practice has grown dramatically as scientists increasingly learn of old growth's irreplaceable ecological and economic values to society (including ameliorating the impacts of climate change) and recognize that old growth has become an endangered ecosystem. . . .

To continue clear-cutting Tongass old growth for the next 15 years (as specified in the Plan's preferred alternative) is simply not reasonable nor scientifically supportable.

I strongly recommend that you modify the preferred TLMP alternative and complete the transition out of old growth on the Tongass within the next three years as recommended by the joint scientific societies' letter. . . .

For decades, scientists have been urging the Forest Service to end high-grading (i.e., disproportionate harvest of rare forest communities) the most valuable stands of large-tree old growth on the Tongass. . . .

I strongly recommend revising the Plan amendment to immediately terminate the high-grading of large-tree old growth on the Tongass. High-grading rare forest communities is incompatible with the goal of maintaining the natural range of forest diversity across the Tongass and ensuring adequate habitat for those plants and animals that depend on those communities.

At the end of the TLMP amendment process, I was disappointed that the Forest Service did not have a clear date for transitioning out of clear-cutting old growth and shifting their harvest focus to second growth. Recall that in 2010, the secretary of agriculture announced that the Forest Service would quickly make this transition. But eight years later, the Tongass National Forest is still clear-cutting old growth and the Forest Service's plan to "quickly transition" out of clear-cutting old growth seems to have been forgotten.

CLIMATE CHANGE

By 2000, I was becoming increasingly aware of the growing concerns about climate change and how it could impact Alaska. However, we did not explicitly address this issue in our research or conservation work on the Tongass. According to the 2018 US Climate Assessment,[19] annual average temperatures have increased by 1.8 degrees Fahrenheit across the contiguous United States since the beginning of the twentieth century. The Climate Assessment further reports that Alaska "is warming faster than any other state, and it faces a myriad of issues associated with a changing climate."

Although air and ocean temperatures in Southeast are relatively moderate compared to the rest of Alaska, the annual temperature of mainland Southeast is predicted to increase 1.6 to 2.3 degrees by 2049.[20] Over the next sixty years, Colin Shanley and colleagues project increasing mean annual temperature and precipitation, and decreasing snow throughout North America's northern coastal temperate rainforest.[21] These authors further state:

> These projected changes are anticipated to result in a cascade of ecosystem-level effects including: increased frequency of flooding and rain-on-snow events; an elevated snowline and reduced snowpack; changes in the timing and magnitude of stream flow, freshwater thermal regimes, and riverine nutrient exports; shrinking alpine habitats; altitudinal and latitudinal expansion of lowland and subalpine forest types; shifts in suitable habitat boundaries for vegetation and wildlife communities; adverse effects on species with rare ecological niches or limited dispersibility; and shifts in anadromous salmon distribution and productivity.

One of the observable effects that climate change has already had in Southeast is the decline of yellow-cedar because the lack of snow cover has resulted in the freezing of yellow-cedar roots.[22] And in my experience over the last four decades, I have seen remarkable changes in the coverage and retreat of glaciers throughout the mainland coast of Southeast Alaska.

Human-caused global climate change is real. The 2018 Climate Assessment states:

> Ecosystems and the benefits they provide to society are being altered by climate change, and these impacts are projected to continue. Without substantial and sustained reductions in global greenhouse gas emissions, transformative impacts on some ecosystems will occur; some coral reef and sea ice ecosystems are already experiencing such transformational changes.[23]

Although the scientific community has published compelling evidence of climate change and has overwhelmingly identified this as a major concern, the current political climate in the US has not supported decisive national action on this issue. In fact, as I write this section in November 2019, the Trump Administration has just notified the United Nations that it is formally withdrawing from the Paris Climate Agreement. This announcement was made in the face of indisputable scientific evidence that human-induced climate change is occurring, including five months in a row of near or record-breaking temperatures.

The denial of climate change by some industry and political leaders is, unfortunately, reminiscent of the historical denials of health risks from the tobacco and chemical industries. This also parallels agency and industry denial of the ecological harm caused from liquidating old-growth forests. According to research forester Tara Barrett, "The Tongass National Forest stores massive amounts of forest carbon, more than any other national forest in the United States. The estimated above ground average carbon density in the forest was 70 tons per acre."[24] This is estimated to represent 8 percent of the total carbon stored in the conterminous United States.[25] Conserving the old-growth forest on the Tongass will aid in ameliorating climate change, and it will increase the ecological resilience of this temperate rainforest. Conserving our nation's last remaining stands of old growth will also provide critical habitat for fish and wildlife populations dependent on old-growth forests as well as many of the ecological services these forests provide the American public.

THE BATTLE OVER THE TONGASS CONTINUES

Over the last decade, the Roadless Rule remained controversial and unsettled. Strong resistance to the Roadless Rule had come from the Bush Administration and a number of western states, including Idaho, Wyoming, and Alaska, along with most timber and mining industry advocates. Earthjustice, led by attorney Tom Waldo, and the Natural Resources Defense Council were very effective in coordinating years of legal actions for a coalition of environmental groups and Native and other interests. The Roadless Rule was one of the most broadly reviewed and supported public land management policies in the history of our nation. It received over 600 public hearings across the nation and more than 1.6 million public comments. In July 2015, the Tongass exemption issue was again addressed by the Ninth Circuit Court when it upheld a lower court decision that overturned the Tongass exemption to the Roadless Rule. However, the State of Alaska, Alaska Forest Association, and others litigated this decision. In September 2017, the US District Court for the District of Columbia ruled against the Tongass exemption to the Roadless Rule.

However, in August 2018, the Department of Agriculture signed a memorandum of understanding with the State of Alaska to prepare an Alaska-specific

version of the Roadless Rule. That same year, the Forest Service released their final record of decision to allow a sale of 235 million board feet of old-growth forest on Prince of Wales Island over the next fifteen years. This new timber sale would be the largest in decades and focused on an area that had already been extensively clear-cut and is covered by a vast network of logging roads.

In October 2019, the Forest Service issued a plan and draft environmental impact statement to completely exempt the Tongass National Forest from the 2002 Roadless Area Conservation Rule, thus lifting the prohibition on timber harvest and road construction on 9.2 million acres of inventoried roadless areas of the Tongass Forest. The combination of the Prince of Wales timber sale and exemption of the Roadless Rule will result in further high-grading of the rarest, most valuable old-growth habitat, lead to unsustainable forest management, and risk significant impacts to fish and wildlife, as well as jeopardize subsistence fishing and hunting and two of Southeast's most significant economic drivers: fisheries and tourism.

Only time will tell what kind of future lies ahead for the Tongass National Forest. However, with each year that old-growth forests continue to be clearcut, many of the unique ecological elements of this forest will be irretrievably lost, and the conservation options for future generations will be foreclosed forever (Fig. 3.35).

FIG. 3.35.
A commercial fishboat cruising north up Sitka Sound.

4
PERSONAL REFLECTIONS

CONSERVATION

I can't recall when I first began thinking about it, but I suspect my conservation philosophy began to emerge when I was a teenager on Orcas Island, hunting deer in the forest behind our home, digging clams and collecting oysters off our beach, or diving for abalone and rock scallops in the intertidal waters of the San Juan Islands. Our family's harvesting rule was simple: don't take more than you can use, and don't concentrate your taking in one place. That basic approach describes my place-based conservation strategy. After going to college and majoring in biology, my conservation philosophy evolved; after grad school, I gained the tools to ground my conservation philosophy in ecological theory.

For me, conservation includes protecting and managing natural resources—from berries and fish to trees and deer—so that they are available in perpetuity for others to use and enjoy. In 1905, Gifford Pinchot, appointed by President Theodore Roosevelt as the first chief of the United States Forest Service, described the purpose of conservation as managing resources "to provide the greatest good to the greatest number of people for the longest time." Conservation, in my opinion, includes both preservation and use. But the key is *sustainable* use and enjoyment of those resources over time measured in decades and centuries.

Early in my career with ADF&G, when I was first doing deer research on the Tongass, I was often asked by forest managers and administrators, "How many deer do you need?" Underlying that question was the assumption that there would always be some deer left after harvesting timber—timber was more important because it provided jobs and a strong economy. The conventional wisdom at that time was that logging benefited deer. However, the more we learned about old-growth forests—including differences in various types of old growth—the more we began to understand that many other species also used old-growth habitat, including bears, marten, flying squirrels, bald eagles, marbled murrelets, goshawks, salmon, and many other fish and wildlife species (Fig. 4.1). And those species depended on a variety of old-growth habitat types that were not necessarily the same as optimal winter deer habitat. In the early stages of our research, it became clear to us that conservation on the Tongass was not just about deer. Fundamentally, conservation was about sustaining the natural diversity and integrity—structure, function, and diversity—of the ecosystem.

Aldo Leopold said:

The last word in ignorance is the man who says of an animal or plant, "What good is it?" If the land mechanism as a whole is good, then every part is good, whether we understand it or not. If the biota, in the course of eons, has built something we like but do not understand, then who but a fool would discard seemingly useless parts? To keep every cog and wheel is the first precaution of intelligent tinkering.[1]

I believe strongly in Leopold's tenet that the "first principle of conservation is to preserve all the parts." Keeping all the parts of an ecosystem should be the foundation of any conservation strategy for our public lands. This does not mean that those lands should be protected from any human uses. But it is imperative that all of the ecological parts should be sustained over time. On the Tongass, high-grading the rare, large-tree old growth violates Leopold's first principle of conservation just as much as threatening the existence of individual species—like king salmon, grizzly bears, or spotted owls—that has occurred on public lands and waters south of Alaska's border.

The concept of conservation must be broadened beyond simply protecting rare, threatened, or endangered species. It must encompass sustaining the integrity of ecosystems, including species, distinct populations, discrete habitat types, and the natural diversity, structure, and function of the ecological communities that make up the greater whole. On an ecosystem level, the whole is greater than the sum of the parts.

☙

Many resource uses are compatible with long-term conservation. Hiking, birding, wildlife study and viewing, hunting, and commercial, sport, and subsistence fishing can be accommodated—if managed responsibly—without

FIG. 4.1. The Tongass National Forest has the highest-density nesting population of bald eagles in the world. Preferred nesting habitat is in the tops of large old-growth trees with sturdy branches in close proximity to shoreline habitat.

FIG. 4.2.
The large tidal estuary at the mouth of the Stikine River on the mainland coast southeast of Petersburg is highly productive and also represents a major transboundary river corridor with Canada.

diminishing the resilience and productivity of the land or water. And even some resource extractive activities can occur on nonwilderness public lands without substantially impacting habitat quality if designed and implemented at an appropriate scale. For example, in many regions of North America where the original old growth has been removed and second- and third-growth forests are under forest management, dispersing timber harvests over time and space can be reasonable management tools to maintain and even enhance fish and wildlife habitat values. But as some ecosystems and distinct habitat types become rare, the best management option is to conserve them so they don't lose their functional role in the larger ecosystem. On a broad geographic scale, this would include tallgrass prairies, natural riparian and wetland habitats, and the few remaining old-growth forests. It is also important to recognize that "preserving" small remnants of these ecosystems or habitats is not a viable conservation option. Fragmentation of habitats into smaller, more isolated patches is also a serious threat to maintaining ecological function. Conservation of large contiguous blocks of habitat must be a fundamental goal of conservation.

In Southeast Alaska, rare or uncommon habitats and communities that should receive a strong conservation focus include large-tree old growth, karst forests, riparian floodplains, and tidal estuaries (Fig. 4.2). These habitats provide many species with unique structural and functional attributes not found

in other more common and abundant habitat types. Habitat diversity provides fish and wildlife species greater options for meeting their needs during changing seasons and environmental conditions. For example, deer use a variety of old-growth habitats throughout the year. During deep winter snow conditions, however, they require large-tree old growth at lower elevations to survive those winters. If those rare habitat types are eliminated, fragmented, or reduced in abundance, deer populations will not be as resilient throughout changing environmental conditions.

Even at the species level, it is important to maintain population diversity. Ecological theory suggests that biological diversity stabilizes ecosystems. In natural biological systems, salmon are a perfect example. Scientists have determined that each individual run of native salmon species found in different stream and river systems is a genetically distinct population; they vary in their morphology and the times that they enter freshwater to spawn. This diversity is an important evolutionary mechanism that allows the species to adapt to environmental change. It also has significant economic implications for subsistence, recreational, and commercial fisheries, which are major economic drivers across Southeast (Fig. 4.3).

Five decades of research on sockeye salmon in Bristol Bay, Alaska, have provided clear evidence that population diversity stabilizes overall salmon

FIG. 4.3. Commercial purse seiners fishing the productive marine waters of Southeast Alaska. The Tongass National Forest produces more economic value from fishing than any national forest in the US. Fishing and tourism are major economic drivers in Southeast.

productivity in that region.[2] Dan Schindler and colleagues established that if the Bristol Bay sockeye salmon population was made up of only one population, rather than its several hundred distinct populations, the variability of returns would be twice as high. Their results also demonstrated that this population diversity stabilizes the annual salmon harvest. Without that diversity, they estimated there would be a tenfold increase in fishery closures for Bristol Bay. They call this the "portfolio effect," and it is analogous to maintaining financial stability by creating a diversified portfolio of investments. There is no better example than Alaska salmon to demonstrate the importance of biological diversity and compatibility of habitat conservation with healthy food security and associated economic prosperity.

⚜

The history of protected lands in the United States—and most of the world—reveals that nearly all of these areas were originally of lower biological productivity than the lands that were first chosen for development. Consider our national parks. Most of these areas, though scenic and possessing high recreational and wilderness qualities, do not, for the most part, represent the most biologically productive lands on the continent. They also do not represent the natural distribution of habitats or wildlife that occurred there three centuries ago. Today, for example, the old-growth evergreen-hardwood forests of the Eastern Seaboard and upper Midwest, the tallgrass prairies, and the coastal redwood forests are represented by only fragmented remnants of their natural distribution and diversity. And those fragments no longer function the way they did centuries earlier. Nor do they provide adequate and resilient habitats to sustain viable populations of their original flora or fauna.

Nevertheless, we still have some important conservation opportunities to fill gaps in our public lands' network of protected areas, including state and national parks, refuges, and forests. Filling those gaps must ensure that we include as many of the rare and underrepresented lands and waters as possible. A variety of land use designations—including wilderness areas, preserves, refuges, parks, recreation areas, and multiple use areas—will be critical for successful ecosystem conservation. And adequate funding is also necessary for enforcement, management, research, and public education. On Alaska's Tongass National Forest, we still have outstanding opportunities to conserve the full range of natural diversity within the north Pacific temperate rainforest. But those opportunities continue to be inexorably foreclosed by incremental development, resulting in ultimate death by a thousand cuts.

⚜

A significant but often overlooked problem in natural resource conservation is that of the shifting baseline. Daniel Pauly at the University of British Columbia developed this concept and applied it to fisheries management.[3] It emphasizes the importance of identifying the appropriate baseline from which to measure change. What may appear stable over the course of the last ten to twenty years may, in fact, represent significant change when measured over five to ten decades or more. Many marine fisheries, from the Atlantic salmon and cod to salmon and herring stocks of the Pacific Coast, provide good examples of changing baselines. The abundance and harvest of those species is today but a fraction of what was harvested a century or more ago, but the slow, incremental changes proceeded without adequate management measures to sustain healthy stocks.

I was raised in western Washington and did my graduate work on the west slope of the Cascade Mountains. But I never had an opportunity to see Washington's once-magnificent stands of giant conifers. In 1900s, immense spruce, hemlock, cedar, and Douglas fir trees were abundant throughout these productive lowland forests. Darius and Tabitha Kinsey photographed the forests and timber operations in western Washington during the 1880s through 1920s.[4] Their photographs documented redcedar trees that were twenty to thirty feet in diameter as well as Douglas fir trees sixteen feet in diameter and over 350 feet tall. When I was a young child, I recall driving by a twenty-foot-diameter redcedar stump at a rest area along the I-5 highway north of Everett (Fig. 4.4). That stump is still there, but there are virtually no trees like this left in western Washington today except for a few individual relics in Olympic National Park. Over the last century, the shifting baseline of Washington State's giant evergreen trees left us with an entirely different forest before most people recognized what was happening. Then it was too late to reverse the eradication of those once magnificent forests.

My late friend Don Schmiege, former director of the US Forest Service's Forest Sciences Lab in Juneau, once told me that in the early 1960s he had asked Forest Service timber managers to set aside, for scientific and educational purposes, some of the large-tree forests of Sitka spruce and redcedar that measured over ten to twelve feet in diameter and were still abundant in the big lowland valleys on Prince of Wales Island. Don told me they just laughed at him. For the last forty years, I have observed forest managers discount small incremental changes in the abundance of old growth, and particularly large-tree stands, over the course of five to ten years—often the life of a timber sale. This lack of establishing clear scientific baselines is further exacerbated by the relatively short-term tenure of many agency managers, who after five or six years may transfer to another location, and never personally see or be held accountable for the long-term results of their management decisions.

THUJA PLICATA
GIANT ARBORVITAE
COMMONLY CALLED WESTERN REDCEDAR

FIG. 4.4.
Redcedar stump in a rest area on I-5 just north of Marysville, Washington. Trees like this used to occur throughout the productive lowlands of western Washington but now occur only as fragmented relics of ancient old-growth stands.

The most recent amendment to the Tongass Land Management Plan continues to schedule clear-cutting of the forest's rare large-tree old growth. As recently as 2018, the Forest Service released a record of decision for a massive old-growth timber sale on Prince of Wales Island. And the 2019 plan to exempt the Tongass from the National Roadless Rule will further liquidate those rare forest habitats. Over the next five to ten years, this may not seem significant compared to the current baseline. However, when compared to a baseline prior to initiation of industrial-scale forestry in the early 1950s, that change is highly significant. The result is an increased risk of losing key elements of the ecological structure and function of this forest. Recall that on northern Prince of Wales Island, contiguous large-tree old growth has been reduced by 94 percent since 1954. By any standard, that is not *sustainable* forest management, nor does it meet the fundamental conservation principle of preserving all the parts.

Successful conservation will ultimately be judged by our ability to maintain functional and resilient ecosystems over a time horizon of centuries for the benefit of multiple generations of Americans. That requires a focus on maintaining natural ecosystem integrity, ensuring sustainability, and safeguarding all the individual parts of each ecosystem. To do that, resource managers must recognize the perils of ignoring shifting baselines.

GOVERNMENT RESOURCE AGENCIES

I have learned that the first rule of agency leadership is to maintain the status quo. There are important exceptions to this rule, and fortunately I have had the opportunity to work under some innovative and courageous agency leaders who kept up with current research, supported their professional staffs, and placed a strong emphasis on science-based conservation. Many political appointees, however, believe that the safest course of leadership is not making waves that rock the agency boat. Most ADF&G and federal agency biologists I met during my career were well-trained scientists, had good knowledge of the resources they managed, and demonstrated a strong conservation ethic. Although administrations come and go, and agency missions often creep in the direction of the current political winds, most agency scientists and managers work diligently to maintain their ethical standards and earn the public trust.

So how should agency biologists navigate the shifting political winds? I strongly believe that each person—regardless of rank—has an important role to play in ensuring the integrity and honesty of government agencies and the *sustainable* management of our public lands. For agency scientists, publishing in peer-reviewed scientific journals is very important. This lays down a scientific record and builds a solid foundation that natural resource managers can use in their decision-making. But I believe that scientists also have an obligation beyond publishing in esoteric journals. Scientists have a responsibility to share their research findings with the broader public. The results and management implications of our science should be made readily available for agency managers, decision makers, and the general public, who seldom read the scientific literature. Although, in most cases, science does not provide direct answers to policy questions, science can inform managers and decision makers about the trade-offs associated with their management decisions. And those trade-offs should be explained in clear, understandable language free of technical jargon.

Scientific publications alone rarely create political pressure. That comes from popular publications, public presentations, and formal testimony where science is translated into management implications that heighten public interest in agency policies concerning public resources. When I found myself involved in those cases, I tried to avoid making value judgments and instead focused on describing the trade-offs associated with different management approaches. In such public settings, it is essential to present scientific findings clearly and objectively, and always avoid exaggeration. When in doubt, my rule of thumb is to err on the side of understatement. The public has a right to know what kinds of trade-offs will likely result from management decisions. It is the responsibility of resource agencies to make that information available to the people who own those resources.

All agency scientists, managers, and administrators have a responsibility to ensure that the agencies for which they work function with integrity and honesty. Although it may not be possible to change an agency position, each person has a personal duty to push their concerns up the chain of authority and make sure their supervisor understands the issues and trade-offs. Clear, concise memos make good paper/electronic trails and, ultimately, can lead to accountability.

Most government bureaucracies operate under a standard time horizon of the next election (generally two to four years). Responsible management of natural resources, however, requires a time perspective of decades and centuries. A decision to clear-cut an old-growth forest, for example, will affect the habitat values of that landscape and associated public use opportunities for centuries, if not forever.

Sometimes changing administrations can exert profound influence on agency missions and regulatory oversight. We are seeing this today as the leaders of some federal agencies have exerted pressure on their staffs to avoid using certain words such as *climate change* or science-based terminology; some agencies have even removed scientific information from their websites. These are chilling examples of a political agenda controlling the use of science. In such circumstances, it may be risky for professional scientists and resource managers to provide their expertise to decision makers and the public. However, it is clearly not acceptable, or honest, for political appointees to overrule scientists on the presentation of peer-reviewed, empirical data. Science and facts matter and should always be part of the decision-making process. Professional societies—such as the American Fisheries Society, Ecological Society of America, Society for Conservation Biology, and The Wildlife Society—can play important roles in peer-reviewing natural resource policies and making scientific findings and their management implications available to both decision makers and the public. Working through those scientific organizations can also insulate individual scientists and resource managers from political retribution.

I also encourage agency scientists and managers to take the time to work constructively with all stakeholders, including environmentalists, tribes, municipalities, industry, and the general public. In general, the professional staff of resource agencies have tremendous knowledge and interest in the conservation of the resources they manage. I believe that much perceived conflict is the result of ineffective communication and misunderstanding of terminology. It is also imperative that agency professionals are consistent and honest in their communication. And, finally, it is critical that elected public officials work to adequately fund research and management programs that underpin the stewardship of our public lands and resources. In addition, the public must exert oversight on elected officials to prevent political decisions that benefit special interests at the expense of the long-term public interest.

ENVIRONMENTAL ORGANIZATIONS

When I was growing up on Orcas Island, neither my family nor I were members of an environmental organization. When I began graduate school, I joined several professional organizations, including The Wildlife Society and the American Society of Mammalogists, but I did not actively participate in the environmental community. After we moved to Juneau and I was working as a research biologist with ADF&G, I interacted with many of the environmental organizations working on the Tongass, including the regional group SEACC as well as several national groups like the National Audubon Society and The Wilderness Society. However, to maintain my scientific credibility, I purposely avoided actively participating in any of those groups as a member.

I have used the terms *environmental* and *conservation* somewhat synonymously here, but I need to further clarify how these terms were perceived by many Alaskans. As a practicing wildlife scientist, I have always considered myself to be a conservationist, and conservation was always the foundation for my professional work. Conservation is explicit in the missions of both ADF&G's Division of Wildlife Conservation and Audubon Alaska. Many Alaskans, however, have a negative view of environmentalism and consider "environmentalists" to be a threat to their economic prosperity. This always puzzled me, because there is so much shared common ground among fishers, hunters, birders, hikers, subsistence resource users, and most outdoor-oriented Alaskans. Some of this environmental bias grew out of President Carter's use of the Antiquities Act in setting aside national monuments in Alaska, followed by passage of the Alaska National Interest Lands Conservation Act (ANILCA) in 1980.

ANILCA provided special protections to over 157 million acres of Alaska land, including national parks, wildlife refuges, national forests, and new designated wilderness areas. Many longtime Alaskans resented this so-called "lockup" of federal lands. Alaskans who considered ANILCA a lockup resented the federal government dictating how they could use and access those new parks, refuges, and wilderness areas, and they laid the blame on environmentalists. Thus, I found that it was easier and less divisive to simply describe myself as a "conservationist" as opposed to an "environmentalist." While this distinction may not make sense, it was a fact of life in Alaska forty years ago when you could see bumper stickers saying "Sierra Club kiss my axe." It is still somewhat true today.

After I began my Southeast Alaska deer research, one of my first interactions with the environmental community was contentious. Sometime around 1977–1978, a local environmentalist quoted me incorrectly about our initial research. I was very cautious about how I framed our preliminary research findings, but this individual deliberately played loose with the facts and basically hung me out to dry in order to score a short-term win. I was very disappointed in that kind of environmental activism that purposely misrepresented our research. Soon after that, however, I developed a cordial and honest working relationship with a number of environmentalists who understood the importance of science. Jim Stratton became director of the Southeast Alaska Conservation Council (SEACC), and Steve Kallick was their new attorney. Jim was later followed by Bart Koehler and then John Sisk. In those early days, I gained a solid appreciation for the conservation leadership at SEACC, and their integrity and willingness to base their conservation advocacy on a solid foundation of science. This led to increased trust and respect. Another organization that gained my early respect was the Audubon Society, led in Alaska by David Cline, a former wildlife scientist in Alaska with the US Fish and Wildlife Service.

During the Tongass battles of the 1980s leading up to passage of the Tongass Timber Reform Act of 1990, I was impressed with Bart Koehler and the SEACC staff's effectiveness in building their conservation message around Alaskans' common interest in maintaining habitat to support productive populations of salmon, deer, and other wildlife. These values were shared by commercial, sport, and subsistence fishermen; Native subsistence hunters and sport hunters; tourism operators; and a wide variety of other Alaska outdoor enthusiasts. A recognition of shared values brought these diverse groups together to support needed conservation measures on the Tongass.

In 1997, after I retired from the Alaska Department of Fish and Game and began working for Audubon Alaska, I remained engaged in many of the same conservation issues. As a conservation/environmental leader, I continued to base my conservation work on a solid foundation of science. I soon recognized, however, that some environmentalists used science when it supported their goals but ignored it when it was inconvenient. In the resource agency culture, there were often political pressures to ignore science, but most of the staff biologists consistently pushed back against those pressures. In the environmental community, staff scientists were the exception rather than the rule during the 1990s.

The subtle differences in organizational culture between natural resource agencies and environmental organizations generated stress that I dealt with throughout my career. At ADF&G, I was often pushing the envelope on conservation and resisted political pressures to minimize public discussion of the management implications of our research. I strongly believed that conservation was a fundamental part of the job, and we had a responsibility to share our scientific findings with the public. In contrast, I sometimes felt like I was swimming upstream within the environmental community when I insisted upon sticking to the facts and avoiding hyperbole and exaggeration about environmental impacts. As a scientist, my credibility has always been my stock-in-trade, and I guarded that fervently throughout my career, regardless of the organization I worked for.

In recent years, more environmental organizations have been using science to guide their conservation advocacy. On the other hand, there are some industries and corporations that are notorious for cherry-picking the science that best supports their agenda, and even some public agencies and political leaders that are either ignoring or rejecting peer-reviewed scientific findings (e.g., climate change). If you use science as a foundation to inform policy decisions, you need to respect the science and stick to the facts. This is the way to build credibility and support within a broader coalition of interests. If you adjust science to support your own ends, your credibility is lost. It is important to understand that science informs decisions. It does not necessarily lead one to a decision.

I understand the frustrations that many environmentalists have when working with agency decision makers, politicians, and industry leaders who misrepresent facts and environmental impacts. History, of course, is replete with examples of industrial and government opposition to environmental regulations (such as the National Environmental Policy Act) that could affect an industry's bottom line. I always thought it was curious that industry—with its clear financial stake—often receives the benefit of doubt from resource agencies in environmental disputes with NGOs. The environmental community has a critical and important role to play as watchdogs in the management of our public lands and waters, and there are many dedicated environmentalists working very hard, with relatively minimal compensation, to protect the public interest. A friend of mine who worked for the oil industry in Alaska once told me how important it was to have environmental oversight. He said that industry always makes decisions based on their bottom line. Environmental groups need to insist that, where environmental regulations are needed, they must be rigorously enforced, even if that results in more cost to the company. The public interest depends on those checks and balances.

When I served as a conservation representative on the Tongass Futures Roundtable, we considered a compromise solution that would provide for the permanent protection of many intact watersheds with the highest biological values on the forest. The trade-off was providing the timber industry with more certainty and access to areas they could harvest that had lower fish and wildlife values. This was a controversial proposal that was opposed by several representatives from both environmental and timber interests. In retrospect, one of the problems associated with our approach, within the environmental community, was identifying lower-priority lands where timber could be harvested. Some environmental groups assumed we were advocating for logging those areas, rather than seeking a solution that would protect the highest-priority conservation and restoration watersheds. Solving big conservation problems by consensus is never easy. In a stakeholder process such as the Tongass Futures Roundtable, it comes down to the ability of individual people—not organizations—to build trust through honest and open dialogue from which agreement can be forged.

In a resource-based economy like Alaska, it is unlikely that we will, in the near term, enjoy a conservation majority. However, I believe there are opportunities to expand the support for pragmatic conservation. One such opportunity is to work collaboratively with more stakeholders—Native communities, fishers, hunters, guides, tourism businesses, and others—who depend on and use Alaska's fish, wildlife, and wild lands, both personally and in their business ventures. Building those alliances is a long-term process that requires humility, effort, and cross-cultural skills of all kinds.

SCIENCE

As I reflect over the last four decades, I have seen a growing popular rejection in the United States of scientific expertise. Nowhere is this more apparent than in the widespread denial of climate change by many political leaders and a substantial segment of the general public. In a 2015 *National Geographic* article, "The Age of Disbelief," Joel Achenbach wrote, "Empowered by their own sources of information and their own interpretations of research, doubters have declared war on the consensus of experts."[5] In that same article, Dr. Marcia McNutt, director of the National Academy of Sciences, stated, "Science is not a body of facts. Science is a method for deciding whether what we choose to believe has a basis in the laws of nature or not."

I think there is generally a broad public misunderstanding of what constitutes science, or the scientific method, and of how public land managers can use science to inform their decision-making. The scientific method involves gathering objective observational and measurement data that serves as evidence to use in experiments that test hypotheses from which conclusions can be derived. Other key elements in the scientific method are replication, peer review, and publication.

Many people believe that different scientists may have access to different facts or "alternative facts." This concept often leads to the dilemma of dueling scientists, such as those industry-sponsored scientists who disregarded warnings about the health risks of toxic chemical pesticides, tobacco, or addictive prescription drugs. But we need to recognize that science is based on a rigorous methodology. A political change of administration does not, and should not, change the science upon which policies are based. Science is a skeptical, questioning process. Hypotheses are crafted and then submitted to rigorous and systematic testing to disprove or accept them.

For centuries, there has been a tension between scientists' new theories and the cultural and political status quo. Proving that the Earth is round and that it orbits the sun was anathema to many religions and existing cultural beliefs, just as Darwin was considered heretical because of his theory of evolution through natural selection. Today, in the United States, we face similar battles over the compelling scientific evidence, accumulated by interdisciplinary scientists from around the world, that the climate is changing as a result of human activity, that this change has grave risks to all life on Earth, and climate change will have huge economic costs. The question now is: How many conservation options will be foreclosed before decision makers and the public step beyond their political tribalism and respond to facts based on rigorous scientific methodology and peer review?

When I began my professional career in Alaska, I naively thought we could use science and common sense to find reasonable solutions to our conservation challenges. However, science doesn't give you the answer. Instead, it provides tools and information for making informed decisions. But all too frequently, it seems like money and power politics trump facts, reason, and sometimes the broader public interest. In the long run, however, I believe that science and fact-based decision-making will remain a fundamental and critical part of our American culture and democratic process. It is imperative today that scientists provide the public with an understanding of their scientific results and the management implications of their work. Admittedly, translating scientific findings for the public without being labeled as an advocate for a specific policy is a fine line to walk. Each scientist must find their own balance in making their science more broadly available while also maintaining their credibility.

BALANCING RESOURCE MANAGEMENT IN SOUTHEAST ALASKA

Seeking balance in resource management is not easy, particularly when it involves public lands and waters of both local and national interest that many stakeholders care deeply about but also have varied perspectives for how those resources should be managed. The Tongass Forest encompasses about 80 percent of the land base of Southeast. Because it is a national forest, managing this public resource must account for regional, state, and national interests.

A review of the Southeast Conference's 2018 report[6] on the regional economy of Southeast Alaska provides the following statistics. Southeast's population was 72,915 in 2017. The top economic sectors were government (35%), visitor industry (11%), commercial fishing and seafood industry (10%), and health care (9%). The total labor force in 2017 was 45,640. The visitor industry and commercial fishing and seafood industry accounted for 17 and 8 percent of the labor force respectively, while the timber industry accounted for less than 1 percent. Tourism is a vibrant and growing industry in Southeast, and commercial, sport, and subsistence fishing continue to be mainstays of the economy. These important economic drivers depend on maintaining a healthy, productive forest ecosystem. Compared to other economic sectors, the timber industry in Southeast has declined significantly from its peak in the 1990s. According to a recent report from Taxpayers for Common Sense, over the last twenty years, the Tongass National Forest has lost an average of $30 million annually on its timber management program, or about $600 million over the last twenty years.[7]

⚜

It is instructive to review the mission of the US Forest Service: "To sustain the health, diversity, and productivity of the Nation's forests and grasslands to meet the needs of present and future generations." Under the Multiple Use-Sustained Yield Act of 1960, national forest lands are to be managed in trust for the American public for "outdoor recreation, range, timber, watershed, and wildlife and fish purposes." The National Forest Management Act (NFMA) of 1976 (and its planning regulations of 2012) requires that forest plans must provide for "ecological sustainability" and "ecosystem integrity." In addition, forest plans "must provide for the diversity of plant and animal communities."

The Forest Service definitions for sustainability and ecological integrity are as follows:

Sustainability. The capability to meet the needs of the present generation without compromising the ability of future generations to meet their needs. For purposes of this part, 'ecological sustainability' refers to the capability of ecosystems to maintain ecological integrity . . .

Ecological integrity. The quality or condition of an ecosystem when its dominant ecological characteristics (for example, composition, structure, function, connectivity, and species composition and diversity) occur within the natural range of variation and can withstand and recover from most perturbations imposed by natural environmental dynamics or human influence.

These definitions are critical for understanding how the Forest Service is meeting its forest management and conservation mandates. If we consider that productive old growth on the Tongass is a nonrenewable resource under standard timber harvest schedules, it is clear that the historical pattern of logging throughout Southeast Alaska and the Tongass National Forest has had a major impact on the "composition, structure, function, and connectivity" of this ecosystem. Arguably, the integrity of this ecosystem is at risk, particularly in heavily harvested regions of the Tongass like northern Prince of Wales Island, where the diversity, structure, and connectivity of plant communities (a requirement of NFMA) have been significantly altered from their natural range of variation. At the same time, the resilience of this ecosystem is also being stressed by climate change.

FINAL THOUGHTS ON FOUR DECADES OF MY TONGASS ODYSSEY

Few places on Earth have large intact landscapes that still function much as they have for millennia. The Tongass National Forest contains the largest expanse of old-growth forest in the United States. Together with the forests of the northern British Columbia coast, this region encompasses the greatest intact temperate rainforest remaining on Earth. But this rainforest's ecological integrity is at risk.

After serving on the Tongass Futures Roundtable for five years, commenting on the most recent Tongass Plan Amendment, watching the Forest Service fail to follow through on their transition out of old-growth logging (promised in 2010), and seeing plans to significantly increase old-growth clear-cutting on Prince of Wales and exempt the Tongass from the National Roadless Rule, I no longer consider a compromise solution involving continued clear-cutting of Tongass old growth to be scientifically justifiable or ecologically and economically sustainable. The science is definitive. It is past time to end old-growth clear-cutting on the Tongass—as it has been stopped on all other national forests in the United States.

At what point do we recognize that continued exploitation of a limited natural resource—a population, species, or ecological community—has gone too far? In the early 1800s, the passenger pigeon was common and numbered in the hundreds of millions; a century later, it was extinct.[8] The plains bison of North America numbered in the tens of millions in the first half of the 1800s, but commercial incentives for hunting bison, together with the settlement of the American West, brought bison to the precipice of extinction in the 1880s.[9]

Today only one free-ranging herd persists—in Yellowstone National Park. By the early 1900s, nearly all the expansive tallgrass prairies were gone from the American plains. By the mid-1900s, small fragments of old-growth forests were all that remained across much of their original distribution in the contiguous United States. Today, these species and ecosystems no longer play a functional role across their historic range. Instead, they are either gone or have become relics of the past—functionally extinct in terms of their natural role in the ecosystem.

Salmon were once abundant throughout the northern Atlantic and Pacific Oceans, and spawned in tremendous numbers throughout the rivers and streams of Europe, much of the East Coast of North America, and the Pacific Northwest. University of Washington professor David Montgomery has documented that, for all intents and purposes, wild Atlantic salmon have become functionally extinct over most of their former range, and the Pacific salmon has declined dramatically in the Pacific Northwest, where many populations are now listed as threatened or endangered.[10] He noted that for over 100 years, fisheries managers knew what was necessary to conserve salmon. However, the market forces of dams, logging, habitat loss, water pollution, and overfishing precluded conservation of this valuable renewable resource.

The clear-cutting of old growth is an archaic and unsustainable timber practice. This appraisal was clearly articulated in 2014 when many scientists—including two former chiefs of the Forest Service—wrote the president, requesting "a national old growth conservation policy that fully protects the remaining old growth on national forests throughout the United States." The many sustainable resource uses on the Tongass—from subsistence harvesting of fish and wildlife to commercial and sportfishing, tourism and outdoor recreation, and carbon storage—are at risk from continued logging of old growth.

As I reflect on the last forty years, I am gratified to see many positive changes in forest management. But at the same time, I am disappointed that many needed conservation measures are still slow in coming. How have I come to terms with my inability to effect more critical and enduring conservation on the Tongass? Fundamentally, I don't want to become a zealot, lose my scientific credibility, or substantially erode my quality of life. I wanted to attain a balanced life of passion for my personal interests and family and friends while also aspiring to meet my personal responsibilities and ethics as a scientist and citizen. The challenge for me was in identifying what I could reasonably accomplish, work toward achieving those goals, and accept what I was unable to change. Although this is easy to articulate, it is difficult to achieve, and often led to significant highs and lows in my emotional outlook. Throughout these years, it was critically important for me to seek balance between professional work and spending time outdoors—exploring the backcountry, observing and photographing wildlife, hiking, skiing, fishing, hunting, and sharing quality time with family and friends. When I am able to maintain that balance, I remain optimistic, happy, and effective.

Ultimately, my goal in writing this memoir was to document the shifting baseline of forest management on the Tongass and what we learned over the last four decades of scientific research. As Winston Churchill allegedly said, in a 1948 speech to the House of Commons, "Those who fail to learn from history are condemned to repeat it." It is important that people recognize that for over thirty years, scientists and forest managers understood the ecological values of old-growth forests and realized that clear-cutting those forests was not sustainable. But national and regional leadership of the Tongass National Forest was slow to change and failed to integrate new science into their forest management. Why did this happen? Political influence by the timber industry and the Alaska congressional delegation pressured the Forest Service to disregard both science and public opinion, and continue clear-cutting old growth for short-term economic gain—although highly subsidized—at the expense of the broader, long-term public interest. I hope this story will provide a realistic baseline and explicit notice to the stewards of our public lands that they must become more transparent and accountable if they are "to provide the greatest good to the greatest number of people for the longest time."

Six principles have been the foundation for my conservation work in Alaska.

1. **Conservation is Job #1.** The trees, deer, bears, birds, salmon, and other wildlife do not have a voice. As conservation practitioners, it is our responsibility to evaluate the consequences of management of our public lands and waters and the long-term effects that management has on our nation's fish and wildlife heritage. Our overarching goal—supported by legal mandates—is to ensure that this natural heritage will endure long after we are gone.

2. **It's all about the ecosystem.** Today, habitat loss and fragmentation are two of the most significant causes of species extinction. Wildlife exist in complex relationships within their ecological communities. Protecting *all the parts* of the ecosystem—distinct populations, species, habitat types, ecological communities, and ecosystem structure, function, and processes—is a fundamental principle of conservation.

3. **Science matters.** Science provides indispensable tools for making informed decisions about management of our public resources. We have a *responsibility* to ensure that peer-reviewed science is part of the decision-making process, and that scientific findings are made accessible and clearly explained to decision makers and the public.

4. **Integrity is fundamental.** When we don't know, we must be honest and

say we don't know and never exaggerate for effect. Credibility is our most important asset, and we must steadfastly protect it.

5. **Speak truth to power.** Whether it's a congressperson, a regional forester, an agency director, corporate attorney, or conservation activist, our basic message and facts should not change. They may not agree with us, and decisions may not go as we would like, but we should not be intimidated by positions of power.

6. **Seek balance in life.** It's difficult to be effective and maintain a passion for work on something you don't understand and value. The restorative quality of getting outdoors and maintaining a connection with nature enhances job effectiveness and the joy of living well. Sharing experience in nature with family and friends is priceless.

RAINFOREST DREAM

I have a dream. In my dream, it's 2028 and I'm hiking up the Kadashan River with my grandchildren, fifteen-year-old Maya and twelve-year-old Toby. (My first visit to Kadashan, on Chichagof Island, was in 1977 when I started my Alaska deer research [Fig. 4.5].) It's early July, and we're sitting on a big, shaggy beach log at the high-tide line just below a stringer of Sitka spruce trees. We're looking northwest across the river delta over a dense patch of beach rye. I explain to Maya and Toby that fifty years ago I used to fly a small airplane from Juneau to Kadashan and land on this strip of beach. I studied wildlife here to try and understand how they make their living in this coastal rainforest. In my dream, it's midtide and very noisy with flocks of gulls and crows scattered up and down the river along with a few ravens and eagles. All these birds and myriad other creatures are beginning to congregate here as they prepare for another summer's bounty of Pacific salmon—the priceless gift that returns from the sea like clockwork each summer. We see a gaggle of geese dispersed across the flats grazing on sedges that grow on these upper tidelands just below the zone of beach rye. We hike into the woods, to the old abandoned Kadashan road. It is slowly being reclaimed by a thick growth of alder and hemlock. The Kadashan cabin and weir are long gone, but the salmon still make their way upriver by the tens of thousands, feeding the bears and the eagles and the giant trees themselves. Young people are veritable sponges for soaking up nature's secrets. And building awareness of nature and its value to our lives will, I believe, lead to future actions to conserve our wildland heritage. Memories flood through my mind as I recall past experiences of discovery and the joy of doing fieldwork in this rich rainforest ecosystem.

FIG. 4.5. The Kadashan River winds its way up through the extensive wetland delta into riparian spruce old-growth forest. Three species of salmon plus steelhead spawn in this river and provide important food for bears and many other mammals and birds. There are few intact coastal watersheds left in the world that still maintain their natural ecological integrity like the Kadashan. Places like this have priceless value to current and future generations of Americans.

I am lucky. In my dream, Maya and Toby indulge their eighty-one-year-old grandpa with their interest and enthusiasm for this great northern rainforest and the fish and wildlife it supports. I tell them that when their Daddy and Auntie were little, they also visited Kadashan when I was doing research here on brown bears. Of course, they want to see bears. We hike up the river's east bank, following a well-used bear trail that meanders in and out of the ragged edge of the old-growth forest. We hear the occasional melodic song of the hermit thrush and electric trill of varied thrush. With my new hearing aids, I can once again enjoy this forest symphony. In places along the trail, we could see distinctive, enormous depressions in the moss made from the footprints of bears that have for centuries ambled over the same trails we're walking on today.

We also gaze at the dark shadows moving through the deeper river eddies as dense schools of pink and chum salmon begin their ancestral migration up their natal streams to dig their redds and spawn. Both grandchildren know a great deal about salmon and their cycle of life because their dad is a fisheries scientist. But in spite of their knowledge, they are excited about being here and observing this impressive spectacle of nature. In my experience, it is rare to find anyone who is not impressed by this primordial cycle of life that occurs in such abundance beneath the canopy of ancient trees.

In some of the shallow riffles, we watch large numbers of individual fish and are able to sort out the smaller pink salmon from the chums. The male pinks have grotesque humped backs while the larger chums have purple and green banding on their sides. We also see occasional salmon with large holes ripped out of their backs. As we move farther into the forest, we see partially eaten carcasses scattered along the gravel bars, up along the riverbanks, and well into the forest below majestic spruce trees. The stink of rotten fish envelops us like the smoke from a smoldering woodfire. All these carcasses provide critical, life-sustaining nutrition to many species of birds, mammals, insects, and plants. I explain that scientists have discovered that marine nitrogen—derived from salmon—has been found in the needles of spruce and the leaves of devil's club and other plants. You can also identify this marine nitrogen in the hair of bears that partake each summer and fall in nature's bountiful smorgasbord of Pacific salmon (Fig. 4.6).

My grandchildren love the adventure of our hike and stick close in anticipation of the possibility—likelihood—of glimpsing a bear. They ask me about the trees. We sit on the riverbank again and look at a large spruce five to six feet in diameter. It is surrounded by devil's club and stink currant. There are also big patches of salmonberry scattered in forest openings, and next to a giant spruce is a large oval depression in the earth where a bear has made a day bed. Few limbs occur below twenty-five feet, but deep mounds of moss encrust the larger branches, and gray lichens hang like shaggy beards from the outer limbs. This tree towers at least 150 feet above us. They ask how old it is. Without tak-

FIG. 4.6. A coastal brown bear feeding on a spawning salmon. Salmon anchor the productivity of the coastal rainforest ecosystem. Salmon provide over 100 species of birds, mammals, fish, and invertebrates with valuable food resources.

ing an increment core to count the annual rings, I can't be sure, but I guess it's probably at least 400 years old. I tell them that this tree was a seedling around the time that Jamestown, Virginia, was established. And at that time, Haida and Tlingit communities were thriving in what is now the Tongass National Forest, and had existed there for millennia without impacting the integrity of the forest ecosystem including its salmon and large trees. This tree was about 150 years old when our country declared its independence from England. The first Russian colony at Sitka began when it was about 180 years old, and it was over 300 years old when Alaska gained statehood. And this spruce is not one of the ancient trees of Southeast. The oldest trees approach 1,000 years of age—about the time that brown bears and most of the original forests were extirpated from the British Isles. In my dream, my grandkids are impressed with our back-of-the-envelope history lesson, and I am grateful that they are interested in the natural history of Southeast.

As we hike farther through the riparian spruce forest, we encounter a small wetland meadow full of skunk cabbage with enormous leaves and upright yellow flowers. Some of these have been dug out of the boggy muck, their white roots partially consumed by bears that were also foraging on a variety of berries and sedges. But now the bears are focused largely on salmon. We next discover a huge pile of gray, sloppy bear dung. This bear was clearly gorging on fish. Because my grandkids are young and relatively untainted by peer pressure, this kind of stuff is still cool. I'm on a roll, sharing my knowledge and love of this place with my grandchildren. Mary Beth and I raised our own children, Erik and Sarah, this same way. I think these kinds of early childhood experiences are becoming increasingly rare today as we enter the era of urban living and pervasive digital entertainment. And I suspect our society will be the poorer for the loss of these encounters with the natural world.

Our next surprise is the glimpse of a Sitka black-tailed doe foraging on bunchberry and five-leaved bramble near the base of a large hemlock tree. I suggest that she probably has a young fawn hidden somewhere nearby. We watch her as she glides daintily through the forest. The wind is light, but she picks up our scent and bounds into the understory vegetation and out of sight. I ask my grandkids if they can see a difference between this forest stand and the one where we found the bear scat and day bed. They are surprisingly perceptive as they describe the forest here as more open, with fewer bushes and different trees. Yep, this is a hemlock-spruce forest with blueberry shrubs and lots of herbaceous understory plants that deer prefer over the devil's club and salmonberry that dominate the riparian spruce forest. I explain how the spruce with their scaly gray bark tend to be larger than the hemlocks, which have shaggier brown bark. But the best trick for learning to distinguish the two is feeling their needles. They both agree that spruce needles are sharp and hemlock are soft and lacy. Simple differences but easily remembered.

FIG. 4.7. A dark chocolate brown bear standing on the edge of the old-growth spruce forest along the Kadashan River delta that I encountered at close range over thirty years ago while hiking downstream in the late afternoon.

We sit on an old nurse log with dozens of young hemlock seedlings popping out of the moss and admire the forest spread out before us. The sizes and ages of these trees are amazingly variable, and, looking through the stand, you get a sense of layered vegetation with soft, gentle shafts of sunlight streaming at an angle through the forest canopy. We talk about the variety and beauty of this forest, and how it changes quickly from one acre to the next. I'm excited because they are learning to recognize the unique character of an old-growth forest. We continue walking.

As we poke our heads out through the edge of the beach-fringe forest, we see a mother bear and two yearling cubs grazing on sedges 200 yards across the delta. We sit quietly on the bank and watch the bears through our binoculars. "Wow, this is really cool." We sit quietly for many minutes just absorbing the nature, wildness, and charm of Kadashan. Half an hour later, as we walk downstream through chest-high beach rye, we encounter a single bear less than fifty yards away watching us at the forest edge. We stop. The bear stands up to get a better look at us. There are three of us, and there are no surprises, no threats. This is the magic hour. We watch this bear for perhaps a minute in the early-evening light until it drops down and dissolves like an apparition beneath ancient spruce trees. We continue to stand there as the evening sun slips toward the mountains behind Tenakee Inlet. No one says anything at first; then both kids excitedly recall their experience watching this bear up close. They think that Kadashan is magical—and so do I. Later that evening, I describe to my grandchildren the small but rewarding role I played in keeping Kadashan wild (Fig. 4.7).

Appendix I:
Southeast Alaska and
Tongass National Forest Facts

» Coastal temperate rainforests are rare and represent less than 2 percent of the Earth's forest cover.

» The Pacific Northwest temperate rainforest, from northern California to southern Alaska, is the largest temperate rainforest on Earth. Most of this temperate rainforest south of central British Columbia has had extensive logging and road development.

» The most significant area of intact coastal temperate rainforest in the world occurs along the coast of northern British Columbia through Southeast Alaska.

» Southeast Alaska extends north from the Canadian border at Dixon Entrance over 450 miles to Yakutat Bay and encompasses about 21.6 million acres. This region is dominated by the Alexander Archipelago and a narrow ribbon of mainland bounded by coastal mountains along the Canadian border and the Gulf of Alaska.

» Southeast Alaska encompasses approximately 18,000 miles of marine shoreline and more than 5,500 islands.

» More than 1,000 glaciers occur in Southeast Alaska covering about 5,600 square miles.

» More than 12,000 estuaries are distributed throughout Southeast Alaska.

» Over 5,500 streams, rivers, and lakes extending over 17,000 miles support spawning runs for five salmon species plus steelhead trout; about

80 percent of the commercial salmon catch in Southeast spawns on the Tongass Forest.

» The Tongass National Forest represents about 80 percent of Southeast Alaska and at 16.8 million acres is the largest national forest in the US. Glacier Bay National Park represents 12 percent of Southeast. The remainder of land in Southeast is state, municipal, or private.

» Approximately 73,000 people live in Southeast Alaska; Juneau, the largest city and state capital, has a population of about 30,000 people.

» Annual precipitation is high and is distributed throughout the year. Most places in the region receive over 60 inches per year (double that of Seattle). The wettest weather stations get over 200 inches a year. Higher elevations (above 2,000 feet) receive two to three times the precipitation at sea level.

» Deep winter snow accumulations are common at elevations above 1,500 feet and at sea level along the northern mainland coast.

» The Tongass Forest encompasses about 30 percent of the Earth's remaining old-growth, coastal temperate rainforest and the vast majority of old-growth forest remaining in the United States.

» Old growth includes trees of all ages from seedlings and sapling to old trees (some as old as 1,000 years); age of dominant trees generally exceeds 300 years. These forests have a multilayered canopy of tree limbs which allows sunlight to penetrate the forest, resulting in a lush forest floor plant community of herbs, ferns, mosses, and shrubs. This complex forest structure provides a variety of habitats that support an abundance and diversity of fish and wildlife populations.

» In second-growth forests (the result of clear-cutting) all the trees are the same age and approximate size, and, because the dense forest canopy heavily shades these forests, there is little plant growth on the forest floor. Second-growth forests provide lower habitat values for most species of fish and wildlife. Because it takes several centuries for a clear-cut forest to develop the ecological characteristics of old-growth forests are essentially nonrenewable when managed for clear-cutting every 100 years.

» Only about half of the Tongass National Forest is actually forested, with the rest of the lands consisting primarily of rock, ice, alpine tundra, shrubs, and muskeg bogs.

» Productive old-growth forest (of potential commercial timber quality) represents less than 30 percent of the entire Tongass land base.

» Over 450,000 acres have been clear-cut on the Tongass, as well as an additional 320,000 acres on state and private lands in Southeast Alaska.

» Large-tree old-growth forests (with a mean diameter greater than 21 inches) are rare on the Tongass (representing less than 3 percent of the land base), and about half of the original stands of large-tree old growth have already been logged. The most productive stands of ancient spruce and hemlock trees (with some individual trees ranging from four to ten feet in diameter) were the target of much early logging and have become very rare today.

» Congressionally protected areas of the Tongass represent 6.6 million acres. Glacier Bay National Park consists of another 2.7 million acres. Much of the land base in these protected areas is dominated by nonforest lands and scrub or small-tree forest.

Appendix 2:
Historical Benchmarks in Southeast
Alaska and the Tongass National Forest

» 2.6 million years before present: During the Pleistocene glaciation
(2.6 million to 12,000 years ago), most of Southeast Alaska was covered
by ice. At the end of the Pleistocene, the ice sheet began retreating to the
east, and many plant and animal species began to colonize or recolonize
this coastal region. The dynamic glacial history of this area, sea level
changes, an archipelago of thousands of islands, and a fragmented coast
with many large, coastal fjords have molded a distinctive assemblage of
species and subspecies of plants and animals on different islands.

» 10,000 years before present: Southeast Alaska's lands and waters have
been the ancestral home of Indigenous Tlingit and Haida peoples for
approximately 10,000 years (since retreat of the last major ice cover).
Much of Southeast Alaska was inhabited by the Tlingit people. The range
of the Haida was centered on Haida Gwaii (Queen Charlotte Islands) on
the northern British Columbia Coast, but the northern Haida also lived
on Prince of Wales Island. The Tsimshian people from northwestern
British Columbia have occupied Annette Island since 1887. Southeast
Alaska's abundant fish, wildlife, and forest resources were the foundation
upon which the Indigenous people lived and developed a rich cultural
heritage.

» 1741: The Vitus Bering Expedition from Russia made sightings of land in
Southeast Alaska.

- » 1775: The Spanish expedition under command of Captain Quadra anchored in Krestof Bay near present-day Sitka.
- » 1778: The English expedition under Captain Cook visited northern Southeast Alaska.
- » 1793: Captain Vancouver explored much of Southeast Alaska.
- » 1799: Russia established a post in Sitka. Small-scale logging for local and regional use began during the early Russian occupation and continued under American settlement through the first half of the 1900s. Most early timber harvest was done by hand, logging selected high-value trees along the shoreline.
- » 1867: The United States purchased Alaska from Russia.
- » 1878: First salmon cannery was built in southeastern Alaska. Commercial fishing was the major economic driver of Southeast Alaska from the 1880s through the mid-1950s.
- » 1879: John Muir visited Glacier Bay.
- » 1899: Harriman Expedition traveled through southeastern Alaska.
- » 1902: Alexander Archipelago Forest Reserve established by President Theodore Roosevelt.
- » 1907: Alexander Archipelago Forest Reserve expanded to 15 million acres by President Roosevelt and renamed the Tongass National Forest.
- » 1923: Six small saw mills were processing Tongass timber for local regional use and some export.
- » 1925: President Coolidge designated much of Glacier Bay as a National Monument.
- » 1940s: During World War II, Sitka spruce was logged from Kosciusko Island to provide strong, lightweight timber for aircraft construction.
- » 1947: Congress passed the Tongass Timber Act, which authorized long-term (fifty-year) timber contracts to supply Tongass wood to pulp mills in Southeast Alaska.
- » 1951: The Tongass Forest signed the final fifty-year contract with Ketchikan Pulp Co. for timber on Prince of Wales and Revillagigedo Islands. The mill began operation in 1954, initiating the industrial-scale timber industry in Alaska.
- » 1957: The Alaska Lumber and Pulp Co. of Sitka was granted a fifty-year contract for timber harvest on Baranof and Chichagof Islands in northern Southeast Alaska.
- » 1959: Alaska was granted statehood. Fish and wildlife management became the state's responsibility.
- » 1960: Forest Service's plan for the Tongass was to clear-cut 95 percent of the forest as expeditiously as possible to establish new stands of second-growth trees. Pulp was exported to Japan and the Pacific Northwest, while the highest-quality lumber went primarily to Japan.

» 1965: Maximum timber harvest on the Tongass forest occurred between 1965 and 1981, with peak annual harvests averaging about 20,000 acres.

» 1971: Congress passed the Alaska Native Claims Settlement Act (ANCSA) which established a regional Native corporation (Sealaska) and twelve Native village corporations in Southeast Alaska. In total, these corporations were granted approximately 660,000 acres (including surface and subsurface estate) to select from the Tongass Forest. The corporations largely focused their selections on the best timberlands of the Tongass with the intent of exporting timber.

» 1976: A long-term timber sale planned for Admiralty Island to supply a third pulp mill in Southeast Alaska was canceled largely as a result of public opposition based on concern over impacts to fish and wildlife.

» 1978: President Carter, using his power under the Antiquities Act of 1906, established Misty Fiords and Admiralty Island National Monuments.

» 1979: The Tongass Forest completed the Tongass Land Management Plan. This was the first forest plan in the national forest system, and it charted the course of timber management on the Tongass for the next eighteen years.

» 1980: Congress passed the Alaska National Interest Lands Conservation Act (ANILCA), which designated wilderness on 5.5 million acres of the Tongass National Forest. ANILCA identified subsistence use of fish and wildlife resources as a priority use of federal lands in Alaska. Section 705 of ANILCA also authorized the Forest Service to offer 450 million board feet of timber per year for sale from the Tongass and provided a minimum $40 million per year to build logging roads. These targets were designed to maintain timber jobs in Southeast Alaska.

» 1990: The year of maximum overall timber harvest in Southeast Alaska. From the mid-1980s through the early '90s, logging was near its peak on both Forest Service and Native Corporation lands, approaching one billion board feet of timber in 1990.

» 1990: Congress passed the Tongass Timber Reform Act largely as a result of environmental concern over the impacts of clearcut logging on fish and wildlife habitat. An additional 280,483 acres of wilderness was established plus 727,762 acres of Land Use Designation II (roadless fish and wildlife habitat areas closed to logging). The act also repealed the mandated timber harvest target and the $40 million subsidy, and required that harvest of high-volume old-growth timber stands not exceed their proportional occurrence on the forest. This last requirement basically prohibited high-grading of the best (high-volume or large-tree) old-growth stands.

» 1990s: The long-term timber contracts were ended in the 1990s (ALP in 1993, KPC in 1997) and logging on national forest land substantially declined by the mid-1990s at which time Native corporation logging became the major source of wood from Alaska.

» 1997: The Tongass Forest completed the second Tongass Land Management Plan. It included a set of large, medium, and small old-growth reserves, designed to maintain viable, well-distributed populations of vertebrate wildlife across the Tongass Forest.

» 2001: The US Forest Service included the Tongass National Forest in President Clinton's Roadless Rule. This affected 109 inventoried roadless areas, encompassing 9.3 million acres of the Tongass that would be removed from road-based development projects including commercial logging.

» 2003: The Bush Administration exempted the Tongass from the Roadless Rule.

» 2006: Inaugural meeting of the Tongass Futures Roundtable convened.

» 2007: *Conservation Assessment of the Coastal Forests and Mountains Ecoregion of Southeastern Alaska and the Tongass National Forest* was published by Audubon Alaska and The Nature Conservancy.

» 2007: The Sealaska lands bill (Southeast Alaska Native Land Entitlement Finalization Act) was first proposed by Congressman Don Young and introduced in both the House and Senate through 2013. This bill would amend ANCSA to provide Sealaska Corporation with new land selections for logging, including a significant portion of the remaining large-tree old-growth forest.

» 2008: The Forest Service revised the Tongass Land Management Plan.

» 2008: The Tongass Science Cruise was organized by Audubon and TNC.

» 2009: The Tongass Science Workshop and Conference was held in Juneau.

» 2009: Tongass Futures Roundtable considered and rejected a compromise solution for balancing timber and conservation on the Tongass.

» 2010: The Forest Service announced the Tongass Transition, which described a shift from harvesting old growth to second growth and a renewed focus on forest restoration.

» 2013: The Tongass 77 congressional proposal was launched by Trout Unlimited and partners, including Audubon Alaska, Alaska Conservation Foundation, and others.

» 2013: Tongass Forest released its record of decision on the Big Thorne Project on Prince of Wales Island. This large timber sale allowed the harvest of 149 million board feet of timber, including 6,186 acres of old growth and 2,299 acres of second growth and allowed construction of 46 miles of new logging roads.

» 2013: *North Pacific Temperate Rainforests: Ecology and Conservation* was published by the University of Washington Press.

» 2014: A group of North American scientists (including two former chiefs of the Forest Service) wrote a letter to President Obama recommending a national policy prohibiting the logging of old growth on National Forest system lands.

» 2014: Congress passed the Sealaska Lands Bill in which Sealaska Corporation received 68,400 acres from the Tongass National Forest for timber development.

» 2015: Seven scientific societies sent a letter to the secretary of agriculture asking him to end old-growth clear-cutting on the Tongass within the next three years.

» 2015: The Ninth Circuit Court upheld a lower court decision that over-turned the Tongass exemption to the Roadless Rule.

» 2016: The Tongass Land Management Plan was amended and included a decision to continue clear-cutting old-growth forests on the Tongass.

» 2019: The Forest Service record of decision allowed 235 million board feet of old-growth timber sale on Prince of Wales Island over the next fifteen years.

» 2019: The Forest Service Draft Environmental Impact Statement identi-fied a preferred alternative to exempt the Tongass National Forest from the National Roadless Rule.

Appendix 3:
Glossary of Technical Terms

Many of these definitions have been excerpted or adapted from US Forest Service documents, including the 2016 Tongass National Forest Land and Resource Management Plan, and various ecology textbooks.

Alexander Archipelago: The offshore islands of southeastern Alaska from Glacier Bay to the Canadian border.

Alluvial soils: Recent soil deposits from rivers and streams, laid down along river beds, stream sides, flood plains, and estuaries. These well-drained alluvial soils provide a productive substrate for trees and other vegetation.

Anadromous fish: Fish, including salmon and steelhead, that mature and spend much of their adult life in the ocean, returning to freshwater streams to spawn.

Biogeographic provinces: Twenty-two ecological subdivisions of southeastern Alaska that are identified by generally distinct ecological, physiographic, and biogeographic features. Examples include Admiralty Island, North Prince of Wales Island, and Stikine River.

Biological diversity: The variety of life, including diversity of gene pools, species, communities, landscapes, and ecological processes like predation, decomposition, parasitism, and nutrient cycling.

Biological hot spots: Geographical areas with particularly high habitat values for fish and wildlife and areas with high levels of species diversity and/or abundance.

Canopy: The top or overstory of a forest stand, including treetops and limbs that intercept sunlight and snow, resulting in shade and snow-free patches on the forest floor.

Canopy gaps: Natural openings in the forest overstory created from the loss of single trees or small groups of trees caused by windthrow, insects, or disease.

Carrying capacity: The concept that there is a maximum population size an ecosystem can sustain without causing long-term habitat damage and a reduction in the population size.

Clear-cut: Forest harvesting method in which all trees are cleared in one cut. Clear-cuts produce an even-aged stand of second-growth timber.

Climate change: Since the industrial revolution, climate change across the Earth has been documented by climate scientists as a result of the increasing release of greenhouse gases (such as CO_2 and methane) that trap heat within the Earth's atmosphere. Increasing temperatures have led to significant changes in weather patterns and the distribution and behavior of species and the function of ecosystems.

Conservation: The management of natural resources to prevent overexploitation or destruction. The management of human uses of fish, wildlife, or other natural resources to yield the greatest sustainable benefit to current generations while maintaining options for future generations. This definition of conservation encompasses preservation, maintenance, sustainable use, restoration, and enhancement.

Conservation Area Design: A proposal to identify, on a map, watersheds of high ecological value that should be protected from logging and road construction, as well as identifies high-value watersheds that had previously been logged that should be restored, watersheds with lower ecological values (e.g., non-forest icefields and mountainous, muskeg bogs, scrub forests), and lower-value watersheds that had previously been logged that could be available for further logging.

Conservation assessment: An ecological report prepared by Audubon Alaska and The Nature Conservancy that assessed the ecological resources and development infrastructure across Southeast Alaska. It also ranked the ecological values of watersheds in each biogeographic region of Southeast and developed a conservation strategy for Southeast and the Tongass.

Conservation Priority Watersheds: Intact watersheds in Southeast that have the highest ecological values for fish, wildlife, and old-growth forest communities.

Ecological parts: All the parts of an ecosystem, including individual plant, animal, and other species, habitat types, and ecological processes such as predation, parasitism, and nutrient cycling.

Ecology: The relationships of organisms to their physical environment and interactions among organisms.

Ecosystem: An interacting ecological community together with its physical environment, considered as a unit. Ecosystems can be defined at various scales from a small pond to a large region like southeastern Alaska.

Ecosystem integrity: The maintenance of an ecosystem's biological diversity (e.g., genes, species, populations, communities, landscapes) and ecological processes (e.g., predator-prey relationships, herbivory, decomposition, nutrient cycling) within their natural range of variability over time.

Ecosystem services: Ecosystem services include the full range of goods and services that are vital to humans, including clean air and fresh water, energy, food, fuel, forage, climate regulation, water filtration, soil stabilization, flood control, pollination, seed dispersal, soil formation, and nutrient cycling, as well as educational, aesthetic, spiritual, and recreational values.

Endemic: Distribution restricted to a specific locality (for example, the Prince of Wales flying squirrel and Alexander Archipelago wolf).

Estuary: An ecological system at the mouth of a stream where freshwater and saltwater mix and where salt marshes and intertidal mudflats are present.

Floodplain: The relatively flat land with alluvial soils on either or both sides of a stream or river that is subject to flooding.

Focal species and systems: Species like salmon, brown bear, and marbled murrelets, and ecological systems like estuaries or large-tree forests, that are used as indicators of ecological values.

Geographic information systems (GIS): Data about the location and types of lands, resources, and uses within a specific area that are used to make computer-generated maps.

Habitat: The physical and biological resources required by an organism for its survival and reproduction; these requirements are species specific. Food and cover are major components of habitat and must extend beyond the requirements of the individual to include a sufficient area capable of supporting a persistent population.

Habitat fragmentation: Process by which habitats are increasingly subdivided into smaller, more isolated units.

High-grading: The disproportionate harvest of a specific forest type. For example, targeting rare, high-value forest stands in greater proportion than their occurrence on the forest.

High-volume old growth: Large-diameter trees that grow on well-drained, or karst, soils and are synonymous with large-tree old growth. These old-growth stands are rare on the Tongass but have historically been the focus of timber harvest. These stands provide important habitat for many species of fish and wildlife.

Intact watersheds: Watersheds that maintain their natural abundance and diversity of native species and natural habitats and that have had minimal or no significant resource development activities, including roads and timber harvest.

Integrated management watersheds: Watersheds that have previously been logged but still have important biological values.

Island biogeography: The theory and study of the biogeography of islands in which each island is considered an ecosystem different than surrounding islands or nearby mainlands. Island biogeography posits that islands will have fewer species than the adjacent mainland, and larger islands will have a greater number of species than a smaller island. The Tongass encompasses more than 1,000 islands, many of which have distinct species assemblages compared to the adjacent mainland and other islands of the archipelago.

Karst: A type of topography that develops in areas underlain by soluble rocks, primarily limestone. Dissolution of the subsurface strata results in areas of well-developed surface drainage that are sinkholes, collapsed channels, or caves.

Keystone species: Species that have a disproportionately large influence on other species and the ecosystem in which they occur, such as Pacific salmon, beavers, and bears.

Large-tree old growth: Large-diameter, old-growth trees that grow on well-drained productive soils. Classified by the Forest Service as SD-67 stands. Considered somewhat synonymous with high-volume old growth. Relatively rare on the Tongass Forest and have historically received disproportionate harvest pressure.

Low-volume old growth: Small-diameter, old-growth trees that grow on poorly drained soils. Classified by the Forest Service as SD-4 stands. Relatively common on the Tongass Forest and have much less economic value and thus have received less harvest pressure than high-volume old growth.

Old growth: Ecosystems distinguished by the later stages of forest development. Old growth is characterized by a patchy, multilayered canopy; trees of uneven age; large trees, snags, and woody debris on the forest floor; dominant trees over 300 years old; and a diverse and productive understory of herbs, shrubs, and ferns on the forest floor.

Old-growth reserve: A contiguous unit of old-growth forest habitat managed to maintain the integrity of the old-growth forest. Beach-fringe forest, riparian buffers, and habitat conservation areas all contain old growth reserves.

Productive old growth: Old-growth forest capable of producing at least 20 cubic feet of wood fiber per acre per year, or having greater than 8,000 board feet per acre.

Regrowth forest: Synonymous with second-growth forests.

Resilience: The ability to recover from change.

Restoration: The process of restoring to an original or natural condition.

Restoration watersheds: Managing and restoring degraded watersheds to near-natural condition. For example, restoring damaged salmon spawning habitat to original conditions.

Riparian: The streamside area including a stream channel, lake or estuary bed, and the plants that grow in the water and the land next to the water.

Science: A disciplined methodology for gathering objective observation and measurement data that serves as evidence to use in experiments that test hypotheses from which conclusions can be derived. Key elements in the scientific method are replication, peer review, and publication.

Scrub old growth: Forested lands with small stunted trees that are of no commercial value, such as trees occurring in or on the periphery of muskeg bogs.

Second growth: Young forest growth that has regenerated naturally, or has been planted, after some extreme removal of the original forest (for example, clearcut harvest, substantial forest fire, or insect attack).

Southeast Alaska: The narrow mainland coast and nearshore islands from the Canadian border south of Ketchikan to Yakutat Bay. Also termed Southeast.

Sustainable use: Management that ensures that human use of resources can be maintained indefinitely without harm to the resource.

Temperate rainforest: High-precipitation, generally coastal forests occurring across the Earth's temperate latitudes.

Umbrella species: A species selected to achieve broader conservation objectives because management that protects that species will indirectly protect other species and the ecological community they inhabit.

Viable population: For forest planning purposes, a fish or wildlife population that has the estimated number and distribution of reproductive individuals to ensure its continued existence is well distributed in a national forest. A population of a species that continues to persist over the long term with sufficient distribution to be resilient and adaptable to stressors and likely future environments.

Watershed: A distinct area bounded by ridges where all surface waters drain to a common point. Watersheds can range from less than 100 acres to more than 100,000 acres. In the Tongass Land Management Plan, Value Comparison Units (VCUs) are often analogous to watersheds or make up segments of watersheds.

Wilderness: Areas designated by congressional action under the 1964 Wilderness Act or subsequent acts. "Wilderness" is defined as undeveloped federal land retaining its primeval character and influence without permanent improvements or human habitation. Wilderness areas are protected and managed to preserve their natural conditions, which generally appear to have been affected primarily by the forces of nature, with the imprint of human activity substantially unnoticeable. On the Tongass National Forest, wilderness has been designated by the Alaska National Interest Lands Conservation Act of 1980 and Tongass Timber Reform Act of 1990.

Wildlife: The natural fauna of the region made up of birds, mammals, fish, and other organisms.

Windthrow: The act of trees being uprooted by the wind. A common natural forest disturbance in Southeast.

Appendix 4:
Scientific Names of Wild Plants, Mammals, Birds, and Fish

COMMON NAME   SCIENTIFIC NAME

Plants

Beach rye (or dunegrass)	*Elymus mollis*
Blueberry	*Vaccinium* sp.
Bigleaf maple	*Acer macrophyllum*
Bracken fern	*Pteridium aquilinum*
Bunchberry	*Cornus canadensis*
Cow parsnip	*Heracleum lanatum*
Deer cabbage	*Fauria crista-galli*
Devil's club	*Oplopanax horridus*
Douglas fir	*Pseudotsuga menziesii*
Fern-leaved goldthread	*Coptis asplenifolia*
Five-leaved bramble	*Rubus pedatus*
Labrador tea	*Ledum groenlandicum*
Lyngby sedge	*Carex lyngbyei*
Mountain hemlock	*Tsuga mertensiana*
Red alder	*Alnus rubra*
Redwood	*Sequoia sempervirens*
Salmonberry	*Rubus spectabilis*
Shore pine	*Pinus contorta*
Sitka spruce	*Picea sitchensis*
Skunk cabbage	*Lysichiton americanum*
Stink currant	*Ribes bracteosum*
Thimbleberry	*Rubus parviflorus*
Western hemlock	*Tsuga heterophylla*

COMMON NAME	SCIENTIFIC NAME
Plants	
Western redcedar	*Thuja plicata*
Willow	*Salix* sp.
Yellow-cedar	*Chamaecyparis nootkatensis*
Mammals	
Beluga whale	*Delphinapterus leucas*
Bison	*Bison bison*
Black bear	*Ursus americanus*
Bobcat	*Lynx rufus*
Brown (grizzly) bear	*Ursus arctos*
Caribou	*Rangifer tarandus*
Chipmunk	*Eutamius townsendii*
Cougar	*Felis concolur*
Coyote	*Canis latrans*
Dall porpoise	*Phocoenoides dalli*
Deer mouse	*Peromyscus maniculatus*
Gray whale	*Eschirichtius glaucus*
Gray wolf	*Canis lupus*
Harbor seal	*Phoca vitulina*
Humpback whale	*Megaptera novaeangliae*
Marten	*Martes americana*
Meadow vole	*Microtus townsendii*
Mountain goat	*Oreamnos americanus*
Mule deer	*Odocoileus hemionus*
Pacific white-sided dophin	*Lagenorhynchus obliquidens*
Polar bear	*Ursus maritimus*
Prince of Wales flying squirrel	*Glaucomys sabrinus griseifrons*
Rabbit (introduced European species)	*Oryctolagus cuniculus*
River otter	*Lutra canadensis*
Rocky mountain elk	*Cervus canadensis*
Sitka black-tailed deer	*Odocoileus hemionus sitchensis*
Steller sea lion	*Eumetopias jubata*
Vagrant shrew	*Sorex vagrans*
Voles	*Microtus pennsylvanicus; M. longicaudus*
Walrus	*Odobenus rosemarus*
Birds	
Ancient murrelet	*Synthliboramphus antiquus*
Arctic tern	*Sterna paradisaea*
Bald eagle	*Haliaeetus leucocephalus*
Belted kingfisher	*Ceryle alcyon*
Black-footed albatross	*Phoebastria nigripes*
Black-legged kittiwake	*Risa tridactyla*
Black oystercatcher	*Haematopus bachmani*
Bonaparte gull	*Larus philadephia*
Canada goose	*Branta canadensis*
Common raven	*Corvus corax*

COMMON NAME	SCIENTIFIC NAME

Birds

Fork-tailed storm petrel	*Ocenodroma furcata*
Glaucus-winged gull	*Larus glaucescens*
Hermit thrush	*Catharus guttatus*
Kittlitz's murrelet	*Brachyramphus brevirostris*
Long-tailed duck	*Clangula hyemalis*
Marbled murrelet	*Brachyramphus marmoratus*
Northern fulmar	*Fulmarus glacialis*
Northern goshawk	*Accipiter gentilis*
Northwestern crow	*Corvus caurinus*
Pacific wren	*Troglodytes troglodytes*
Pigeon guillemot	*Cepphus columba*
Passenger pigeon	*Ectopistes migratorius*
Queen Charlotte goshawk	*Accipiter gentilis laingai*
Red-necked phalarope	*Phalaropus lobatus*
Red-throated loon	*Gavia stellata*
Sheerwater	*Puffinus* sp.
Sooty grouse	*Dendragapus obscurus*
Spotted owl	*Strix occidentalis*
Spotted sandpiper	*Actitis mcularia*
Thayer's gull	*Larus thayeri*
Tufted puffin	*Fraturcula cirrhata*
Vancouver Canada goose	*Branta canadensis fulva*
Varied thrush	*Ixoreus naevius*

Fish

Atlantic salmon	*Salmo salar*
Chum salmon	*Oncorhynchus keta*
Cod	*Gadus* sp.
Coho salmon	*Oncorhynchus kisutch*
King salmon	*Oncorhynchus tshawytscha*
Pacific halibut	*Hippoglossus stenolepis*
Pacific Herring	*Clupea pallasii*
Pink salmon	*Oncorhynchus gorbuscha*
Red salmon	*Oncorhynchus nerka*
Steelhead trout	*Oncorhynchus mykiss*

Endnotes

PART 1
1. E. O. Wilson, *The Naturalist* (Island Press, 1994).

PART 2
1. O. C. Wallmo, ed., *Mule and Black-tailed Deer of North America* (Wildlife Management Institute, 1981).

2. S. MacDonald and J. Cook, *The Mammal Fauna of Southeast Alaska* (University of Alaska Museum, 1999); J. Cook and S. MacDonald, "Island Life: Coming to Grips with the Insular Nature of Southeast Alaska and Adjoining British Columbia," in *North Pacific Temperate Rainforests: Ecology and Conservation*, ed. G. Orians and J. Schoen (University of Washington Press, 2013).

3. E. Kellogg, ed., *The Rainforests of Home: An Atlas of People and Place* (Interrain, 1995).

4. P. Alaback, "Biodiversity Patterns in Relation to Climate in the Temperate Rainforests of North America," in *High-Latitude Rain Forests and Associated Ecosystems of the West Coast of the Americas: Climate Hydrology, Ecology, and Conservation*, ed. R. Lawford, P. Alaback, and E. Fuentes (Ecological Studies, 1996).

5. D. DellaSala, ed., *Temperate and Boreal Rainforests of the World: Ecology and Conservation* (Island Press, 2011).

6. Alaback, "Biodiversity Patterns in Relation to Climate in the Temperate Rainforests of North America"; DellaSala, *Temperate and Boreal Rainforests of the World*; G. Orians and J. Schoen, eds., *North Pacific Temperate Rainforests: Ecology and Conservation* (University of Washington Press, 2013).

7. L. Crone and J. Mehrkens, "Indigenous and Commercial Uses of the Natural Resources in the North Pacific Rainforest with a Focus on Southeast Alaska and Haida Gwaii," in *North Pacific Temperate Rainforests: Ecology and Management*, ed. G. Orians and J. Schoen (University of Washington Press, 2013).

8. A. Harris and W. Farr, *The Forest Ecosystem of Southeast Alaska: 7. Forest Ecology and Timber Management* (Pacific Northwest Forest and Range Experiment Station, Forest Service. Portland, Oregon, PNW-25, 1974).

9. J. Sisk, "The Southeastern Alaska Timber Industry: Historical Overview and Current Status," in *The Coastal Forests and Mountains Ecoregion in Southeastern Alaska and the Tongass National Forest*, ed. J. Schoen and E. Dovichin (Audubon Alaska and The Nature Conservancy, 2007); US Forest Service, *Tongass Land Management Plan Revision: Final Supplemental Environmental Impact Statement* (R10-MB-48a, USDA Forest Service Alaska Region, Juneau, 2003); US Forest Service, *Timber Supply and Demand 2000: Alaska National Interest Lands Conservation Act Section 506(a) Report to Congress* (Report 20, R10-MB-521, Alaska Region, Juneau, 2004).

10. Sisk, "The Southeastern Alaska Timber Industry."

11. Crone and Mehrkens, "Indigenous and Commercial Uses of the Natural Resources in the North Pacific Rainforest with a Focus on Southeast Alaska and Haida Gwaii"; Sisk, "The Southeastern Alaska Timber Industry."

12. M. Smith, ed., *Ecological Atlas of Southeast Alaska* (Audubon Alaska, Anchorage, 2016): http://bit.ly/2cL9obi; US Forest Service, *Tongass Land and Resource Management Plan Amendment. Final EIS* (R10-MB-769e,f, Ketchikan, 2016).

13. Alaska Lumber & Pulp Company, "Why Clearcutting Is Nature's Way" (ad in a local Southeast newspaper, 1979).

14. R. Young, "Last Chance for Admiralty," *Field and Stream*, May 1964.

15. R. Young, *My Lost Wilderness* (Winchester Press, 1983), 190.

16. F. Dufresne, *No Room For Bears* (Holt, Rinehart and Winston, 1965), 11.

17. H. Merriam, *Deer Report. Progress Rept., Federal Aid in Wildlife Restoration Project W-17-2 and 3* (Alaska Dept. of Fish and Game, Juneau, 1971).

18. A. S. Leopold and R. H. Barrett, *Implications of Wildlife of the 1968 Juneau Unit Timber Sale: A Report to U.S. Plywood Champion Papers, Inc* (1972).

19. A. Bloom, "Sitka Black-Tailed Deer Winter Range in the Kadashan Bay Area, Southeast Alaska," *Journal of Wildlife Management* 42 (1978): 108–112.

20. D. McKnight, "History of Deer Research in Alaska," in *Sitka Black-Tailed Deer: Proceedings of a Conference in Juneau, Alaska*, ed. O. C. Wallmo and J. W. Schoen (US Forest Service, Alaska Department of Fish and Game, 1979).

21. J. W. Schoen and O. C. Wallmo, "Timber Management and Deer in Southeast Alaska: Current Problems and Research Direction Black-Tailed Deer," in *Sitka Black-Tailed Deer: Proceedings of a Conference in Juneau, Alaska*, ed. O. C. Wallmo and J. W. Schoen (US Forest Service, Alaska Department of Fish and Game, 1979).

22. J. W. Schoen and O. C. Wallmo, "Deer and Logging Relationships in Southeast Alaska," *Alaska Fish Tales and Game Trails* 11 (1978): 2–3.

23. September 5, 1997, Forest Service Memo T975 from regional forester John A. Sandor to PNW director's representative Don Schmige at the Forestry Sciences Laboratory in Juneau, AK. This memo was in O. C. Wallmo's personal file documenting the history of the manuscript review of our 1980 Forest Science paper on Southeast Alaska deer. When Wallmo retired, he gave me that file, which I have in my personal files.

24. O. C. Wallmo and J. W. Schoen, "Response of Deer to Secondary Forest Succession in Southeast Alaska," *Forest Science* 26 (1980): 448–462.

25. Harris and Farr, *The Forest Ecosystem of Southeast Alaska*.

26. Joint Resolution by the Alaska Boards of Fisheries and Game. #80-80-JB, 12-7-1980, Juneau, Alaska.

27. P. Alaback, "Dynamics of Understory Biomass in Sitka Spruce-Western Hemlock Forest of Southeast Alaska," *Ecology* 63 (1982): 1932–1948.

28. C. Rose, "Deer Response to Forest Succession on Annette Island, Southeast Alaska," in *Proceedings of the Symposium on Fish and Wildlife Relationships in Old-Growth Forests*, ed. W. Meehan, 285–290 (Juneau, 1984).

29. J. W. Schoen, O. C. Wallmo, and M. D. Kirchhoff, "Wildlife–Forest Relationships: Is a Reevaluation of Old Growth Necessary?," *Transactions of the 46th North American Wildlife and Natural Resources Conference* (1981): 541.

30. J. W. Schoen and M. D. Kirchhoff, *Habitat Use by Mountain Goats in Southeast Alaska. Final Report* (ADF&G, Juneau, 1982).

31. J. W. Schoen and M. D. Kirchhoff, "Seasonal Distribution and Home Range Patterns of Sitka Black-Tailed Deer on Admiralty Island, Southeast Alaska," *Journal of Wildlife Management* 49 (1985): 96–103.

32. J. W. Schoen and M. D. Kirchhoff, "Seasonal Habitat Use by Sitka Black-Tailed Deer on Admiralty Island, Alaska," *Journal of Wildlife Management* 54 (1990): 371–378.

33. M. D. Kirchhoff and J. W. Schoen, "Forest Cover and Snow: Implications for Deer Habitat in Southeast Alaska," *Journal of Wildlife Management* 47 (1987): 497–501.

34. J. W. Schoen and M. D. Kirchhoff, *Seasonal Distribution and Habitat Use by Sitka Black-tailed Deer in Southeastern Alaska. Progress Rept. W-22-1, Job 2.6R* (ADF&G, Juneau, 1983).

35. J. W. Schoen and M. D. Kirchhoff, "Little Deer in the Big Woods," *Natural History* 97, no. 8 (1988): 52–55.

36. J. W. Schoen, S. D. Miller, and H. V. Reynolds, "Last Stronghold of the Grizzly," *Natural History* 96, no. 1 (1987): 50.

37. J. Trevino and C. Jonkel, "Do Grizzly Bears Still Live in Mexico?," *International Conference on Bear Research and Management* 6 (1986): 11–13.

38. J. Schoen and S. Gende, "Brown Bear," in *The Coastal Forests and Mountains Ecoregion in Southeastern Alaska and the Tongass National Forest*, ed. J. Schoen and E. Dovichin (Audubon Alaska & The Nature Conservancy, 2007).

39. J. Schoen and L. Beier, *Brown Bear Habitat Preferences and Brown Bear Logging and Mining Relationships in Southeast Alaska. Final Report. Project W-23.3, Study 4.17* (ADF&G, Juneau, 1990).

40. J. Schoen, L. Beier, J. Lentfer, and L. Johnson, "Denning Ecology of Brown Bears on Admiralty and Chichagof Islands, Southeast Alaska, and Implications for Management," *International Conference on Bear Research and Management* 7 (1987): 293–304.

41. Schoen et al., "Denning Ecology of Brown Bears on Admiralty and Chichagof Islands, Southeast Alaska, and Implications for Management."

42. B. Richards, "A Place Apart: Alaska's Southeast," *National Geographic* 165, no. 1 (1994): 65.

43. Schoen et al., "Denning Ecology of Brown Bears on Admiralty and Chichagof Islands, Southeast Alaska, and Implications for Management."

44. E. Hellgren, "Physiology of Hibernation in Bears," *Ursus* 10 (1998): 467–477; O. Toien, J. Blake, D. Edgar, D. Grahn, C. Heller, and B. Barnes, "Hibernation in Black Bears: Independence of Metabolic Suppression from Body Temperature," *Science* 331 (2011): 906–909.

45. J. Schoen, J. Lentfer, and L. Beier, "Differential Distribution of Brown Bears on Admiralty Island, Southeast Alaska: A Preliminary Assessment," *International Conference on Bear Research and Management* 6 (1986): 1–5.

46. J. Peek, M. Pelton, H. Picton, J. Schoen, and P. Zager, "Grizzly Bear Conservation and Management: A Review," *Wildlife Society Bulletin* 15 (1987): 160–169.

47. Oversight Hearing before the Subcommittee on Public Lands of the Committee on Interior and Insular Affairs, House of Representatives, Ninety-Ninth Congress, Second Session on Management of the Tongass National Forest. Hearing Held in Washington, DC, May 8 and 9, 1986 (US Government Printing Office, 1986, Serial No. 99-26), 132–147.

48. S. Miller et al., "Brown and Black Bear Density Estimation in Alaska Using Radiotelemetry and Replicated Mark-Resight Techniques," *Wildlife Monograph* 133 (1997).

49. Schoen and Beier, *Brown Bear Habitat Preferences and Brown Bear Logging and Mining Relationships in Southeast Alaska*.

50. Schoen and Beier, *Brown Bear Habitat Preferences and Brown Bear Logging and Mining Relationships in Southeast Alaska*.

51. Schoen and Beier, *Brown Bear Habitat Preferences and Brown Bear Logging and Mining Relationships in Southeast Alaska*; J. Schoen, R. Flynn, L. Suring, K. Titus, and L. Beier, "Habitat-Capability Model for Brown Bear in Southeast Alaska," *International Conference on Bear Research and Management* 9, no. 1 (1994): 327–337; K. Titus and L. Beier, *Population and Habitat Ecology of Brown Bears on Admiralty and Chichagof Islands. Progress Report* (ADF&G, Juneau, 1994).

52. G. Hilderbrand, S. Jenkins, C. Schwartz, T. Hanley, and C. Robbins, "Effect of Seasonal Differences in Dietary Meat Intake on Changes in Body Mass and Composition in Wild and Captive Brown Bears," *Canadian Journal of Zoology* 77 (1999): 1623–1630.

53. S. Gende, T. Quinn, and M. Willson, "Consumption Choice by Bears Feeding on Salmon," *Oecologia* 127 (2001): 327–382; S. Gende, T. Quinn, M. Willson, R. Heintz, and T. Scott, "Magnitude and Fate of Salmon-Derived N, P, and Energy in a Coastal Stream Ecosystem," *Journal of Freshwater Ecology* 19 (2004): 149–160.

54. Miller et al., "Brown and Black Bear Density Estimation in Alaska Using Radiotelemetry and Replicated Mark-Resight Techniques."

55. Schoen, Lentfer, and Beier, "Differential Distribution of Brown Bears on Admiralty Island, Southeast Alaska."

56. M. Ben-David, K. Titus, and L. Beier, "Consumptions of Salmon by Alaskan Brown Bears: A Trade-off Between Nutritional Requirements and the Risk of Infanticide?," *Oecologia* 138 (2004): 465–474.

57. Schoen, Beier, Lentfer, and Johnson, "Denning Ecology of Brown Bears on Admiralty and Chichagof Islands, Southeast Alaska, and Implications for Management."

58. J. Schoen, "Bear Habitat Management: A Review and Future Perspective," *International Conference on Bear Research and Management* 8 (1990): 143–154.

59. Schoen and Beier, *Brown Bear Habitat Preferences and Brown Bear Logging and Mining Relationships in Southeast Alaska*.

60. Titus and Beier, *Population and Habitat Ecology of Brown Bears on Admiralty and Chichagof Islands*.

61. R. Flynn, S. Lewis, L. Beier, and G. Pendleton, *Brown Bear Use of Riparian and Beach Zones on Northeast Chichagof Island: Implications for Streamside Management in Coastal Alaska. Final Report* (ADF&G, Juneau, 2007).

62. M. Shephard, B. Winn, R. Flynn, et al., *Southeast Chichagof Landscape Analysis. Technical Report R10-TP-68* (US Forest Service, Sitka, 1999).

63. R. Noss, H. Quigley, M. Hornocker, T. Merrill, and P. Paquet, "Conservation Biology and Carnivore Conservation in the Rocky Mountains," *Conservation Biology* 10 (1996): 949–963; S. Trombulak and C. Frissell, "Review of Ecological Effects of Roads on Terrestrial and Aquatic Communities," *Conservation Biology* 14 (1999): 18–30; B. McLellan, "Relationships Between Human Industrial Development Activity and Grizzly Bears," *International Conference on Bear Research and Management* 8 (1990): 57–64.

64. K. Titus and L. Beier, *Population and Habitat Ecology of Brown Bears on Admiralty and Chichagof Islands. ADF&G Progress Report* (ADF&G, Juneau, 1991).

65. K. Titus and L. Beier, *Population Habitat Ecology of Brown Bears on Admiralty and Chichagof Islands. ADF&G Progress Report* (ADF&G, Juneau, 1993).

66. Schoen and Beier, *Brown Bear Habitat Preferences and Brown Bear Logging and Mining Relationships in Southeast Alaska.*

67. J. Schoen, M. Kirchhoff, and J. Hughes, "Wildlife and Old-Growth Forests in Southeastern Alaska," *Natural Areas Journal* 8 (1988): 138–145.

68. Tongass Timber Reform Act, *Hearing before the Subcommittee on Public Lands, National Parks and Forests of the Committee on Energy and Natural Resources United States Senate, One Hundredth Congress, First Session on S. 708. November 3 and 5, 1987* (US Government Printing Office, 1988), 83–212.

69. J. Schoen, M. Kirchhoff, and M. Thomas, *Seasonal Distribution and Habitat Use by Sitka Black-tailed Deer in Southeastern Alaska. Final Report* (ADF&G, Juneau, 1985).

70. "Editorial: Paying Twice to Ruin a Rain Forest," *New York Times*, June 25, 1997.

71. Schoen, Miller, and Reynolds, "Last Stronghold of the Grizzly."

72. "Of Time and the Forest," *Natural History* 97, no. 8 (August 1988).

73. Schoen and Kirchhoff, "Little Deer in the Big Woods."

74. J. W. Thomas, L. F. Ruggiero, R. W. Mannan, J. W. Schoen, and R. A. Lancia, "Management and Conservation of Old-Growth Forests in the United States," *Wildlife Society Bulletin* 16 (1988): 252–262.

75. Schoen, "Bear Habitat Management."

76. US Forest Service, *Record of Decision for Kelp Bay Timber Sale, Tongass National Forest* (Juneau, 1992).

77. M. Kirchhoff, J. Schoen, and T. Franklin, "A Model for Science-Based Conservation Advocacy: Tongass National Forest Case History," *Wildlife Society Bulletin* 22 (1995): 358–364.

78. K. Titus and J. Schoen, "A Plan for Maintaining Viable and Well-distributed Brown Bear Populations in Southeast Alaska." Unpublished paper submitted to the Tongass National Forest TLMP Planning Team, 1992.

79. L. Suring, D. Crocker-Bedford, F. Flynn, et al., "A Process for Conserving Wildlife Species Associated with Old-Growth Forests in Southeast Alaska" (submitted to the Tongass National Forest TLMP Planning Team, Juneau, 1993), 214.

80. R. Kiester and C. Eckarhardt, *Review of Wildlife Management and Conservation Biology on the Tongass National Forest: A Synthesis with Recommendations* (Pacific Northwest Research Station, USDA Forest Service, Corvallis, Oregon, 1994).

81. D. Swanston, C. Shaw III, W. Smith, K. Julin, G. Cellier, and F. Everest, *Scientific Information and the Tongass Land Management Plan: Key Findings from the Scientific Literature, Species Assessments, Resource Analyses, Worships, and Risk Assessment Panels. General Technical Report PNW-GRR-386* (US Department of Agriculture, Forest Service, Pacific Northwest Research Station, 1996).

82. R. Powell, D. McCullough, C. Benkman, et al., "Joint Statement of Peer Review Committee Members on Tongass National Forest Planning for Old Growth Associated Wildlife Species," October 1996.

PART 3

1. ADF&G, "Alaska Wildlife Action Plan" (2015): http://www.adfg.alaska.gov/static/species/wildlife_action_plan/2015_alaska_wildlife_action_plan.pdf.

2. K. Durbin, *Tongass: Pulp Politics and the Fight for the Alaska Rain Forest* (Oregon State University Press, 1999).

3. Peer Review Committee of Scientists: R. Powell, D. McCullough, A. Hansen, et al., "Joint statement of members of the Peer Review Committee concerning the inadequacy of conservation measures for vertebrate species in the Tongass National Forest Land Management Plan of Record, September 1997."

4. S. Trombulak and C. Frissell, "Review of the Ecological Effects of Roads on Terrestrial and Aquatic Communities," *Conservation Biology* 14 (1999): 18–30; J. Strittholt and D. DellaSala, "Importance of Roadless Areas in Biodiversity Conservation in Forested Ecosystems: Case Study of the Klamath-Siskiyou Ecoregion of the United States," *Conservation Biology* 15 (2001): 1742–54.

5. J. Schoen and S. Senner, *Alaska's Western Arctic: A Summary and Synthesis of Resources* (Audubon Alaska, 2002).

6. M. Smith, E. Myers, and J. Schoen, *Habitat Conservation Strategy for the National Petroleum Reserve—Alaska* (Audubon Alaska, 2011).

7. M. Dombeck and J. Thomas, "Declare Harvest of Old-Growth Forests off Limits and Move On," *Seattle Post-Intelligencer*, August 24, 2003.

8. D. Albert and J. Schoen, "A Conservation Assessment for the Coastal Forests and Mountains Ecoregion of Southeastern Alaska and the Tongass National Forest," in *The Coastal Forests and Mountains Ecoregion of Southeastern Alaska and the Tongass National Forest: A Conservation Assessment and Resource Synthesis*, ed. J. Schoen and E. Dovichin (Audubon Alaska and The Nature Conservancy, 2007).

9. D. Albert and J. Schoen, "A Comparison of Relative Biological Value, Habitat Vulnerability and Cumulative Ecological Risk Among Biogeographic Provinces in Southeastern Alaska," in *The Coastal Forests and Mountains Ecoregion of Southeastern Alaska and the Tongass National Forest: A Conservation Assessment and Resource Synthesis*, ed. J. Schoen and E. Dovichin (Audubon Alaska and The Nature Conservancy, 2007).

10. Roundtable members included the Sitka Tribe, Goldbelt Inc., the First Alaskans Institute, Tlingit Haida Central Council, and the Ketchikan Indian organization. Several national, regional, and local environmental groups participating in the roundtable included The Nature Conservancy (one of the key conveners of the Roundtable), Alaska Rainforest Campaign, Alaska Wilderness League, Audubon Alaska, Natural Resources Defense Council, Southeast Alaska Conservation Council, The Wilderness Society, and Trout Unlimited. Other environmental groups—including Greenpeace and the Sierra Club—consistently attended all roundtable meetings as observers. Foundations that participated in and helped fund the roundtable included the Gordon & Betty Moore Foundation, National Forest Foundation, Pew Charitable Trusts, Campion Foundation, and Wilburforce Foundation. In addition, the Forest Service, Alaska Department of Fish and Game, and Alaska Department of Natural Resources participated in the roundtable.

11. D. Chadwick, "The Truth about Tongass," *National Geographic* 212, no. 1 (July 2007): 125.

12. J. Schoen and E. Dovichin, *A Conservation Assessment and Resource Synthesis for the Coastal Forests and Mountains Ecoregion in Southeast Alaska and the Tongass National Forest* (Audubon Alaska and The Nature Conservancy, 2007): http://www.conservationgateway.org/ConservationByGeography/NorthAmerica/UnitedStates/alaska/seak/era/cfm/Pages/default.aspx.

13. M. Smith, ed., *Ecological Atlas of Southeast Alaska* (Audubon Alaska, 2016).

14. US Forest Service, *Tongass Land and Resource Management Plan, Final Environmental Impact Statement, Plan Amendment, Record of Decision* (Washington, DC, 2008).

15. The Tongass Conservation Collaborative included Audubon Alaska, The Nature Conservancy, Alaska Wilderness League, Southeast Alaska Conservation Council, Trout Unlimited, Sitka Conservation Society, Alaska Conservation Foundation, and the Alaska Region of The Wilderness Society.

16. TCW Economics, *Economic Contributions and Impacts of Salmonid Resources in Southeast Alaska. Final Report to Trout Unlimited Alaska Program* (2010): http://www.americansalmonforest.org/uploads/3/9/0/1/39018435/econreportfull.pdf.

17. G. Orians and J. Schoen, eds., *North Pacific Temperate Rainforests: Ecology and Conservation* (University of Washington Press, 2013).

18. D. Albert and J. Schoen, "Use of Historical Logging Patterns to Identify Disproportionately Logged Ecosystems Within Temperate Rainforests of Southeast Alaska," *Conservation Biology* 27 (2013): 774–784.

19. US Global Change Research Program, *Fourth National Climate Assessment* (2018): nca2018.globlchange.gov.

20. Smith, *Ecological Atlas of Southeast Alaska.*

21. C. Shanley, S. Pyare, M. Goldstein, P. Alaback, et al., "Climate Change Implications in the Northern Coastal Temperate Rainforest of North America." *Climate Change* (2015): DOI:10.1007/s10584-1355-9.

22. P. Hennon, D. D'Amore, P. Schaberg, D. Wittwer, and C. Shanley, "Shifting Climate, Altered Niche, and a Dynamic Conservation Strategy for Yellow-Cedar in the North Pacific Coastal Rainforest," *BioScience* 62 (2012): 147–158.

23. US Global Change Research Program, *Fourth National Climate Assessment.*

24. T. Barrett, *Storage and Flux of Carbon in Live Trees, Snags, and Logs in the Chugach and Tongass National Forests. General Technical Report PNW-GTR-889* (Pacific Northwest Research Station, US Forest Service, 2014).

25. W. Leighty, S. Hamburg, and J. Caouette, "Effects of Management on Carbon Sequestration in Forest Biomass in Southeast Alaska," *Ecosystems* 9 (2006): 1051–1065.

PART 4

1. A. Leopold, *Round River* (Oxford University Press, 1993), 146.

2. D. Schindler, R. Hilborn, B. Chasco, C. Boatright, T. Quinn, L. Rogers, and M. Webster, "Population Diversity and the Portfolio Effect in an Exploited Species," *Nature* 465 (2010): 609–613.

3. D. Pauly, "Anecdotes and the Shifting Base-Line Syndrome of Fisheries," *Trends in Ecology and Evolution* 10 (1995): 430.

4. D. Bohn and R. Petschek, *Kinsey Photographer: A Half Century of Negatives by Darius and Tabitha Kinsey* (Chronicle Books, 1982).

5. J. Achenbach, "The Age of Disbelief," *National Geographic* (March 2015): 30–47.

6. Southeast Conference, *Southeast Alaska by the Numbers 2018* (2018).

7. Taxpayers for Common Sense, *Cutting Our Losses: Twenty Years of Money-Losing Timber Sales in the Tongass* (October 2019).

8. G. Meffe and C. Carroll, *Principles of Conservation Biology* (Sinauer Associates, 1994), 192; D. Blockstein and H. Tordoff, "Gone Forever—a Contemporary Look at the Extinction of the Passenger Pigeon," *American Birds* 39 (1985): 845–851.

9. E. Bolen and W. Robinson, *Wildlife Ecology and Management* (Prentice Hall, 1999).

10. D. Montgomery, *King of Fish: The Thousand-Year Run of Salmon* (Westview Press, 2003).

Index

Page numbers in italics refer to figures, those followed by m refer to maps.
Those followed by n refer to notes, with note number.

near author's Smuggler's Cove home, 48, 66

and old-growth forest, 42, 123

at Port Houghton Salt Chuck, 217

Baranof Island

author's tour of, with National Geographic writer, 217–18, *219*

Kelp Bay timber sale, 175

road construction and timber harvesting on, 200

South Baranof Wilderness, 201

See also ABC Islands

Barrett, Reginald, 34, 35, 50

Barton, Mike, 154, 175

Basket Bay, author's conservation assessment of, 208, *209*

Bay of Pillars

author's conservation assessment of, 204

as potential rainforest restoration area, 236

Bear Creek watershed, author's conservation assessment of, 204

"Bear Habitat Management: A Review and Future Perspective" (Schoen), 166–67

Beaudin, Dave, 62–63

Beier, LaVern

background of, 85

bear safety talk to miners, 151

and brown bear research, 85, *87*, 90, 102

aerial telemetry location of bears, 116, *117*, 124, 137

bear density studies, 107–8, 150

capture and collaring of bears, 88, 99, 105, 106–7, 112–13, 115

den inspections, 94–97

ground observation of bears, 125–26, 142

and impact of mining, 109

National Geographic article on, 106

study on forest type preferences, 145

walking tours of habitat, 97–98

friendship with author, 99

Bennett, Lynn, 56, 66–67, 99, 106–7, 113

Berry-Frick, Anissa, 203–4, *205*

Between Pacific Tides (Ricketts), 10

biodiversity, complex interconnected parts necessary for, 192

biogeographic provinces of Southeast Alaska, 199*m*

evaluation with Audubon-TNC GIS database, 198–201

biology, author's college study of, 10–11

black oystercatchers, 239, *239*

black-tailed deer, *36*

decline of population, with old-growth logging, 106, 254

importance of, 35

types of forest preferred by, 288

black-tailed deer conference (Juneau, 1978), 39

black-tailed deer research

and discovery of importance of old-growth forest, 266

early studies, 34–35

and habitat diversity, value of, 269

management implications of, 80–81

political obstacles to implementing recommendations of, 80

publications on, 161–62

studies after author's research, 81

black-tailed deer research phase one (Admiralty and Chichagof islands), 33–55

ADF&G Hood Bay research station, 28, 37, *37*

arrival at island, 25, 26, 28

author's pleasure in being part of, 28

boats used in, 33, 40

and characteristics of Alaskan forests *vs.* forests in lower 48 states, 41

determining effects of logging as goal of, 33, 36

difficulty of travel in study areas, 37, 38

first field season, 36–39

field crew, 37

methodology, 36–37

sites surveyed, 38

on nonrenewability of old-growth forest under current system, 52, 55, 133

peer review of results, 50

pushback from timber industry and Forest Service, 46, 69, 97

research team for, 25

results

on detrimental effects of logging on deer populations, 38, 39, 40, 41–46, 43–46

on differences between old-growth and second-growth forests, 41–46, 43–46

publication of, 46, 50

subsequent research verifying, 52–53

black-tailed deer research phase one (*cont.*)
  second field season, 39–41
  weather as challenge in, 33
  See also "Response of Deer to Secondary
    Forest Succession in Southeast
    Alaska" (Wallmo and Schoen)
black-tailed deer research phase two
  (Admiralty Island), 61–81
  aerial telemetry data on deer movement
    author's training to fly plane for,
      67–68
    collection of, 64–65, 66–68, 72
  capturing and radio-collaring of deer,
    61–65, 68, 69
  on deer deaths in winter, 79
  deer migrations documented in, 68, 72,
    72
  methodology, 76
  objectives of, 61, 63
  overlap with brown bear research, 97
  results on deer habitat preferences,
    69–79
    on deer's avoidance of areas with
      snow accumulation, 70, 71, 71, 73,
      73–76, 74, 75, 77, 79
    on deer's wintertime preference for
      mid- and high-volume old-growth
      forest, 73–76, 73–78, 79
    on food availability as central attrac-
      tion of old-growth forest, 44, 45,
      74–76, 76, 77, 79
  publication of, 78–79, 80–81
  on seasonal deer distribution, 76–79, 77
  testimony on, to House Subcommittee
    on Public Lands, 132–34
  and types of old-growth forest, distin-
    guishing between, 63, 69–74, 70, 71, 74,
    74, 75, 76, 77, 78–79
  sites for, 61, 61–62, 62
  subsequent studies, 79
Blind Slough, author's conservation assessment of, 204
Bloom, Art, 34, 35
British Columbia Coast, heavy logging on,
  246
brown bear(s), 289
  on ABC islands, 83
  active elimination of, by some loggers,
    150
  as adaptable generalists, 125, 145
  avoidance of humans, 126, 151
  and bear safety talks for miners, 151

day beds of, 147, 147
at Glacier Bay, 240, 241
human-caused mortality as major
  problem in, 124, 125, 126–27, 148–50,
  166–67
impact of timber harvesting on, 106
in Kadashan watershed, 230
as keystone species, 84
killing in defense of life or property,
  Alaska law on, 109
permanent trails used by, 81, 82
problem bears, as product of improper
  human garbage disposal, 109, 109,
  126–27, 148–49, 150, 151, 152
range and populations, two hundred
  years ago, 81
salmon as food for, x, 78, 81, 83, 83, 84,
  84, 88, 118, 141, 141–43, 142, 146, 147,
  286, 287
as term, *vs.* grizzly bear, 81
as threatened species in lower 48 states,
  83
transfer of marine nutrients inland, 84,
  232, 286
as umbrella species, 83
vulnerability to population decline, 148
brown bear research (Admiralty and
  Chichagof Islands), 81–127, 137–52
  aerial telemetry location of bears, 115–18,
    117, 124, 137
  aircraft used in, 116
  data collected during, 116
  frequency of flights and bear identifica-
    tions, 115, 116–18
  average home range size, 138
  bear density estimate methods, 137, 150
  bear density in three study areas, simul-
    taneous flights to compare, 107–8
  benefits *vs.* risks to animals, 100
  boats used in, 98
  capturing and radio-collaring of bears,
    87, 88–90, 89, 97–98, 105, 112–14, 115,
    125
    and challenge of identifying bear's
      sex from the air, 107
    data collected on captured bears,
      89–90
    moments of danger in, 113
    and risk of killing bear, 100
dens
  inspection of, 94–97
  types on Admirality island, 92, 92,
    96, 97

types on Chichagof Island, *93*, 97
typical locations of, 97, 145, *146*
on displacement of bears, "musical
chairs" effect in, 151
on distribution of female bears, to avoid
injury to cubs, 139
on distributions from shoreline to
ridges, 116, 124, 138, 139, *139*, 146
ecological importance of bears and,
83–84
family accompanying author in, aboard
Orca II, 114–15, 118, 121
on feeding and types of food, 138, 139,
140, *140*, *141*, 141–43, *142*, *143*, 146
on feeding times and places, 86–88, 94,
95, 107, 109
field notes from, 106–9, 112–13, 114–15
and forest type preferences
clear-cut forest, minimal use of,
145–47
old-growth forest as critical habitat,
145, 147
second-growth forest, lack of nutritious food in, 147
and getting a feel for the habitat, 97–98
ground observation of bears in, 118–21
moments of danger in, 118–21, 125–26
on hibernation
body state during, 110
emergence from, 93–94, 138, *146*
start, factors affecting, 109–10, 145,
146
time spent in, 138
high bear densities observed on
northern Admiralty Island, 107,
137–38, 150
on improper garbage disposal, impact
of, *109*, *109*, 126–27, 148–49, 150, 151,
152
and increased human-bear interaction,
detrimental effects of, 147–48
in Kadashan Watershed (Chichagof
Island), 101–5
on litter size, 93–94
and logging's impact on bears, 108–9,
109
author's affidavit in lawsuit over,
111–12
effects on habitat, 145–47
logging roads, and increase in dangerous human contact, 125, 126,
147, 148
long workdays in, 98, 106, 124

losses of tracked bears to human-caused
fatalities, 122, 148–49
and mining's impact on bears, 108, *108*,
150–52
as multidecade study, 88
number of bears tracked, 89, 99
objectives, 85, 86
overlap with deer research, 97
pleasure of conducting, 106, 122
previous studies, 84–85
on reduction of human contact as key to
bear survival, 148, 149, 152
results
on effect of forest clear-cutting,
124–25
final report, 166
publications of, 128, 163, 166–67
on road construction
displacement of bears by, 150–52
and increase in dangerous human-
bear contact, 125, 126, 147, 148
need for decrease in, 127
seasonal distribution and habitat use,
138–45, *146*
in Spring, 138–39, *146*
in Summer, 139–40, *146*
in late Summer, *141*, 141–43, *146*
in Fall, 143–45, *146*
study areas, 85, 86, 87
weather as complication in, 124
"Buried Treasures" (Maser), 162
Bush, George H. W., 174, 191, 260

Camp Nor'Wester, author and wife's
employment at, *17*, 17–18
Caouette, John, 192, 193
Cape Fanshaw, author's conservation
assessment of, 203–4
Carstensen, Richard, 192, 220
Carter, James E. "Jimmy," 159, 172, 275
Catherine Island logging site, author as
ADF&G representative at, 28–29
Chadwick, Doug, 214–15, 217, 219, 220
Chaik Bay, *139*
Chantey (boat), 3–4, 7–8
Chichagof Island, 86
author's conservation assessment of,
206–8, *207*
black-tailed deer research on, 34, 40
logging on, *35*
in east, *200*, *201*
effect on bears, 108–9, *109*, 148–49

Chichagof Island (*cont.*)
  as selective harvesting type, 231
  logging roads on, 87, 101, 102, 106, 110,
    118, 147
    author's affidavit in lawsuit over,
      111–12
  old-growth forest on, 43, 71
  science cruise to (2008), 229–31
  See also ABC Islands; black-tailed deer
    research phase one (Admiralty and
    Chichagof islands); brown bear
    research; Kadashan watershed
    (Chichagof Island)
Chilkat Peninsula, cruise to (2009), 243
climate change
  in Alaska, 239, 240, 259
  and carbon storage by old-growth forest,
    257, 260
  downplaying for political reasons, 274
  expected effects of, 259
  scientific consensus on, 279
  U.S. failure to act on, 259–60
  widespread denial of, 278, 279
Cline, David, 132, 183–84, 251, 276
Clinton, William J. "Bill," 186, 190–91, 208
coastal forest, as patchwork of forest types,
  63, 69–71, 70, 71, 74
Collinsworth, Don, 112, 154
Congress
  Alaska delegation's support of logging
    industry, 129, 136, 158–59, 172, 173–74,
    186, 283
  fact-finding tours of Tongass, author's
    involvement with, 154, 167–68, 170–71,
    171
  See also House Subcommittee on Public
    Lands hearings on Tongass forest
    management; Senate Bill 708, hear-
    ings on; Tongass Timber Reform Act
conservation
  author's personal philosophy on, 265
  as compatible with managed human
    use, 266–68
  definition of, 265
  fragmented habitats as inadequate for,
    268
  and habitat diversity, value of, 269
  habitat types requiring conservation,
    268
  land use designations as central to, 270
  as legal requirement for Tongass man-
    agement, 280–81

limited functionality of fragmented
  habitats in modern U.S., 270
opportunities to fill gaps in public lands'
  network, 270
"preserving all parts" as basic rule in,
  266, 283
principles for, 272–73, 283–84
shifting baseline problem in, 271–72
in Southeast Alaska, habitats requiring
  strong conservation focus, 268–69
success of, as judged across centuries,
  272
sustainability as key concept in, 265
well-managed resource extraction as
  compatible, 268
Conservation Area Design for Southeast
  Alaska, 221–22, 223*m*
  benefits over other plans, 235
  Tongass Conservation Collaborative
    based on, 235
*Conservation Assessment and Conservation
  Strategy* (Audubon-TNC), 224, 226
*A Conservation Assessment and Resource
  Synthesis for the Coastal Forests and
  Mountains Ecoregion in Southeastern
  Alaska and the Tongass National Forest*
  (Audubon-TNC), 220–22
  publication of, 220
  recommendations in, 220–22
  and Tongass 77 proposal, 252
conservation assessment of Southeastern
  Alaska (Audubon-TNC), 196–210
  aerial reconnaissance of watersheds,
    203–10
  Audubon-TNC joint development of,
    194–96
  and biogeographic provinces of
    Southeast, evaluation of, 198–201
  and Conservation Area Design, 221–22,
    223*m*
  and environmental activists' opposition
    to choosing areas to prioritize, 198
  and evidence of greatest damage to
    regions of greatest biological value,
    200–201, 200–202
  focus on most important areas, neces-
    sity of, 198
  GIS database
    development of, 196
    testing of, 197–210
    uses of, 196–97
  goals of, 196–97

Juneau ice field, 168, *169*

Kadake Bay, author's conservation assessment of, 204–5
Kadashan watershed (Chichagof Island), 71, *285*
   author's conservation assessment of, 208
   author's vision for future of, 284–90
   counting of salmon in, 114, *114*
   field observation of bears at, 147
   fish weir, 114, *114*, 115
   large brown bear population in, 113–14
   large salmon population in, 113
   logging plans, dispute over, 102–3, 110
     ADF&G involvement in, 110–12
     author's affidavit in lawsuit, 111–12
     lawsuit in, 110–11
     and political pressure on ADF&G, 112
   logging road construction, 111–12
   river delta, *87*, *101*
   science cruise to (2008), 229–30
Kallick, Steve, 111, 276
Kasaan Peninsula, author's conservation assessment of, 206
Kelp Bay timber sale, 175
Kelso, Denny, 112, 130, 154
Kenai Brown Bear Stakeholder Group, 211
Kenai Fjords National Park, 249
Kessler, Wini, 192
Ketchikan Pulp Company (KPC), 30–31, *31*, 177
King Salmon River delta (Admiralty Island), *96*
Kirchhoff, Matthew
   and Audubon forest diversity workshop (Juneau, 2002), 192
   background of, 53
   basketball games with author, 53–54
   capturing and radio-collaring of deer, 66, 69
   and deer research, 75, 79, 81
   hiring for author's research team, 53
   home of, *54*
   and lawsuit to force Forest Service compliance with Tongass Timber Reform Act of 1990, 175
   "Little Deer in the Big Woods," 78–79, 161–62
   move next door to Schoen, 66
   and political pressure on research, 112
   research in Glacier Bay National Park, 238–42
   and science cruise of Tongass (2008), 226, 229
   "Silent Music," 160–61
   testimony to Congress, 159
   and value of old-growth forest, efforts to publicize, 153–54
   and VPOP, 176
Kirchhoff, Patty, 53–54, *54*, 66
Klein, David R., 34, 50, *53*, 164
Klukwan Lake, author's conservation assessment of, 206
Koehler, Bart, 131, 276
Kook Lake, author's conservation assessment of, 208, *209*
Koskuisko Island, second-growth forest on, *43*
KPC. *See* Ketchikan Pulp Company
Kuiu Island
   author's conservation assessment of, 204
   potential rainforest restoration areas on, 236
Kupreanof Island
   author's conservation assessment of, 204, *204*
   effect of logging on wildlife, 33
   road construction and timber harvesting on, 200

Lake Eva, as potential fish and wildlife management area, 235
Landmark Trees Project, 192, 228
land-sea interface, importance in Tongass, 232
"Last Stronghold of the Grizzly" (Schoen, Miller, Reynolds), 160
Lentfer, Jack
   affidavit in Kadashan logging lawsuit, 111
   and black-tailed deer conference (Juneau, 1978), 39
   and black-tailed deer research, 38–39
   career of, 38, *38*
   and purchase of *Orca II*, 104
   testimony before Congress, 134, 136, 159
Leopold, Aldo, 25–26, 35, 266
Little Basket Bay watershed, author's conservation assessment of, 208
"Little Deer in the Big Woods" (Schoen and Kirchhoff), 78–79, 161–62

local knowledge, value for public outreach, 203

logging. *See* roads, logging; timber harvesting in Tongass; timber industry in Southeast Alaska

Long Bay
   author's tour of, with National Geographic writer, 218–19
   science cruise to (2008), 226–28

Long Island, author's conservation assessment of, 206

Lynn Canal (Admiralty Island), 99, 99

MacKinnon, Andy, 226, 228, 229, 230, 234

"Management and Conservation of Old-Growth Forests in the United States" (Wildlife Society), 162–63

Mansfield Peninsula, 86
   as potential rainforest restoration area, 236

McKnight, Don, 34–35, 111, 112

media
   interest in Alaska wilderness, 105–6, 159
   and Senate Bill 708 hearings, 159

Mendenhall Glacier, 47, 56

Miller, George, 167–68

Miller, Sterling, 137, 160

mining
   impact on bears, 108, 108, 150–52
   well-managed, as compatible with conservation, 268

Misty Fjords National Monument, 201

Mitkof Island
   author's conservation assessment of, 204
   road construction and timber harvesting on, 200

Montague Island, cruise to (2009), 245–46

mountain goat(s), 57, 58, 60

mountain goat research, 56–61
   aerial telemetry data, collection of, 56–57
   assignment of author to, 57
   capturing and radio-collaring of goats, 57–59, 58
   conclusions of, 59–61
   location of, 56, 56
   objectives of, 57

Mount Edgecumbe National Volcanic Monument, proposal for, 237

Mount Fairweather, 86, 99, 99

Mud Bay, author's conservation assessment of, 207, 208

Multiple Use-Sustained Yield Act of 1960, 280

murrelets, 229
   Kittlitz's, 238, 239, 240
   marbled, 238
   Sarah Schoen's research on, 244–45, 245

muskeg bogs, characteristics of, 69, 70

National Audubon Society
   appeal of TLMP, 187–88
   conservation as goal of, 275
   testimony before Congress, 132

National Audubon Society, Alaska Office
   appeal of Tongass Land management Plan of 2008, 224
   author as Director of, 179, 183, 224
      and defining of priorities, 185
      fundraising as burden, 183, 185
      responsibilities and goals, 183–84
   author as senior scientist at, 183
   author's respect for, 276
   author's retirement from, 250–51
   author's transition to part-time senior scientist, 224, 250
   author's work with
      development of conservation assessment of Southeastern Alaska, 194–96
      as difficult and stressful, 222–24
      and key salmon watersheds, identification of, 251–52
      and study plan reviews, 100
      and Tongass Conservation Collaborative, 235–37
      and Tongass Land Management Plan, 224–25
      and Tongass science cruise, 225–33, 227
      and Tongass Science Workshop (2009), 233–35
      and work based on science, 276
   conservation assessment of Alaska's Western Arctic, 194, 197
   forest diversity workshop (Juneau, 2002), 192–93
   and Roadless Conservation Rule, 189–91
   Senner as Director of, 185–86
   staff and colleagues, 183–84
   and Tongass Futures Roundtable, 212

black-tailed deer's wintertime preference for, 73–76, 73–78, 79
carbon storage by, 257, 260
complex structure of, 161
and cumulative effect of storm damage,
41, 42
and deer management, debate over,
80–81
distinguishing between types of, 63,
69–74, 70, 71, 74, 74, 75, 76, 77, 78–79
as drastically reduced, 81
importance to numerous animal
species, 43, 44, 266
large spruce found by author, 219–20,
228, 229
as largest remaining old-growth forest,
256, 257
Natural History magazine special issue
on, 160–62
as nonrenewable under current system,
52, 55, 133, 156, 255, 257
plans for harvesting of, 123
scientific management, political obstacles to, 80
as small percentage of Tongass National
Forest, 122, 160–61, 192, 196, 227
suppression of author's conclusions
about, 153
Wildlife Society position statement on,
122–23
old-growth forest in Tongass, clear-cutting
of, xiii, 256
amount cut per year, 35
calls for ending of, 195, 253
as contrary to Forest Service policy,
281
as contrary to legal requirements for
Tongass management, 281
cumulative effect of, 157
damage to wildlife from, 162–63
and decline in deer populations, 157
and decline in wildlife populations, 254
Forest Service decision to stop, 250, 281
new logging contracts despite, 256,
260–61, 272
and habitat fragmentation, 163, 177, 221,
254
as poor conservation practice, 266
TLMP of 2015-16 and, 258, 272
Tongass as last national forest allowing,
255, 258
as unjustifiable, 281–82
as unsustainable practice, 272

old-growth forest in Tongass, loggers'
targeting of (high-grading), 106, 147,
156–57, 168–69, 170–71, 177, 192, 196, 205,
232–33
Albert and Schoen article on, 253–54
as ongoing practice, 261
prohibition of, in Tongass Timber
Reform Act of 1990, 174
refusal of some to acknowledge, 253
See also high-grading of old-growth
forest
old-growth forest in U.S., as mostly gone,
xiii, 55, 133, 162, 256, 257
Olson, Sig, 34, 172
Orca II (boat), 104
author's family accompanying research
trips in, 114–15, 118, 121
cruises along North Pacific Coast, 246
last family cruise on, 164–66, *165*
purchase and early cruises, 104–5
sale of, 172
use in research, 105
Orcas Island, author's childhood home on,
4, 5, 7
See also Schoen, John, childhood on Orcas
Island
Orcas Power and Light, author's work for,
15
Orians, Gordon
as author's professor at University of
Washington, 21
and book from Tongass Science
Workshop, 250, 252–53
on Tongass science cruise (2008), 226,
229
and Tongass Science Workshop, 231, 233,
235

Pacific coastal temperate rainforest
as largest on Earth, 30
Tongass as part of, 30
Pamplin, Lew, 110–11, 112, 130
parents of author
and author's conception, 3–4
conservatism of, 9
father's lessons, 7–8, 67–68
father's pilot training, 13
home on Orcas Island, 4, 5, 7
honeymoon, 3–4
Paris Climate Agreement, 260
"Paying Twice to Ruin a Rain Forest"
(*New York Times*), 159

Schoen, Mary Beth Lewis (wife), *12, 115*
    and aerial reconnaissance of watersheds, 203, 206
    in Alaska, first trip, *15, 15–16*
    birth of Erik, 65
    birth of Sarah, 100
    at Camp Nor'Wester, *17, 17–18*
    cruise of Tongass with writer from *National Geographic*, 214–20, 219
    and cruises of coastal Alaska (2009), *238*, 242, 243, 328
    dating and marriage, 12, 15, 17
    education of, 12, 15–16, 17
    as full-time mom, 65–66
    parents of, 12, 14
    and research trips in *Orca II*, 114–15
    second pregnancy, 97
    visit from parents, 100
Schoen, Sarah (daughter), *105, 115*
    birth of, 100
    career of, 244–45, *245*
    and research trips in *Orca II*, 114–15
Schoen, Steve (brother), *4, 5, 105*
science
    author's reliance on, 276
    corporations misusing, 277
    growing popular rejection of, in U.S., 278
    history of tension between cultural status quo and, 279
    as informing but not leading to decisions, 277, 279
    as key element in conservation, 283
    as method rather than body of facts, 278–79
    misuse by some environmentalists, 276
    vs. politics, in policy-making, 273, 274, 275, 279
    and scientist's integrity, importance of, 112, 275, 277, 283–84
    scientists' responsibility for educating public on, 279
science cruise of Tongass (2008), 225–33, 227
    goals of, 226
    grant funding, 225–26
    initial aerial survey, 226, 227
    return to large spruce found on *National Geographic* cruise, 228, 229
    scientists aboard, 226
    Tongass Science Workshop following, 231, 233–35

trip summary and scientific consensus of, 232–33
scientific names, 307–9
scientific organizations, value to agency scientists, 274
SEACC. *See* Southeast Alaska Conservation Council
Sealaska Corporation, 213, 214
Secord, David, 226, 228, 229, 231
Security Bay, author's conservation assessment of, 204–5
Seiberling, John, 128, 129–32, 134–36
Seirra Club, legal challenge to 1997 TLMP, 189
Senate Bill 708, hearings on, 154–59
    author's testimony at, 156–57
    media interest in, 159
    testimony by Southeast Alaska residents, 157–58
Senate Subcommittee on Public Lands, National Parks and Forests. *See* Senate Bill 708, hearings on
Senner, Stan, 185–86, *186*, 190–91, 224
Sheridan, Walt, 168–69
Sitka Sound, *261*
Smith Island, cruise to (2009), 246
snow accumulation
    deer's avoidance of areas with, *70, 71, 71, 73,* 73–76, *74, 77,* 79, 269
    as greater in second-growth than old-growth forests, *45,* 45–46, *46,* 73, *74,* 77, 79, 156
sounds of Alaska wilderness, 90–92
South Baranof Wilderness, 201
Southeast Alaska
    declining quality of forests and wildlife diversity north of, 247–48, *248*
    facts about, 291–93
    habitats requiring strong conservation focus, 268–69
    historical benchmarks, 295–99
    timber industry in, history of, 30–31
    topography of, *27m*
Southeast Alaska Conservation Council (SEACC), 110, 111, 131, 275, 276
Southeast Conference, 213
2018 report, 280
South Prince of Wales Wilderness, 201, 207
Spasski and Hoonah Totem Corp., 230
Spasski Bay, and science cruise, 226